RECENT ADVANCES IN SUSTAINABLE DEVELOPMENT

EDITORS

DR. MAMTA SHARMA   **DR. HUKAM SINGH**

DR. UPENDRA SINGH

PUSTAK BHARATI

TORONTO CANADA

Editors : Dr. Mamta Sharma
Dr. Hukam Singh
Dr. Upendra Singh

Book Title : Recent Advances in Sustainable Development

Cover Picture : By Dr. Anil Kumar Chhangani, D.Sc

Published by :
Pustak Bharati (Books India)
180 Torresdale Ave, Toronto Canada M2R 3E4
email : pustak.bharati.canada@gmail.com
Web : www.pustak-bharati-canada.com

Published for
Raj Rishi Government Autonomous College,
Alwar, Rajasthan, India

Financial Assistance
Rashtriya Uchchatar Shiksha Abhiyan
(RUSA-2.0)

Copyright ©2023

ISBN 978-1-989416-47-1

9 781989 416471

90000

ISBN : 978-1-989416-47-1

Preface

"Our planet is slowly dying, and if we don't do anything about it soon enough, it would eventually begin to deteriorate and everything would be used. The world would become a barren place without any resources. We need to cater to the needs of our planet, and we need to change our life styles so that it becomes beneficial to the planet. We need to become much more eco-friendly, so that no harm is dealt to the planet by our existence. Many people don't realize that they waste large amounts of energy and other resources in various unnecessary things that could otherwise be saved."

This series of books is an extension of the 3 days international conference on **Multidisciplinary Approach Towards Sustainable Development and Climate Change for A Viable Future (ICMSDC-2022)** held from 12th-14th August 2022 at Raj Rishi Government Autonomous College, Alwar, Rajasthan.

We are very happy and delighted to publish our series of books which are accumulation of research papers of knowledgeable experts in the field of sustainable development and climate change.

Climate change is the most significant challenge to achieving sustainable development, and it threatens to drag millions of people into grinding poverty. At the same time, we have never had better know-how and solutions available to avert the crisis and create opportunities for a better life for people all over the world. Climate change is not just a long-term issue. It is happening today, and it entails uncertainties for policy makers trying to shape the future.

There is a dual relationship between sustainable development and climate change. On the one hand, climate change influences key natural and human living conditions and thereby also the basis for social and economic development, while on the other hand, society's priorities on sustainable development influence both the greenhouse gas emissions that are causing climate change and the vulnerability.

Climate policies can be more effective when consistently embedded within broader strategies designed to make national and regional development paths more sustainable. This occurs because the impact of climate variability and change, climate policy responses, and associated socio-economic development will affect the ability of countries to achieve sustainable development goals. Conversely, the pursuit of those goals will in turn affect the opportunities for, and success of, climate policies.

With these books, we aim to reach to as many people as we can, and spread awareness about sustainable development and climate change and its in-depth analysis through our didactic research papers. We hope that the thought with which ICMSDC-2022 was executed is taken forward through this series of books and the inception of an idea of saving the environment is rooted in the minds of our readers.

The articles in these books have been contributed by eminent research scholars, scientists, academicians and industry experts whose contributions have enriched this book series. We thank our publisher, Pustak Bharati, Toronto, Canada for joining us in this initiative and helped in publishing this series of books.

Finally, we will always remain indebted to all our well-wishers for their blessings, without which ICMSDC-2022 and series of these book would have not come into existence.

Financial Assistance provided by Rashtriya Uchchatar Shiksha Abhiyan (RUSA-2.0) is gratefully acknowledged.

Dr. Mamta Sharma
Dr. Hukam Singh
Dr. Upendra Singh

Contents

1. High time to Save the Biological Diversity

Dr. Mamta Sharma*,
Dr. Hukam Singh**
Dr. Upendra Singh ***

Introduction

Biodiversity refers to the variety of living organisms present on earth, including all the species of plants, animals, fungi, and microorganisms that inhabit the planet. The environment, on the other hand, encompasses all the physical and natural systems that support life on earth, including the air, water, land, and climate. Biodiversity and environment conservation are two intertwined concepts that are crucial for sustaining life on earth. Biodiversity is essential for the functioning of ecosystems, which provide a range of services that support human wellbeing, such as air and water purification, pollination of crops, and climate regulation. The loss of biodiversity can have devastating impacts on these services, leading to reduced agricultural yields, increased air pollution, and more severe weather events. Furthermore, biodiversity is important for human health, as many of the medicines and foods we rely on come from plants and animals. It is estimated that up to 50% of modern drugs are derived from natural compounds found in plants and animals. Biodiversity is also crucial for cultural, spiritual, and recreational purposes, as it forms the basis of many traditional practices and indigenous knowledge systems. However, biodiversity is under threat from a range of human activities, including habitat destruction, overexploitation of natural resources, pollution, and climate change. These activities have led to the extinction of many species, with up to one million species at risk of extinction in the coming decades.

The term biodiversity refers to the wealth of plants, animals and microorganisms that contain precious genes and formulate delicate ecosystems. Biodiversity is the variety and variability of life on Earth. Biodiversity is typically a measure of variation at the genetic, species, and ecosystem level. Biodiversity refers to variety and variability among the living organisms and ecological complexes in which occur. This includes diversity within species, between species and of the ecosystem. It is defined as the totality of genes, species and ecosystems of a region. Biodiversity or Biological diversity comprises Genetic diversity, Species diversity and Ecosystem diversity (level of biodiversity).

Genetic diversity

It refers to the variation of genes within the species stores as immense amount of genetic information. Genetic variation is seen among the individuals within a species. For instance, in cattle there are many varieties with respect to colour, milk yield, size or disease resistance. The genetic variation may be in alleles, entire genes or in chromosomal structures. It leads to better adaptation of species to the changed environment. New species are formed due to genetic variation.

Species diversity

It refers to the various species found within a region. Variability found within a species or between different species of a community. Species diversity is measured by species richness (number of species per unit area) and evenness or equitability (evenness in the number of individuals of a species). In the case of species richness, higher species diversity represents greater species diversity. In the second case, evenness of species represents higher species diversity.

Ecosystem diversity

It refers to the variations in the biological communities in which the species live. The diversity within a community is called alpha diversity. The diversity between communities is called Beta diversity. Examples are Tropical Rain Forest and Boreal Forest. The present diversity has developed over millions of years of evolution and therefore ecological balance should not be disturbed. The diversity of the habitats over total landscape or geological area is referred to as Gamma diversity (or) Landscape diversity. For example, Forest ecosystem, aquatic ecosystem, Grasslands, Deserts, mangroves etc. Alpha diversity refers to the average species diversity in a habitat or specific area. Alpha diversity is a local measure.

2

Beta diversity refers to the ratio between local or alpha diversity and regional diversity. This is the diversity of species between two habitats or regions. It is calculated by the following equation: (number species in habitat1 (H1) - number of species habitat 2 (H2) & 1 have in common) +(number of species in H2- number of species H1 & H 2 have in common).

Gamma diversity is the total diversity of a landscape and is a combination of both alpha and beta diversity.

Biodiversity Conservation

Environment conservation refers to the efforts to protect and restore the natural systems that support life on earth. This includes actions to reduce pollution, mitigate climate change, and conserve habitats and species. Environment conservation is crucial for maintaining the services that ecosystems provide, as well as for preserving biodiversity and the benefits it provides to human health and wellbeing. One of the key strategies for biodiversity and environment conservation is protected areas, such as national parks, wildlife reserves, and marine sanctuaries. These areas provide habitats for species to thrive, while also serving as important sources of ecological and cultural value. Protected areas are also important for promoting sustainable tourism, which can provide economic benefits to local communities while supporting conservation efforts.

The enormous value of biodiversity emphasizes the need to conserve biodiversity. Biodiversity is a natural reservoir with tremendous economic potential. Wildlife is a gift of nature to be nurtured. Biodiversity is an important resource for man and nation. So, its conservation and rational use are the need of the hour to achieve sustainable development.

 World wide fund for Nature (WWF 1994) works to conserve biological diversity as follows.

➢ Creating and maintaining systems of effective and sustainable protected areas.
➢ Promoting practices of sustainable development
➢ Conserving certain species of special concern.
➢ Promoting environmental education to enable people to manage the natural resources sustainably

Methods of Conservation

There are two methods of conservation of biodiversity.

• In-situ conservation (within habitat)
• Ex-situ conservation (outside habitats)

Biodiversity and its Conservation Methods

Biodiversity refers to the variability of life on earth. It can be conserved in the following ways:

• In-situ Conservation
• Ex-situ Conservation

In-situ Conservation :

In-situ conservation of biodiversity is the conservation of species within their natural habitat. In this method, the natural ecosystem is maintained and protected. The in-situ conservation has several advantages. Following are the important advantages of in situ conservation :

1. It is a cost-effective and convenient method of conserving biodiversity.
2. A large number of living organisms can be conserved simultaneously.
3. Since the organisms are in a natural ecosystem, they can evolve better and can easily adjust to different environmental conditions.

Certain protected areas where in-situ conservation takes place include national parks, wildlife sanctuaries and biosphere reserves.

Ex-situ Conservation :

Ex-situ conservation of biodiversity involves the breeding and maintenance of endangered species in artificial ecosystems such as zoos, nurseries, botanical gardens, gene banks, etc. There is less competition for food, water and space among the organisms.

Ex-situ conservation has the following advantages :

1. The animals are provided with a longer time and breeding activity.
2. The species bred in captivity can be reintroduced in the wild.
3. Genetic techniques can be used for the preservation of endangered species.

4

Conclusion :

One of the most important strategies for biodiversity and environment conservation is sustainable management of natural resources. This involves using resources in a way that meets the needs of the present without compromising the ability of future generations to meet their own needs. For example, sustainable forestry practices can help to maintain forest ecosystems while providing timber for construction and other uses. Similarly, sustainable agriculture practices can help to conserve soil and water resources while producing food for human consumption. Reducing pollution and mitigating climate change are also important for biodiversity and environment conservation. Pollution can have harmful effects on both human health and the environment, leading to reduced biodiversity and ecosystem services. Mitigating climate change is also crucial, as it can lead to changes in weather patterns and the distribution of species, as well as more severe weather events such as hurricanes, floods, and droughts. Finally, education and awareness-raising are crucial for biodiversity and environment conservation. This includes teaching people about the importance of biodiversity and the environment, as well as providing them with the knowledge and skills needed to support conservation efforts. Public participation and engagement are also important, as they can help to build support for conservation initiatives and ensure that they are effective and sustainable. In conclusion, biodiversity and environment conservation are essential for sustaining life on earth. Biodiversity provides a range of services that support human wellbeing, while environment conservation is crucial for maintaining the natural systems that provide these services. Protected areas, sustainable resource management, pollution reduction, climate change mitigation, and education and awareness-raising are all important strategies for achieving biodiversity and environment conservation goals. By working together to protect and restore our planet's natural systems, we can ensure a healthy and sustainable future for ourselves and for future generations.

References

Source of knowledge is the internet and it is highly acknowledged.

*Associate Professor (Zoology)
**Professor
*** Associate Professor (Chemistry)
Raj Rishi Government (Autonomous) College
Alwar, Rajasthan 301001,India.
email : mamta810@gmail.com
drhukamsingh63@gmail.com ;
dr.usingh09@gmail.com

2. Role of Shade Houses for Vegetable Production

Niraj Kumar Prajapati

Abstract

As a result of dramatic technological advancements, human activities pertaining to agricultural growth and productivity are reaching new heights every day. Along with technology, protected structures have entered the agricultural industry, and for forward-thinking growers and farmers around the world, shade net structures are a crucial component. This chapter explains in clear detail some of the technical requirements, planning, applications, material usefulness, and potential future research areas for the shade net structure. Future studies will take a closer look at the significance and range of protected cultivation.

Keywords : Vegetable, shade house, protected cultivation, off-season etc.

Introduction

The largest contribution to a nation's GDP growth is made by horticulture. Due to the importance of agriculture to the national economy, it is crucial that farmers take good care of their crops and put in a lot of effort in the field. Numerous methods exist for protecting crops. The use of technology in this industry has undergone remarkable progress during the last few decades. Insect and weed control for crops has a long history of success. With the use of these technologies, sowing, harvesting, storage, and distribution have improved. Presently, progressive farmers are adopting commercially protected cultivation of high-value vegetables (Maitra *et al.* 2020).

Fresh vegetable demand is constant throughout the year, while supply is only available during the growing season. The growth, physiological process, flowering, fruit setting, and ultimately yield and economic return of the various vegetable crops are all negatively impacted by changes in climatic vagaries like fluctuation in temperature, light, humidity, wind velocity, etc. The unfavourable weather significantly decreased yield or may have caused the entire harvest to fail. The urgent need is to encourage off-season production in order to boost the supply of fresh vegetables outside of the typical growing season.

Under open field conditions, it is impossible to cultivate winter-season vegetables in the summer because of the harmful effects of the hot sun and greater day and night temperatures on vegetative growth, which results in the loss of flowers and fruits. Again, low temperatures, cold waves, and freezing injuries affect summer crop cultivation throughout the winter months in open fields. Crops can be grown off-season by using the right protection technologies and creating a conducive environment. With the advent of shade net, which controls light and temperature to some extent and produces an environment that is beneficial for crop growth, it is possible to raise the crop during the hot summer months with the desired yield and quality.

"Protected cultivation" refers to a set of methods for modifying a plant's natural habitat, which completely or partially modifies the microclimate conditions, in order to increase their productivity. Wind breaks, mulches, low tunnels, direct coverings, high tunnels, and greenhouses are examples of protected cultivation systems. Another goal is to create a microclimate that will improve crops' yield and quality while also promoting more efficient resource usage.

Why a Shade House?

Offers a favourable environment for crops that can be maintained and regulated by the farmer, resulting in a healthy crop with superior quality, good light transmission, and UV protection. Shade houses are crucial for plant growth because they give plants time to "harden off" and become adapted to their environments. Protecting crops from adverse weather conditions such as wind, rain, hail, and snow as well as from pests, diseases, and predators is one of the main goals of protected cultivation. Increasing output per unit area Planting propagation material to increase germination rate and hardening to encourage the growing of high-quality vegetables beneath shade net houses. Year-round production of vegetables grown out of season. Continuous production of disease-free and genetically superior transplants is possible.

Role of Shade Net House

A straight-forward yet effective innovation that helps protect crops is the horticulture shade net. It shields the crops from the sun's heat. Sunlight is a crop's primary need for growth, yet too much of it can cause serious harm. Some crops are delicate, and particular regions are more susceptible to intense sunrays owing to geography and climatic conditions. Shade Net has a crucial role to perform in this situation.

According to Feijuan and Cheng (2012), the amount of light, the moisture in the soil, and the availability of nitrogen are crucial elements impacting the biomass of the crops. These elements also directly affect photosynthesis and growth. Different effects of varied light might be seen in the development of leaf area, growth, and yield.

Additionally, a lack of shade can reduce productivity by increasing the amount of light that hits the plant, which has a negative impact on the system's metabolism. To increase agricultural output, it is vital to research the ideal lighting conditions. Differently coloured shade nets allow for the manipulation of both light amount and quality.

Shahak and Gussakovsky (2004) reported that colour nets are an innovative concept in agricultural technology that combines physical protection with selective solar radiation filtration in order to particularly promote desirable physiological reactions that are light-regulated. While light scattering enhances light penetration into the inner canopy, spectral modification especially aims to promote photo morphogenetic-physiological responses. When the diffuse component of the incident radiation is amplified under shade, radiation efficiency rises. The reactions that are intended to be addressed are those that affect each crop's commercial value, such as yield, product quality, and rate of maturation.

Application of Shade Nets

Aids in the cultivation of vegetables, spices, medicinal plants, flowering plants, and foliage plants. Employed in nurseries for growing fruits and vegetables as well as producing forest species, etc. Promotes the quality drying of a variety of agricultural items. Used to ward off insect invasions. Tissue culture plants have secondary hardening nurseries. Aids in generating an environment that is favourable for the generation of vermicompost. Crops from natural weather disturbances such as wind, rain, hail, frost, snow, birds, and insects. Used in the creation of graft saplings and lowering their mortality during hot summer days.

How Does Shade Net Work?

Shade nets come in a variety of shades, or shade factors, including 15%, 35%, 40%, 50%, 75%, and 90%. For instance, a 35% shade factor means that the net will block 35% of the light intensity and only permit 65% of it to flow through. For a plant to grow at its best, the amount of sunlight and amount of shadow must be specific to each plant. The optimal shade factor selection is crucial to achieving the best possible climatic conditions and maximising plant productivity.

Qualities of an Ideal Shade Net

It must be extremely strong and long-lasting. This guarantees that it will persist for multiple crop lifetimes. UV Stabilization is the most crucial component that you must not overlook. A good shade net must provide the greatest amount of crop-protecting shadow. The shade needs to be technically constructed for greater yield. Large agricultural fields and even kitchen gardens can benefit from the use of shade netting. The shading effect of crops resulted in various changes to both crop microclimate and crop activity. The use of shade nets is done for protecting various horticultural crops against various abiotic factors like scorching insolation, excess wind speed, bird and rodent damage, and for improving the thermal climate (Kittas *et al.* 2009).

Components of Shade Net Houses

Depending on the shade net house, steel, bamboo, or GI pipes are used for the framework, and nuts and bolts are used to secure it at the joints. Special locking profiles made of aluminium secure covering materials to structures. UV-stabilized covering materials, such as insect net or shade net, bear hanging loads of 15 to 25 kg per square metre; vegetable trellising systems. Control System: Manual, Semi-Automatic, or Automatic if a high-priced shade net house is being installed. Planting Material: soilless media like coco peat.

Shade Net Installation

Allow 25% more shade fabric than you will need to completely cover the building. Staple the cloth to the structure every 12 inches, starting with the longest side you will be covering. As you move away from the house, start stapling on the closest short side, keeping the shade cloth uniformly aligned.

Structural Materials

The frame and cladding material make up the two essential parts of a shade house structure. The frame of the shade house serves as support for the cladding material and is built to provide protection from wind, rain, and crop weight. Depending on the weather conditions of the shade house, the agro-shade net or horticulture shade net lasts for 3–5 years. In high-rainfall regions like Orissa, structural frames with modest modifications appropriate to local conditions are advised.

Features and Specifications

Yield increases five to seven times or higher. Uniform and of greater quality. Less fertilizer is needed, which results in a decrease in fertilizer cost. Low water usage results in water savings. Fewer possibilities of disease attack, which lowers the cost of disease control. Greater fertilizer and water efficiency, troublesome soil conditions, and problematic topography when cultivating. Cultivation under unfavourable weather conditions. Requires minimal space to achieve the greatest production and advantages. Simple to control, maintain, and operate.

In shade net houses, shade nets are frequently employed. These shade net dwellings come in three different price ranges depending on the building costs: low cost, medium cost, and high cost.

Low-cost Shade Net House

It has no climate control system and is built with a bamboo supporting frame and UV-stabilized shade net covering. The price per square metre for a low-cost shade net house with all of its components is about Rs 150.

Medium-cost Shade Net House

G.I. pipes, profile springs and wires, and a UV-stabilized shade net are the materials used to construct a medium-priced shade net house. Around Rs 180–250 per square metre is the price range for a medium-priced shade net house that includes all of its components.

High-cost Shade Net House

The lifespan of a high-priced shade net house is about 8 to 10 years. It is built of steel tubes and has numerous amenities, including an auto control mechanism, a heating, cooling, and humidification system, a drip irrigation system, etc. The price per square metre for a high-end shade net house with all of its components is approximately Rs 300.

Types of Shade Houses

Flat Roof Shade Net House

Shade Net for a Flat Roof House was built with the intention of overcoming the issues of intense summertime sunlight, catching CO_2 levels at night, and minimising insect infection. The plant house's top is flat in the flat design, which is the simplest type of design. The net is secured to the framework via a spring. A plant house with a 1-acre lot size is optimal.

Dome-shaped Shade Net House

Dome-Shadow Net houses have a range of technical features. These are recognised for their alluring style, silky finish, and elegant design. They require little upkeep and are simple to install.

Choice of location

A shade house should be situated such that it has easy access to the market for the purchase of input materials and the sale of its products. There shouldn't be any drainage issues at the site. Water of high quality and power should both be available. Wind breakers, however, might be 30 metres from the structure.

Creating a Shadow Structure

The sort of crop that will be cultivated, the materials that are readily available locally, and the local climate should all be taken into account while designing the shade house structure. There ought to be room for future growth.

Orientation
To get the best light possible, a single-span shade house should be located in the east-west or north-south direction, while a multi-span shade house should be located in the north-south direction.

Unit Cost for Different Sizes and Models of Shady Net Houses

Coloured Netting
Crops can be protected from harmful environmental factors such as excessive sun radiation, heat and drought stress, wind and hail, birds, and flying pests using photo-selective, light-dispersive shade nets as an alternative, which would increase crop output, yield, and quality. The reviewed research also makes clear that light quality affects the production, accumulation, and preservation of vegetable phytochemicals as well as the development of degradation during storage. Farmers that grow vegetables should be informed of these new methods for adjusting light quality, which will enable them to meet year-round customer demand for vegetables with high nutritional value while preserving the freshness and post-harvest quality of their produce for a longer length of time. For open-field and greenhouse vegetable production to be sustainable and market-driven in the future, research on light modification in horticulture systems is required. Higher plants respond to changes in light intensity, colour, direction, and regularity. Plants have many photoreceptors, including those that respond to green light: cryptochromes, phototropins, cryptochromes, chlorophylls, and phtyochromes (Batschauer, 1999). Plants can adjust to ambient circumstances thanks to light and other environmental factors. The Colour Net approach was researched in various ornamentals (Nissim-Levi *et al.* 2008), vegetables (Falak *et al.* 2009; 2010), fruit trees (Shahak *et al.* 2004), and vineyards.

Radiation Scattering

It has been demonstrated that diffuse light increases the effectiveness of radiation utilisation, yields (both at the plant and ecosystem level), and even influences plant flowering (timing and amounts). Any shade netting can reflect light, especially ultraviolet light since netting is frequently composed of UV-resistant plastic. Branching, plant compactness, and flower production per plant have

13

all been found to increase with the use of shade netting that enhances light dispersion without altering the light spectrum (Nissim-Levi *et al.*, 2008). In addition to increasing light scattering by 50% or more, coloured shade nets may also have an impact on the growth and development of plants.

Photo Selectivity

The capacity of coloured shade nets to alter the spectrum of radiation reaching crops is the main reason they are being thoroughly tested. They can be used to alter the ratios of red to far-red light that phytochromes detect and the quantities of radiation that can activate the blue and ultraviolet photoreceptors, the blue light involved in phototropic responses mediated by phototropins, and radiation at other wavelengths that can affect plant growth and development. Based on the photosynthetic photon flux density (PPFD) and the a and b chlorophyll content of the leaves, light transmission through various cover materials encourages the differential stimulation of some physiological processes controlled by light, such as photosynthesis.

Using a ceptometer model Sun Scan SS1-UM-1.05 (Delta-T Devices Ltd., UK) with a 64-sensor photodiode linearly sorted in a 100 cm length sword, the effect of nets on the interception of light was assessed annually as a percentage of total photochemically active radiation (PAR) above canopy. Readings are expressed as PAR quantum flux (mol m-2 s-1) units. All measurements were made at noon on clear days. Three times throughout the day, measurements of global radiation were taken every other day.

The Effect of Colour on Plant Growth

Higher plants respond to the type, amount, direction, and regularity of light. Plants have a variety of photoreceptors, including those that respond to green light, cryptochromes, phototropism, and chlorophylls (Batschauer, 1999; Folta and Maruhnich, 2007). Plants can adjust to their surroundings using light and other environmental cues. For decades, researchers have worked to alter the morphology and physiology of plants using photo-selective filters, especially in greenhouse settings that have been widely available for this purpose. Both indoor and outdoor use of these nets is possible. They can guard against physical threats (birds, hail, insects, and extreme radiation), modify the environment (humidity, shadow, and temperature), raise the amount of diffuse (scattered) light, and absorb different spectral bands, all of which have an impact on the quality of the light. These effects can influence crops as well as the organisms associated with them.

Shade Net Colours

Presently, shade nets are available in different colours, i.e., white, black, red, blue, yellow, and green, and in combinations, including:

Green and Black : they cut off unwanted UV rays and give an aesthetic look.

Black on Black : It absorbs and radiates heat inside the shade net house. Used in nursery education.

White x Black : Diffuses the light inside the shade net house. Mainly used for flowers such as Gerbera, Anthurium, etc.

Green x Green : Enhance the process of photosynthesis in plants, resulting in better foliage in ornamental plants.

The Colour Nets are an innovative concept in agricultural technology that combines physical protection with varying sun radiation filters in order to particularly promote desirable physiological reactions that are light-regulated. Due to their capacity to alter the radiation spectrum that reaches crops, coloured shade nets are currently the subject of extensive testing. They can be used to alter the ratios of red to far-red light that phytochromes detect, the quantities of radiation that can activate the blue/ultraviolet-A photoreceptors, the blue light involved in phototropic responses mediated by phototropins, and radiation at other wavelengths that can affect plant growth and development. Coloured shade nets, which have been developed during the last decade to filter selected spectral regions of sunlight while simultaneously inducing light scattering, are designed to specifically modify plant behaviour.

What's different about Shade Plants?

Typically, shade leaves are narrower than sun leaves but larger in area. On a weight basis, sun leaves get thicker than shade leaves, while shade leaves often have more chlorophyll. This is because the palisade cells or additional layer of palisade cells grow longer and have more grana leaves in the chloroplasts. The chloroplasts in shadow leaves migrate about inside the cells to occupy a position where they can absorb the most light without blocking the light from chloroplasts below them. (In sun leaves, the chloroplasts alternate between absorbing bright light and hiding in the shade of others to use it; too much brilliant light would destroy the chloroplasts.) Sun and shade leaves can differ in the amount of photosynthesis by a factor of up to 5 for the same amount of light. Most of these adaptations take place during leaf development; there is little a leaf (or a plant) can do in light conditions.

Shade and the Plant Environment

Air and fruit surface temperatures as well as incoming solar radiation are affected by shade fabric. Reduced levels of solar radiation will result in less sun damage. The overall crop production should stay high when the proper amount of shade is applied. Plant architecture is also changed by shading. Shade-grown plants are higher, more likely to have more nodes, and have larger leaves. Under the building, shading raises the relative humidity and lowers the wind.

Growing of Vegetables under Shade Net

The mean weekly temperature during summer was higher under an open field than in the shade net house. Shade netting increases the availability of net energy for crop growth and also improves the survival of the crop under high temperature and moisture stress conditions.

Deciding what Vegetables can be Grown in the Shade House

Consider which plant component is consumed when selecting the vegetable to grow in your shade house. The best growth conditions for crops like spinach and potatoes, which have edible leaves and roots, are usually partial shade or shadow structures. In contrast, vegetables that are cultivated for their edible fruits, such as tomatoes and cucumbers, do best in full sun, where they need at least 6 hours of sunlight each day. Vegetables that are planted in the shadow typically yield a more succulent crop. Additionally, growing in the shade can reduce bolting in your veggies. Your companion to successfully growing veggies can be a high-quality shade house, which can also provide temporary protection for your plants. Your plants may benefit from a shade house in various ways, such as temporary relief from intense heat. You can effectively grow the proper veggies in the shade house with careful planning. Since you are growing your plant in a shadow house, its watering requirements may differ from those of plants grown in full daylight. Use good soil with nutrient-rich compost for growing your vegetables. So, you might not need to water your plants. Because moisture doesn't evaporate as quickly in the shade house, vegetables are used more frequently.

Production Plan for High-value Vegetables in Shade Net Houses

- Plan 1: Capsicum (July–March) and Cucumber (April–June)
- Plan 2: Cucumber (June-Sept) + Cucumber (Jan-Mar) + Coriander (April-May)
- Plan 3: Beans (May-Aug) + Tomato (Sept-Feb) + Cucumber or Summer Squash (Mar-May)
- Plan 4: Capsicum (July–Dec) + Tomato (Jan–April) + Leafy Vegetables (May–June)
- Plan 5: Cucumber (July–October) + Broccoli/Red Cabbage (Oct–Feb) + Leafy Vegetables/Summer Squash (Mar–June)
- Plan 6: Gerbera (July-March) + Leafy Vegetables (April-June)

Levels of Shade

Full Sun Vegetables

Full-sun vegetables refer to at least six hours (but generally at least eight) of direct sunlight per day. Nearly every day of the season should have at least six hours of direct sunlight hitting the plants. Naturally, days with bad weather and cloudy skies are not included. Nothing manmade (trees, structures, *etc.*) is obstructing the sunlight from reaching full-sun vegetables.

Partial-Sun Vegetables

Vegetables grown in partial sunlight need at least four hours of sunlight each day to grow, but they frequently do well with as few as six hours of direct sunlight. Beans When in a bush variety, these do better with more sun (closer to 6 hours) than in vine varieties, which can do more with less if they're on a trellis. Beets Keep beets partially shaded, and they'll thrive, even in relatively dry conditions.

Light-Shade Vegetables

Vegetables that do well in less sunlight (2 to 4 hours) are often called "light shade" or "shaded" plants. Some "partial shade" plants are also light shade, such as cauliflower and many spices. Suitable Varieties of vegetable crops under shade house conditions: Capsicum: Indra, Orabelle, Bachata, Colour Capsicum Tomato: indeterminate (Hinson, NS-247, NS-537, US-2853) Semi-determinate: (US-618, US-1143, Abhinav, Lakshmi, Anup), Tanuja, and Novara Cucumber: Malini, Seetha, Tripti, US-6125, Valistar, Multi Star, and Kafka French beans: Super King, Classic (NZ) (Pole types): Arka Komal, Arka Suvidha, Contender (Bush types) Red Cabbage: A red jewel Broccoli: Pusa KTS-1, Fantacy, etc.

Conclusion

Any agricultural technique must have a lower cost of cultivation and higher returns to be successful. The value of the crop at the point of consideration is the only factor that influences whether the initial cost of the shade net house is recovered to reach the breakeven point. The essential factors for the stakeholders of protected farming are a longer structure's lifespan, a reduced initial cost for the structure, high-value crops with good storage quality, and measuring market demand. Scope of Future Research: Development of Low-Cost Shade Net Making Materials More climate-resilient and adverse weather-tolerant shade net houses are approaching. breeding aspect of specific cultivars suitable for shade net cultivation. Due attention should be paid to technology transfer activities in regions with limited natural resources. development of alternative growing mediums to the current ones to prevent the formation of nematodes and soil-borne infections The development of an all-in-one kind of instrument to measure various parameters at a stretch Portable shade net houses are being developed with a focus on unstable topographic settings and rapidly changing scenarios like the salinization of fields from seawater intrusion.

References

Batschauer, A. Light perception in higher plants. CMLS, Cell. Mol. Life Sci. **55**, 153–166 (1999).

Fallik, E., Alkalai-Tuvia, S., Parselan, Y., Aharon, Z., Elmann, A., Offir, Y., Matan, E., Yehezkel, H., Ratner, K., Zur, N. and Shahak, Y. 2009. Can coloured shade nets maintain sweet pepper quality during storage and marketing. *Acta Hort.*, **830**: 37-44.

Feijuan, W., Cheng, Z. Effect of nitrogen and light intensity on tomato (*Lycopersicon esculentum* M.) production under soil water control. *African Journal of Agricultural Research*, 2012; **7**(31): 4408- 4415.

Folta, K.M. and Maruhnich, S.A., 2007. Green light: a signal to slow down or stop. *Journal of experimental botany*, **58**(12), pp.3099-3111.

Kittas, C., Rigakis, N., Katsoulas, N. and Bartzanas, T. 2009. Influence of shading screens on micro climate, growth and productivity of tomato. *Acta Hort.*, **807**: 97-102.

Maitra, S., Shankar, T., Sairam, M. and Pine, S. 2020. Evaluation of gerbera (*Gerbera jamesonii* L.) cultivars for growth, yield and flower quality under protected cultivation. *Indian Journal of Natural Sciences*, **10**(60): 20271-20276.

Nissim-Levi, A., Farkash, L., Hamburger, D., Ovadia, R., Forrer, I., Kagan, S. and Oren-Shamir, M. 2008. Light-scattering shade net increases branching and flowering in ornamental pot plants. *Journal of Horticultural Science and Biotechnology*, **83**: 9-14.

Shahak, Y., Gussakovsky, E.E., Cohen, Y., Lurie, S., Stern, R., Kfir, S., Naor, A., Atzmon, I., Doron, I. and Green blat-Avron, Y. 2004. Color Nets: A new approach for light manipulation in fruit trees. *Acta Hort.*, **636**: 609-616

Raj Desh (Eds.) 2019. Floriculture at a glance. 4th Edition, Kalyani Publishers, Ludhiana, India, pp.136-141.

Dept. of Horticulture,
Tilak Dhari Post Graduate College, Jaunpur
U.P.
email : *nkp.ofcl@gmail.com*

3. Environmental Evaluation of Narmada River Water with special reference to Distt. Narmadapuram

Rajul Sharma[1], Noor Ahmad[2], O. N. Choubey[3]

Abstract

Narmada River is considered to be the lifeline and west-flowing river of Narmadapuram, Narmada River plays an important role in the natural, cultural, and economic aspects of the country. Due to pollution in the past few decades, there have been serious changes in aquatic activities and the environment. In recent times, there have been serious concerns about the safe use of river water for drinking water and other purposes. Many pollutants are playing a major role in polluting the river water. A Study was considered for the enhanced Water Quality by Physicochemical Parameters Such as – pH, TDS, Conductivity, Alkalinity, Total hardness, DO, BOD, and COD, etc., All the Parameters were determined by APHA and BIS methods, This was observed that the water quality was found to be poor in the All season because this water condition by humans activity.

Keywords : Narmada River, TDS, DO, BOD, COD, Physicochemical & Biological parameters, APHA, BIS method.

Introduction

Narmada river water is the main source of important activities for domestic, drinking, fisheries, industrial, agricultural, and other purposes. The water of the Narmada River is an important resource for both the natural ecosystem and human development. Water pollution is increasing in rivers. This is due to the massive discharge of industrial waste, domestic sewage, mine drainage, oil spill sand, and extensive fishing techniques. These declines in river waters are caused by both natural and anthropogenic activities, which lead to the deterioration of their quality. Hence the present investigation and action plan are included to monitor the chemical and physical components of the water flow of the Narmada River. The quality of river water pollution status. A study was considered for enhancement of water quality by physicochemical parameters like pH, TDS, conductivity, alkalinity, total hardness, DO, BOD, COD, etc. internationally standard method of sample collection, all parameters APHA and As determined by the BIS method, it was observed that the water quality was found to be poor in all the seasons because of the water condition caused by human activity.

Objective

1. Determine various parameters of Narmada River water.
2. Protection of water quality of Narmada River water from checking the Problems.
3. To determine the physiochemical method to reduce pollution of the Narmada River.

Proposed Work

1. In the present study, water samples will be collected every year from various sites along the Narmada River.
2. The samples will be analyzed for 12 different physicochemical attributes like pH, BOD, COD, Total Coliform, Temp, DO, Alkalinity, Chlorides, Calcium, Magnesium, and Hardness as Calcium Carbonate and TDS.
3. The measurement of the water quality index will be taken into consideration over time.
4. Forecasting the pollution trend for the Narmada river water for the analyzed period.

Proposed Methodology

(i) Area of Study

The study would be conducted in the area of Narmada river district Narmadapuram (M.P.),

(ii) Research design

My research has been carried out to define the water quality and analyzed various physicochemical parameters like Temperature, pH, turbidity, DO, BOD, and COD.

The above physicochemical and biological parameters were determined as per the method suggested by APHA. The Temperature pH and DO were recorded immediately after the collection of the sample, other samples were analyzed in a laboratory within 24hrs. The methods to be adopted for the different parameters are as follows.

Volumetric Method

This method will be used for the following parameter –
Dissolve oxygen, BOD, COD, Total hardness,

Instrumental Method

This method will be used for the following parameter-
Temperature, pH conductivity, turbidity.

Following parameters like DO, BOD, COD, Temperature, pH, Turbidity, and TDS, if the value is very high in river water.

(iii) Statistical Analysis

The Statistical analysis will be performed for correlation and test. The water quality index will be calculated to check the suitability of water for human consumption.

Result : The present study of various physicochemical and Biological parameters on the water of Narmada River Suggested that the values of different parameters depend upon the hydrochemistry of the study area. The results obtained during the present study are tabulated in Table 1. The results are shown by statistical evaluation as Minimum and Maximum values, Average Values, Standard Deviation, Standard Variance, Standard Error, and 95% Confidence Limit of the parameters for Narmada River water are presented in Table 1. The parameter's value is corrected by the WHO Standard value. The resulting value of the below parameters is poor.

Mean Values of Physicochemical & Biological Parameters at Sampling Sites in the Narmada River Water

Table – 1

S. No.	Parameter	Site- I	Site- Ii	Site - Iii	Site - Iv	Site - V	Standard Value of Water WHO
1	pH	7.3	7.6	7.4	7.8	8.0	7
2	Alkalinity mg/L	420	431	423	455	489	20-200 mg/L
3	TDS mg/L	349	362	358	382	391	50-150 mg/L
4	Total Hardness mg/L	125	142	128	151	154	120-170 mg/L
5	DO mg/L	5.7	5.0	5.5	4.5	4.2	4.5 mg/L
6	BOD mg/L	5.3	4.6	4.9	4.4	4.0	3-5 mg/L
7	COD mg/L	58	69	55	77	92	100-250 mg/L
8	Chloride mg/L	187	198	193	206	209	250-1000
9	Phosphate mg/L	0.8	1.0	0.9	1.9	2.4	3 mg/L
10	Nitrate mg/L	0.9	1.1	1.0	1.2	1.3	10 mg/L
11	Zinc (Zn) mg/L	0.161	0.163	0.163	0.169	0.172	5-15 mg/L
12	Coliform count/ml	3200-28300	4000-67200	3100-26500	3600-28600	4100-75300	10000/100 ml

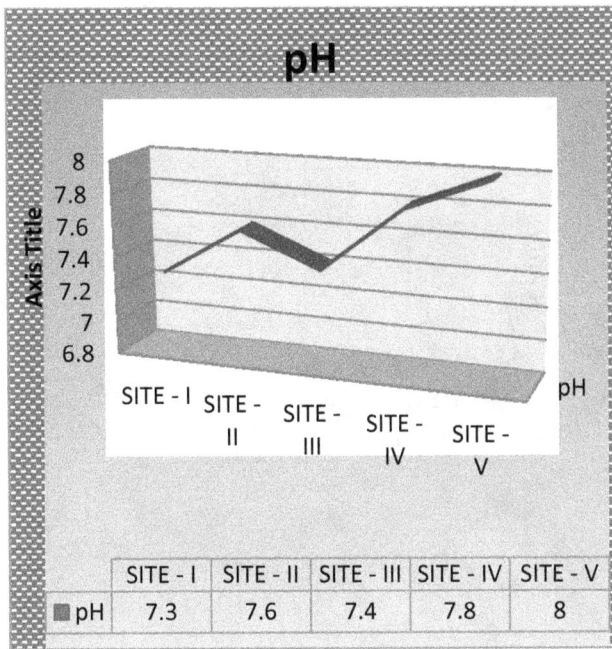

pH

	SITE - I	SITE - II	SITE - III	SITE - IV	SITE - V
pH	7.3	7.6	7.4	7.8	8

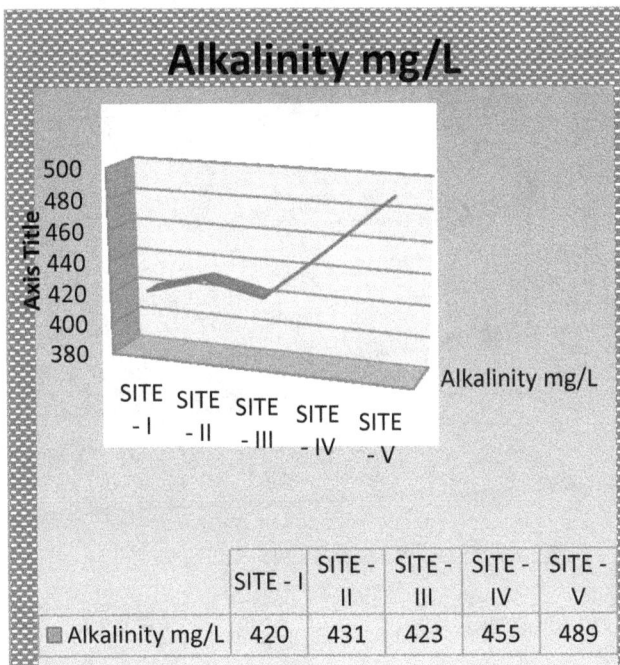

Alkalinity mg/L

	SITE - I	SITE - II	SITE - III	SITE - IV	SITE - V
Alkalinity mg/L	420	431	423	455	489

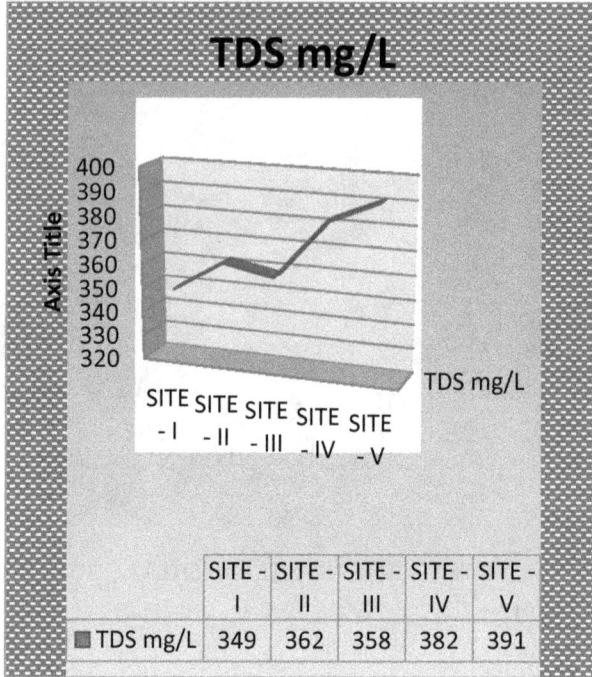

TDS mg/L

	SITE - I	SITE - II	SITE - III	SITE - IV	SITE - V
TDS mg/L	349	362	358	382	391

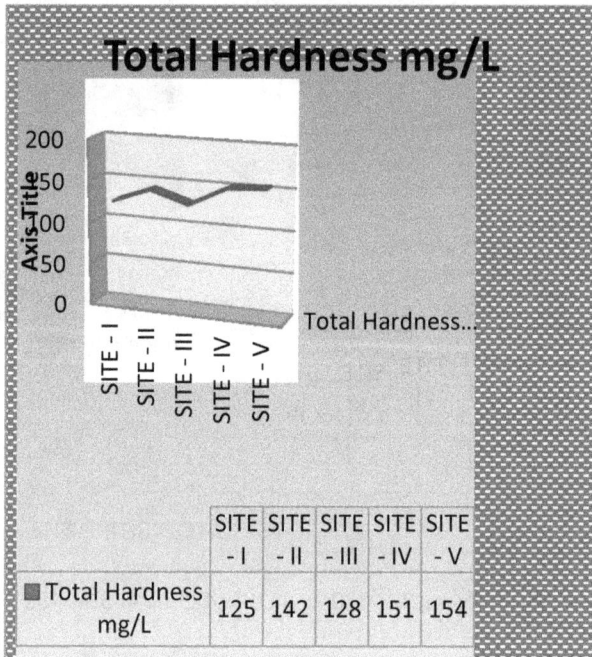

Total Hardness mg/L

	SITE - I	SITE - II	SITE - III	SITE - IV	SITE - V
Total Hardness mg/L	125	142	128	151	154

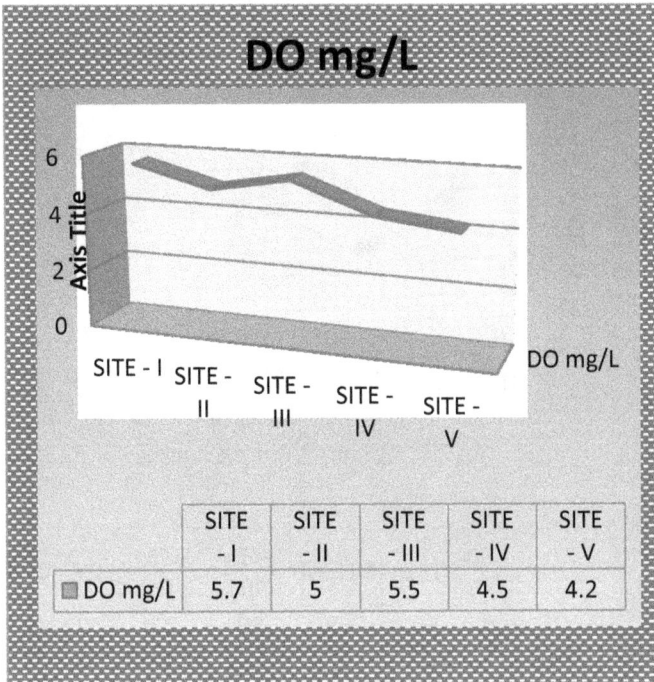

DO mg/L

	SITE - I	SITE - II	SITE - III	SITE - IV	SITE - V
DO mg/L	5.7	5	5.5	4.5	4.2

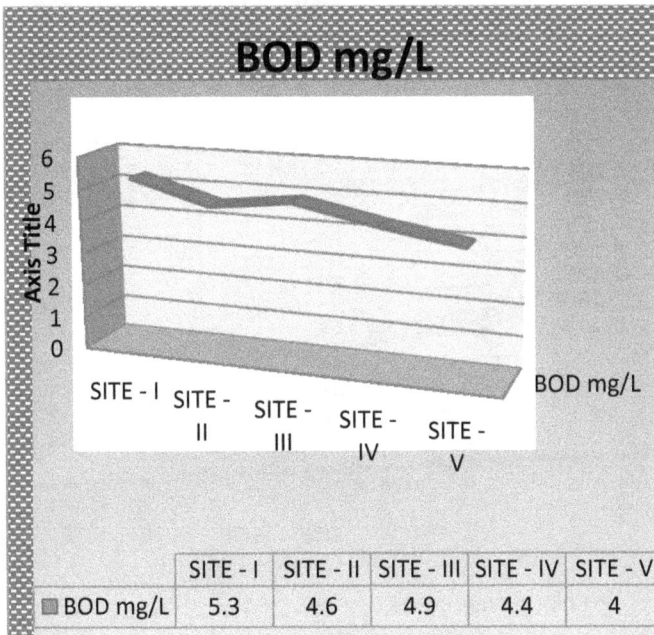

BOD mg/L

	SITE - I	SITE - II	SITE - III	SITE - IV	SITE - V
BOD mg/L	5.3	4.6	4.9	4.4	4

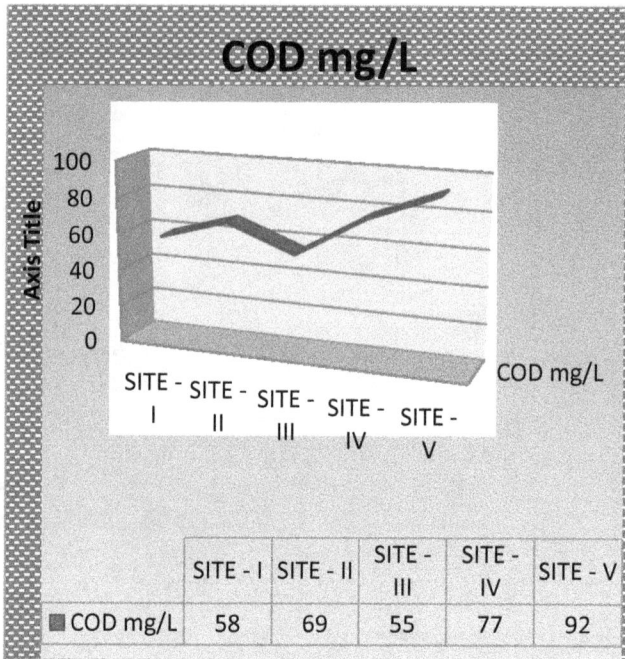

	SITE - I	SITE - II	SITE - III	SITE - IV	SITE - V
■ COD mg/L	58	69	55	77	92

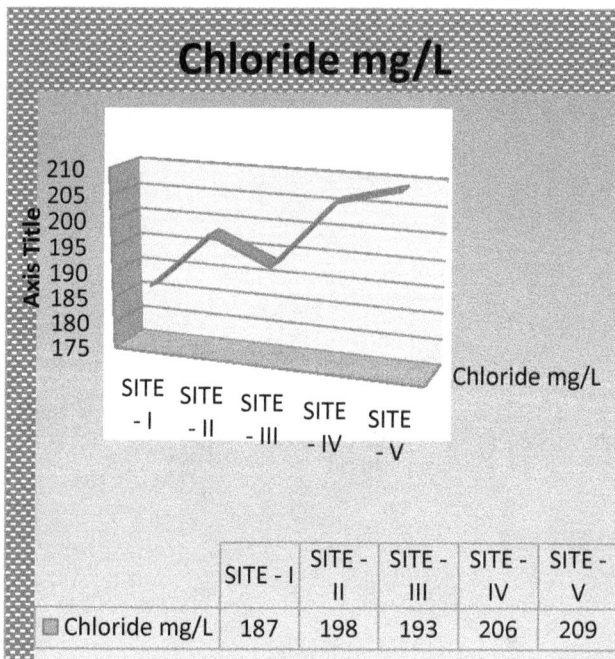

	SITE - I	SITE - II	SITE - III	SITE - IV	SITE - V
■ Chloride mg/L	187	198	193	206	209

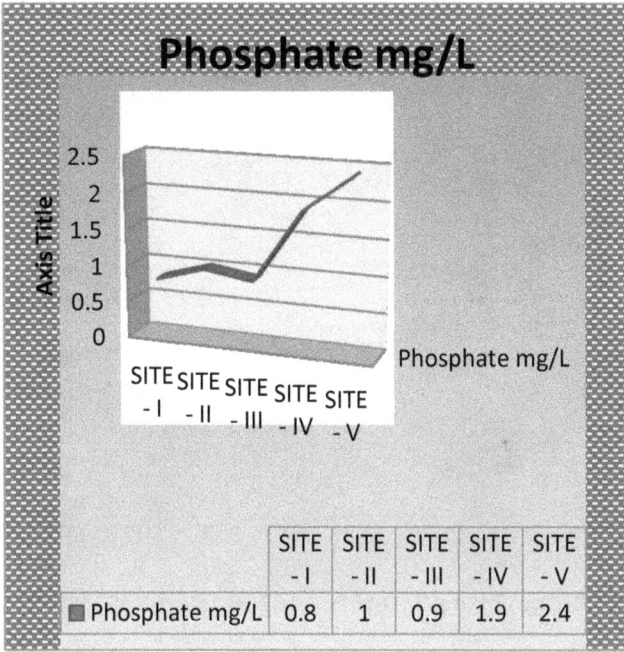

Phosphate mg/L

	SITE - I	SITE - II	SITE - III	SITE - IV	SITE - V
Phosphate mg/L	0.8	1	0.9	1.9	2.4

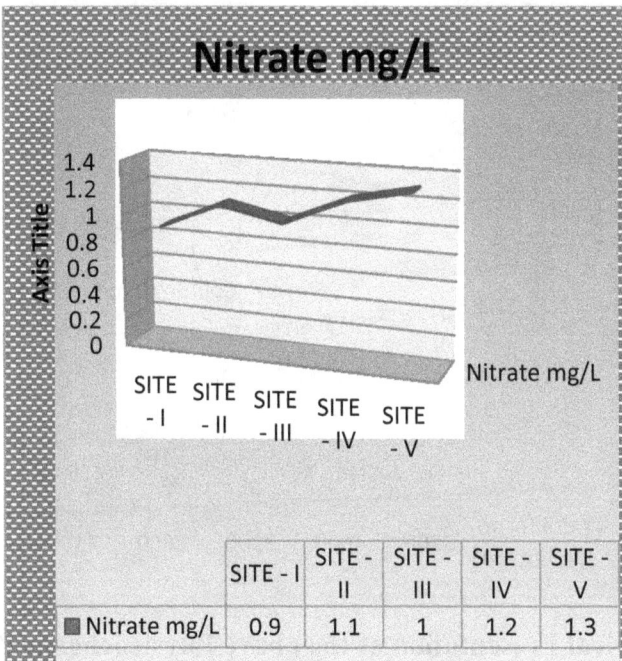

Nitrate mg/L

	SITE - I	SITE - II	SITE - III	SITE - IV	SITE - V
Nitrate mg/L	0.9	1.1	1	1.2	1.3

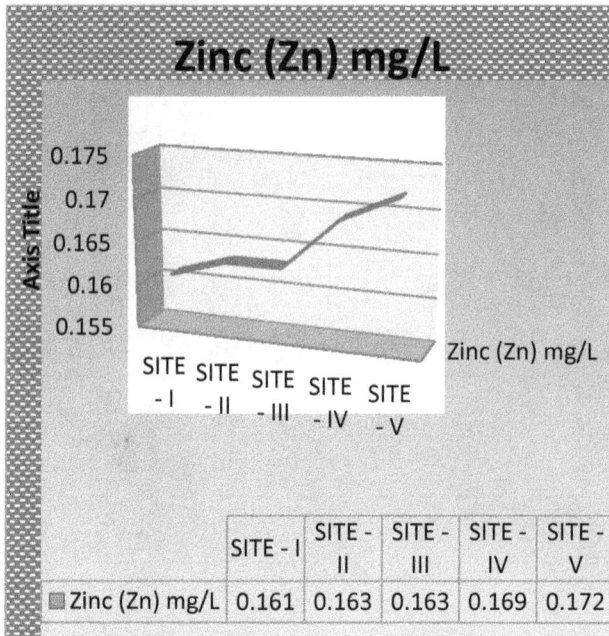

Zinc (Zn) mg/L

	SITE - I	SITE - II	SITE - III	SITE - IV	SITE - V
Zinc (Zn) mg/L	0.161	0.163	0.163	0.169	0.172

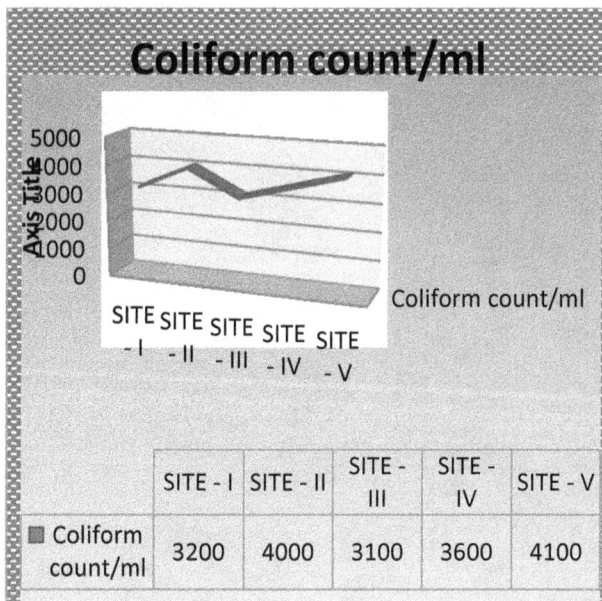

Coliform count/ml

	SITE - I	SITE - II	SITE - III	SITE - IV	SITE - V
Coliform count/ml	3200	4000	3100	3600	4100

Graphical Presentation of the above Physicochemical and Biological Parameters

Conclusion : A Study was considered for the enhancement of the Water Quality by Physicochemical and Biological Parameters Such as – pH, TDS, Alkalinity, Total hardness, DO, BOD, COD, Chloride, Phosphate, Nitrate, Zinc, Coliform, etc. All the Parameters were determined by APHA and BIS methods.

This was observed that the water quality was found to be poor during all seasons because of this water condition by human activity, and municipal and domestic sewage.

References
1. Ashutosh Malviya, S.K. Diwakar, Sunanda, O.N. Choubey, "Chemical assessment of Narmada river water at Hoshangabad city and Nemawar as the navel of the river in Central India", Oriental Journal of Chemistry, Vol. 26(1), 319-323 (2010).
2. Sharma et al. "Analysis of Water Pollution Using Different Physicochemical Parameters: A Study of Yamuna River", Frontiers in Environmental Science Volume 8, 581591 (2020).
3. Nidhi Gupta, Pankaj Pandey, Jakir Hussain, "Effect of physicochemical and biological parameters on the quality of river water of Narmada, Madhya Pradesh, India" Water Sci. Vol. 48, 13 (2017).
4. Saurabh Mishra, Amit Kumar, "Estimation of physicochemical characteristics and associated metal contamination risk in the Narmada River, India", Environ. Eng., Vol.26(1), 190521 (2021).
5. Deepak Gupta et al. "Water quality assessment of Narmada River along the different topographical regions of central India" Water Sci. Vol. 34, 202-212 (2020).
6. Nathan Rickards et al. "Understanding Future Water Challenges in a Highly Regulated Indian River Basin—Modelling the Impact of Climate Change on the Hydrology of the Upper Narmada", Water, Vol. 12, 1762 (2020).
7. Sanjeev Gour, Mamta Gour, "Study on Water quality of Narmada River by analyzing physicochemical and biological parameters using random forest model", IJCSE, Vol.7(1), 2347-2693 (2019).
8. Sabyasachi Swain, S. K. Mishra & Ashish Pandey, "A detailed assessment of meteorological drought characteristics using

simplified rainfall index over Narmada River Basin, India", Environmental Earth Sciences, Vol.80, 21 (2021).

9. Sanjeev Gour, Shailesh Jaloree and Mamta Gour, "Water Quality Assessment using Association Rule Mining for River Narmada", In. J. of sci. abd Tech., Vol. 9 ISSN 0974-6846 (2016).

10. Krishna Kumar Yadav, Neha Gupta, Vinita Kumar, Sudarshana Sharma, Sandeep Arya, "Water Quality Assessment of Pahuj River using Water Quality Index at Unnao Balaji, M.P., India", In. J. of sci.; basic and Applied Res. Ijsbar ISSN 2307- 4531 (2015).

11. Sanjay Kumar Verma, Dr Saleem Akhtar, "Assessment of Water Pollution in Lakes of JABALPUR" Int. J of Adv. Rese. In sci. Engi. And Tech. Vol. 2 ISSN: 2350- 0328 (2015).

12. Anjali Chaurasia, Ankit Kumar and Vipin Vyas, "Study on the ecological status of Chandni nalla- A tributary of River Narmada in the central zone, India" Int. J. of Rese. In Envir. Sci. and Tech. ISSN: 2249-9695 (2015).

13. Sumit Dabral, "An Integrated Geochemical and Geospatial Approach for Assessing the Potential Ground Water Recharge Zones in Mahi -Narmada Inter Stream Doab Area, Gujarat, India" J. of Envi. and Earth science Vol. 3 No 2 ISSN 2224 – 3216 (2013).

14. Soni Virendra, Khwaja Salahuddin, and Visavadia Manish, "Preimpoundmental studies on Water Quality of Narmada River of India" Int. Rese. J. of Envior. Sci. Vol 2 (6) 31-38 (2013).

15. Garg Jaya et al, Water quality management strategies for conservation of Bhopal waters. Environmental conservation Journal 2 (2 & 3) 101-104 (2001).

[1]Research Scholar,
Madhyanchal Professional University, Bhopal (M.P.)
[2]Professor of Chemistry,
Madhyanchal Professional University, Bhopal (M.P.)
[3]Professor of Chemistry,
Govt. Narmada College, Narmadapuram (M.P.)

4. Humanities : Multidisciplinary Aspects of Environmental and Sustainable Development

Dr. Baldev Raj Binawra

Abstract

The Environmental Humanities have broad implications for other fields. They provide historical perspectives on the natural and social sciences, assist in the interpretation of scientific results, clarify societal values, address ethical problems that arise with new technologies, facilitate implementation of public programs, break down barriers between the humanities and the sciences (thereby enhancing the interdisciplinarity of Swedish universities), and foster the values needed to build a sustainable society and the new habits needed for environmental citizenship.

The term "environment" gained currency in the nineteenth century2 and emerged as a focus of global concern only in recent decades. The Environmental Humanities address lacunae in the humanities, which seldom address science and technology in detail, and lacunae in environmental studies, where analysis typically emphasizes science and social science. Several fields that have contributed much to the Environmental Humanities have already begun to bridge this divide, notably cultural geography, anthropology, and the history of technology. As the humanities became democratized in the movement toward mass education, its scholars have gradually become more engaged environmental issues and research.

What are the Environmental Humanities?

The term "environment" gained currency in the nineteenth century2 and emerged as a focus of global concern only in recent decades. The Environmental Humanities address lacunae in the humanities, which seldom address science and technology in detail, and lacunae in environmental studies, where analysis typically emphasizes science and social science. Several fields that have contributed much to the Environmental Humanities have already begun to bridge this divide, notably cultural geography, anthropology, and the history of technology. As the humanities became democratized in the

31

movement toward mass education, its scholars have gradually become more engaged environmental issues and research.

It is difficult to think of a single academic discipline that has not become engaged with the Environmental Humanities. In response to a survey of the field conducted by this committee, Australian scholar Libby Robin, suggested that the phrase Environmental Humanities: "refers to the human sciences that contribute to global change which include environmental concerns such as climate change, global ocean system change, biodiversity and extinctions, and atmospheric carbon. It is an interdisciplinary area that considers the moral and ethical relations between human and non-human others (at all scales up to planetary). Because 'the environment' has been defined by biophysical indicators and studied through 'environmental sciences' (a term that dates back just 50 years) and environmental economics, the moral, political and ethical dimensions of environmental degradation were long neglected as 'outside the expertise' of the dominant discourse. Attitudes and values are not easily measured, nor do they readily yield data that can be incorporated into modeling of future scenarios." Yet environmental problems belong to us all, and the solutions will come from all fields of endeavor, including the humanities. To provide one example, Earth System Science is a dynamic research field dominated by the physical, chemical, geological, and biological sciences, but it must also include societal and human values. Great uncertainties exist in our scientific knowledge of the earth system, and there is much to be learned about clouds, the oceans, the biosphere, geochemical cycles, and other 6 processes. Human behavior is also quite varied and represents an unpredictable variable in the earth system. However, the historical dimension has not received adequate attention from the sciences, despite the fact that historians have studied both the changes in how climate change is conceptualized and the often-misguided actions that societies have taken in response. Ideas and apprehensions have been changing as much as the climate itself. Historians examine not only our conceptual shifts in understanding nature but also transformations in technological capabilities. Moreover, major paradigm shifts are not solely attributable to changes in science and technology, but often are due to social and cultural factors. One essential role for the Environmental Humanities is to identify and understand these changes, so that science has an accurate baseline against which change can be measured.

Three Salient Characteristics

Yet if the emergence of the Environmental Humanities seems inescapably rooted in the many environmental crises of the current era, this does not mean that in response a desirable configuration of institutions and talent will automatically emerge. For the Environmental Humanities have three salient characteristics that need to be considered when considering how they may develop. First, they are inherently interdisciplinary, calling upon expertise in a range of fields, including at a minimum literature, the fine arts, philosophy, history, geography, and anthropology. Not surprisingly, much of the early interesting work in the Environmental Humanities has been done in already existing interdisciplinary fields. Leading practitioners also understand the field in this way. Second, works in the Environmental Humanities often cross national and cultural boundaries. They compare different national responses to similar problems, or engage issues of international concern such as global climate change, acid rain, species extinction, disposal of nuclear waste, or water shortages. While not all studies in the Environmental Humanities are explicitly international or transnational, most are at least implicitly so. Third, its practitioners often seek to be more than observers and critics. They want to be involved, and to have a role in shaping public policy and in shaping the values and the narratives that guide decision-making.

Each of these characteristics poses some problems. Being interdisciplinary runs the risk becoming superficial. Therefore, research teams need to be balanced between the disciplines involved. Because of possible funding constraints, some important disciplinary components of a problem may be under-represented in a research group. For example, work that crosses cultural boundaries risks becoming dismissive of cultural differences. Therefore, it is important that a team have real expertise in each of the cultures involved. Second, the desire to influence public debate requires scholars to simplify complex issues for the media. This process should not be left to chance, but should be built into each project to ensure that the long-term value of the research is communicated clearly, effectively, and at the appropriate level of detail. Third, the teamwork needed in the Environmental Humanities has long been common in the sciences but it has not been a feature of the humanities, where publications and positions have been individualized. Given the multifaceted issues being addressed in the Environmental Humanities, it is necessary to engage this aspect of humanities research, in order to bring together and develop teams of scholars with knowledge of several fields, cultures, and languages and yet still respect the career trajectories of the individual scholars involved. Despite these and other challenges, however, the Environmental Humanities are expanding in almost all parts of the world, particularly in a few areas. The following chapter surveys this growth.

Major Research Centers in the Environmental Humanities

In 2013 there are dozens of university or inter-university centers and national initiatives that support transdisciplinary research in the environmental humanities. Of these a few stand out as especially important centers in Europe, North America, and Australia. They either are institutes of advanced study or they are moving toward being such institutes, with a full range of multidisciplinary faculty, regular programs of visiting scholars, graduate students, conferences, links to museums, publications, and networks of international researchers. Many receive national public funding as well as private foundation grants and therefore are expected to produce research that contributes to solving environmental challenges identified by their governments or intergovernmental organizations.

Conclusions and Recommendations

The Environmental Humanities is an emergent, interdisciplinary field at leading universities. Some excellent scholars distributed among several Swedish universities are presently engaged in the Environmental Humanities, but they do not yet constitute a strongly articulated, self-conscious group who have a primary identification with the field. In this sense, the funding challenge is fundamentally different from that of providing support for a long-established discipline, such as biology, philosophy, or physics. The need is to help a new interdisciplinary field achieve definition and recognition. Research in the Environmental Humanities has great potential for reaching a broad public audience and can participate in the vital "third mission" of Swedish academic institutions by encouraging critical discourse on environmental issues within existing public cultural institutions.

References

- Abram, David. The Spell of the Sensuous: Perception and Language in a More-than-Human World. Vintage, 1997.
- Chakrabarty, Dipesh. "The Climate of History: Four Theses," Critical Inquiry 35 (2009): 197–222. Conway, Jill Ker, Kenneth Keniston, and Leo Marx, eds. Earth, Air, Fire, Water. University of Massachusetts Press, 1999.
- Rose, DB et al. "Thinking Through the Environment, Unsettling the Humanities," Environmental Humanities 1 (2012):1–5, http://environmentalhumanities.org/archives/vol1 Sörlin, Sverker, "Environmental Humanities: Why Should Biologists Interested in the Environment Take the Humanities Seriously?" BioScience 62 (2012): 788–789.
- Haraway, Donna. The Companion Species Manifesto. Prickly Paradigm Press, 2003. Heise, Ursula. Sense of Place and Sense of Planet: The Environmental Imagination of the Global. Oxford University Press, 2008.

Assistant Professor (Education)
S.A.V. Jain Girls P.G.College
Sri Ganganagar (Raj.)

5. Promoting Sustainable Development through Environmental Policy, Green Technologies, and Effective Waste Management : A Comprehensive Review

Deepak Kumar Behera

Abstract

Sustainable development is a critical goal for the world, and it can be achieved by promoting environmentally-friendly policies, green technologies, and effective waste management practices. This article presents a comprehensive review of the literature on these topics, focusing on the importance of environmental policy and governance, green technology and sustainable development, renewable energy sources and their integration into the grid, sustainable urban planning and design, and waste management and recycling. Environmental policy and governance play a vital role in promoting sustainable development by setting standards and regulations that encourage environmental protection. It is essential to have effective policies in place that promote the adoption of environmentally-friendly practices, as well as enforceable penalties for non-compliance. Green technologies are also crucial in promoting sustainable development. These technologies are designed to reduce carbon emissions and promote the efficient use of resources, and they can be implemented in various sectors, including transport-tation, energy, and agriculture. Renewable energy sources, such as solar and wind power, are an essential component of sustainable development. Integration of renewable energy into the grid is critical, and it requires the development of smart grid technologies that can effectively manage the fluctuating nature of renewable energy sources. Sustainable urban planning and design can promote sustainable development by creating livable cities that are designed to be environmentally-friendly. This involves designing buildings that are energy-efficient, creating green spaces, promoting public transportation, and encouraging sustainable waste management practices. Effective waste management and recycling practices are essential for promoting sustainable development. Waste management policies must encourage the reduction, reuse, and recycling of waste, as well as the safe disposal of hazardous waste. Overall, this comprehensive review highlights the importance of promoting sustainable development through the implementation of environmentally-friendly policies, green technologies, and effective waste management practices. Governments, businesses, and individuals all have a role to play in achieving sustainable development, and it is essential to work together to create a sustainable future for all.

Keywords : Sustainable development, Environmental policy, Green technology, Renewable energy, Waste management, Sustainable urban planning.

Introduction

Sustainable development has become a pressing global issue as the world grapples with the interconnected challenges of climate change, environmental degradation, poverty, and inequality (UNEP, 2019). Achieving sustainable development requires a fundamental shift in the way we produce, consume, and govern our economies, societies, and environments. This requires the integration of economic, social, and environmental considerations into decision-making and action at all levels, from local to global (WCED, 1987).

Background and Significance :

The concept of sustainable development emerged in the 1970s as a response to the growing recognition of the environmental and social impacts of economic development. In 1987, the Brundtland Commission released the landmark report "Our Common Future," which defined sustainable development as "development that meets the needs of the present without compromising the ability of future generations to meet their own needs" (WCED, 1987, p. 43).

Since then, there have been significant efforts at the national and international levels to promote sustainable development through the adoption of policies and practices that prioritize the protection of the environment, the promotion of social equity, and the pursuit of economic growth. The United Nations has been at the forefront of these efforts, through initiatives such as the Sustainable

Development Goals (SDGs) and the Paris Agreement on Climate Change.

Despite these efforts, however, the challenges facing sustainable development remain significant. Climate change, biodiversity loss, pollution, and other environmental problems continue to threaten the health and well-being of people and ecosystems around the world. In addition, many people still lack access to basic services such as clean water, sanitation, and energy, while inequalities persist within and between countries.

To address these challenges, a holistic and integrated approach is needed that considers the social, economic, and environmental dimensions of sustainable development. This approach should also involve stakeholders at all levels, including governments, civil society, the private sector, and local communities.

Environmental Policy and Governance :

Effective environmental policy and governance are critical to achieving sustainable development goals. The development and implementation of sound policies, regulations, and guidelines can help to mitigate the impacts of human activities on the environment, while also promoting economic growth and social development (Baker & Schenk, 2020). Strong governance structures and institutions are also key, as they can help to ensure compliance with regulations, facilitate public participation, and promote accountability and transparency (UNEP, 2019).

Environmental policy and governance play a critical role in promoting sustainable development by providing a framework for decision-making and ensuring that environmental concerns are integrated into all aspects of policy and practice. This includes policies related to land use, biodiversity conservation, air and water quality, and climate change mitigation and adaptation.

Effective environmental policy and governance require a range of institutional and legal mechanisms, such as environmental impact assessments, regulatory frameworks, and enforcement mechanisms. They also require robust monitoring and evaluation systems to track progress and identify areas for improvement.

The role of international agreements and organizations is also crucial in promoting environmental policy and governance. The United Nations Framework Convention on Climate Change (UNFCCC), for example, has played a central role in shaping global efforts to address climate change, while the Convention on Biological Diversity (CBD) has helped to promote conservation and sustainable use of biodiversity.

Green Technology and Sustainable Development :

The development and adoption of green technologies are crucial for achieving sustainable development goals, as they can help to reduce the environmental impact of economic activities while also promoting economic growth and job creation (Preston, 2018). Examples of green technologies include renewable energy systems, sustainable agriculture practices, and eco-friendly building materials (Geng et al., 2019). These technologies can help to reduce greenhouse gas emissions, conserve natural resources, and improve the resilience of communities and ecosystems.

Green technology and innovation are essential for achieving sustainable development by promoting the efficient use of resources, reducing pollution and waste, and increasing the resilience of ecosystems and communities. This includes technologies related to renewable energy, energy efficiency, sustainable agriculture, and green infrastructure.

In addition to developing and deploying green technologies, it is also important to promote sustainable consumption and production patterns that prioritize the use of renewable and sustainable resources. This can involve initiatives such as circular economy approaches, which seek to minimize waste and maximize the value of resources through reuse, recycling, and upcycling.

Renewable Energy Sources and Their Integration into the Grid :

Renewable energy sources, such as solar, wind, and hydropower, are increasingly being recognized as key drivers of sustainable development. These sources of energy are renewable, non-polluting, and often cost-competitive with traditional fossil fuels (Baker & Schenk, 2020). The integration of renewable energy sources into the grid can help to reduce reliance on fossil fuels, improve energy security, and promote economic development (IEA, 2019). However, there are also technical and policy challenges associated with the integration of renewables into the grid, including issues related to grid stability, storage, and transmission (IEA, 2019).

Renewable energy sources such as solar, wind, hydro, and geothermal power have the potential to play a significant role in promoting sustainable development by reducing greenhouse gas emissions and increasing energy access for people around the world. However, their integration into the grid presents significant challenges related to variability, reliability, and storage.

To overcome these challenges, it is important to invest in research and development to improve the efficiency and performance of renewable energy technologies, as well as in the development of smart grid technologies and energy storage solutions. It is also important to promote policies and incentives that encourage the deployment of renewable energy technologies, such as feed-in tariffs and tax credits.

Sustainable Urban Planning and Design :

The design and planning of cities and urban areas can have a significant impact on the environment, social equity, and economic development (UN-Habitat, 2016). Sustainable urban planning and design practices can help to promote compact, mixed-use developments, public transportation, and green infrastructure, while also reducing the environmental impact of urbanization (UN-Habitat, 2016). These practices can also help to improve the quality of life for residents, promote economic development, and reduce social inequality.

Sustainable urban planning and design is a critical component of promoting sustainable development in cities and urban areas. Urbanization has led to an increase in environmental issues such as pollution, climate change, and loss of natural habitats. Sustainable urban planning and design seeks to address these issues by incorporating environmental, social, and economic considerations into the planning and design of cities and urban areas.

One of the key principles of sustainable urban planning and design is the promotion of compact, mixed-use development. This involves designing neighborhoods and cities in a way that promotes the efficient use of land and reduces the need for automobile transportation. It also includes creating a mix of residential, commercial, and public spaces to promote a sense of community and reduce the need for long-distance travel.

Another important aspect of sustainable urban planning and design is the incorporation of green spaces and natural habitats into the urban landscape. This includes the creation of parks, gardens, and other green spaces, as well as the preservation of natural habitats such as wetlands and forests. These green spaces provide a range of environmental benefits, including improving air and water quality, reducing the urban heat island effect, and supporting biodiversity.

Sustainable urban planning and design also involves the incorporation of sustainable building practices into the construction and renovation of buildings. This includes the use of energy-efficient materials and designs, the incorporation of renewable energy systems such as solar panels and wind turbines, and the promotion of water conservation practices.

Implementing sustainable urban planning and design requires a range of policy measures and partnerships between government, private sector, and community stakeholders. Some of the policies that can support sustainable urban planning and design include zoning regulations that promote compact, mixed-use development, incentives for the development of green spaces and sustainable buildings, and the establishment of public-private partnerships to fund and manage sustainable development projects.

Waste Management and Recycling :

Effective waste management and recycling practices are crucial for achieving sustainable development goals. These practices can help to reduce the environmental impact of waste disposal, conserve natural resources, and create economic opportunities (UNEP, 2019). The implementation of waste management and recycling programs requires the development of effective policies, regulations, and infrastructure, as well as public education and awareness campaigns (Geng et al., 2019).

Waste management and recycling are essential components of sustainable development. As the global population increases and the amount of waste generated per capita continues to rise, effective waste management and recycling become increasingly important. Ineffective waste management can lead to a range of negative environmental and health impacts, including air and water pollution, greenhouse gas emissions, and exposure to harmful chemicals.

One of the key strategies for effective waste management is the reduction of waste at the source. This involves minimizing the amount of waste generated through strategies such as reducing packaging, using durable goods, and promoting reusable products. The next step in the waste management process is to separate waste into different categories, such as recyclables, organic waste, and hazardous waste. This allows for more efficient processing of waste and reduces the amount of waste sent to landfills.

Recycling is an important component of waste management and involves the collection and processing of materials that would otherwise be disposed of as waste. Recycling helps to conserve natural resources, reduce energy consumption, and reduce greenhouse gas emissions. Common materials that are recycled include paper, plastics, metals, and glass. In addition to traditional recycling programs, there are also emerging technologies for recycling materials such as e-waste and construction and demolition waste.

In order to promote effective waste management and recycling, governments and organizations can implement a range of policies and programs. These can include regulations on waste disposal and recycling, financial incentives for recycling and waste reduction, and education and outreach programs to promote behavior change. Collaboration between different sectors, such as government, industry, and civil society, is also critical for effective waste management and recycling.

Discussion :

The present study aimed to provide a comprehensive review of the role of environmental policy, green technologies, and effective waste management in promoting sustainable development. The findings of the study suggest that a holistic approach is required to achieve sustainable development, which involves the integration of environmental policy, green technologies, and effective waste management.

The study found that environmental policy plays a crucial role in promoting sustainable development. Effective environmental policies such as emission reduction targets, waste management policies, and renewable energy targets can significantly contribute to achieving sustainable development. The study also highlighted the need for stringent monitoring and enforcement of environmental policies to ensure their effective implementation.

Green technologies were also found to be essential for achieving sustainable development. The use of renewable energy sources such as wind, solar, and hydropower can reduce greenhouse gas emissions and promote sustainable energy use. The study also identified other green technologies such as electric vehicles, green buildings, and sustainable agriculture, which can significantly contribute to sustainable development.

Effective waste management was identified as another critical factor in promoting sustainable development. The study highlighted the need for a circular economy approach, which involves reducing waste, reusing materials, and recycling waste. The study also emphasized the need for effective waste management policies, including waste reduction targets, extended producer responsibility, and product design for sustainability.

Conclusion :

In conclusion, the present study suggests that the integration of environmental policy, green technologies, and effective waste management is crucial for achieving sustainable development. Effective environmental policies can provide a framework for promoting sustainable development, while green technologies can significantly reduce greenhouse gas emissions and promote sustainable energy use. Effective waste management policies can also significantly contribute to sustainable development by reducing waste and promoting a circular economy approach.

Limitations :

One of the limitations of the present study is that it is based on a literature review, which may be subject to publication bias. The study also focused mainly on the role of environmental policy, green technologies, and effective waste management in promoting sustainable development and did not consider other factors such as economic and social factors.

Implications :

The findings of the study have several implications for policymakers and stakeholders. Policymakers need to prioritize the integration of environmental policy, green technologies, and effective waste management in their sustainable development strategies. Stakeholders such as businesses and consumers also need to play an active role in promoting sustainable development by adopting green technologies and effective waste management practices.

Policies :

Based on the findings of the study, policymakers need to develop and implement effective environmental policies, including emission reduction targets, waste reduction targets, and renewable energy targets. Policies such as extended producer responsibility and product design for sustainability can also significantly contribute to effective waste management.

Future Study :

Future studies can explore the economic and social factors that contribute to sustainable development. The study can also explore the role of green financing in promoting sustainable development and the potential of emerging technologies such as artificial intelligence and blockchain in promoting sustainable development.

References

Abbas, J., & Sağsan, M. (2019). Impact of knowledge management practices on green innovation and corporate sustainable development: A structural analysis. Journal of Cleaner Production, 229, 611–620. https://doi.org/10.1016/j.jclepro.2019.05.024

Abdul-Wahab, S. A. et al. (2018). Sustainable waste management in developing countries: challenges and opportunities. Obaidi, K.M. Journal of Cleaner Production, 201, 101–110. https://doi.org/10.1016/j.jclepro.2018.08.252

Aldieri, L., & Vinci, C. P. (2018). Green economy and sustainable development: The economic impact of innovation on employment. Sustainability, 10(10), 3541. https://doi.org/10.3390/su10103541

Al-Salem, S. M., Lettieri, P., & Baeyens, J. (2010). Recycling and recovery routes of plastic solid waste (PSW): A review. Waste management, 30(10), 1683-1692. https://doi.org/10.1016/j, wasman.2010.02.008

Ardila-Rey, J. A., Gonzalez-Perez, M. A., & Garcia-Serrano, L. (2019). Barriers and enablers for the implementation of circular economy practices in SMEs. Journal of Cleaner Production, 238, 117889. https://doi.org/10.1016/j.jclepro.2019.117889

Ayu, M., Gamayuni, R. R., & Urba. (2020). nski, M. The impact of environmental and social costs disclosure on financial performance mediating by earning management. Polish Journal of Management Studies, 21, 74–86.

Baker, L. A., & Schenk, T. (2020). Environmental policy and governance. In The Routledge Handbook of Environmental Policy and Politics (pp. 53-66). Routledge.

Baker, S. (2019). Sustainable urban planning: Tackling the climate crisis. Architecture & Design, 30(4), 84–87. https://doi.org/10.1080/00038628.2019.1579562

Boichenko, K. S., Tepliuk, M. A., Rekova, N. Y., Stashkevych, I. I., & Morkunas, M. (2019). Management of fluctuation ¯ of financial and economic integrated development of innovative enterprise. Financ. Credit act. Probl. Theory into Practice, 3, 2306.

Crippa, M., Oreggioni, G., Guizzardi, D., Muntean, M., Schaaf, E., Lo Vullo, E., Solazzo, E., Monforti-Ferrario, F., Olivier, J. G. J., & Vignati, E. (2019). Fossil CO2 and GHG Emissions of all World Countries; Publication Office of the European Union. Luxemburg, IA.

Denneman, A., & Kram, T. (2019). The evolution of environmental policy integration in the European Union: A comparative analysis of EPI policies in the Netherlands and Germany. Environmental

Science and Policy, 97, 25–32. https://doi.org/10.1016/j. envsci. 2019.03.017

Diaz-Sarachaga, J. M., Jato-Espino, D., & Castro-Fresno, D. (2018). Is the Sustainable Development Goals (SDG) index an adequate framework to measure the progress of the 2030 Agenda? Sustainable Development, 26(6), 663–671. https://doi.org/10.1002/sd.1735

Du, B., Liu, Q., & Li, G. (2017). Coordinating leader-follower supply chain with sustainable green technology innovation on their fairness concerns. International Journal of Environmental Research and Public Health, 14(11), 1357. https://doi.org/10.3390/ ijerph14111357

Ellen MacArthur Foundation. (2019). Completing the Picture: How the Circular Economy Tackles Climate Change. https://www.ellenmacarthurfoundation.org/assets/downloads/ce100/ Completing-The-Picture_Online_03-12-19.pdf

European Commission. (2018). A European Strategy for Plastics in a Circular Economy. https://eur-lex.europa.eu/legal-content/ EN/ TXT/PDF/?uri=CELEX:52018DC0280&from=EN

Fankhauser, S., Kazaglis, A., & Srivastav, S. (2017). Green growth opportunities for Asia. In Asian Development Bank economics working paper series No. 508. Asian Development Bank.

Fernando, Y., & Wah, W. X. (2017). The impact of eco-innovation drivers on environmental performance: Empirical results from the green technology sector in Malaysia. Sustain. Prod. Consum., 12, 27–43.

Fujii, H., & Managi, S. (2019). Decomposition analysis of sustainable green technology inventions in China. Technol. forecast. Social Change, 139, 10–16.

Geng, Y., Ren, J., & Wang, Y. (2019). Green technology and sustainable development. In Handbook of Green Development in China (pp. 7-28). Edward Elgar Publishing.

Ghisetti, C., & Quatraro, F. (2017). Green technologies and environmental productivity: A cross-sectoral analysis of direct and indirect effects in Italian regions. Ecological Economics, 132, 1–13. https://doi.org/10.1016/j.ecolecon.2016.10.003

Hambel, C., Kraft, H., & der Ploeg, R. V. (2020). Asset Pricing and decarbonization: Diversification versus climate action. In.

Economics Series Working Papers. SSRN Electronic Journal. Universitat Pompeu Fabra, 901. https://doi.org/10.2139/ ssrn. 3528239

Hao, Y., Wang, Y., Li, L., & Li, H. (2020). Environmental regulation, green technology innovation, and sustainable development: Evidence from China's manufacturing industries. Journal of Cleaner Production, 276, 123266. https://doi.org/10.1016/ j.jclepro.2020.123266

Hu, J., Wang, Z., Lian, Y., & Huang, Q. (2018). Environmental regulation, foreign direct investment and green technological progress—Evidence from Chinese manufacturing industries. International Journal of Environmental Research and Public Health, 15(2), 221. https://doi.org/10.3390/ijerph15020221

Hyung, K., & Baral, P. (2019). Use of innovative public policy instruments to establish and enhance the linkage between green technology and finance. In J. D. Sachs, W. T. Woo, N. Yoshino & F. Taghizadeh-Hesary (Eds.), Handbook of green finance: Energy security and sustainable development (pp. 1–24). Springer.

IEA. (2019). Renewables 2019: Analysis and forecast to 2024. International Energy Agency.

Intergovernmental Panel on Climate Change (IPCC). (2018). Global Warming of 1.5°C. https://www.ipcc.ch/sr15/

Intergovernmental Panel on Climate Change. (1990). Climate change: The IPCC scientific assessment. Cambridge University Press.

International Renewable Energy Agency. (2019). Global renewable energy outlook 2019. https://www.irena.org/publications/2019/Apr/ Global-Renewable-Energy-Outlook-2019

Jansen, J. L. A., and Vergragt Ph. J. (1992). Sustainable development: A challenge to technology. Proposal for the Interdepartmental Research Programme on Sustainable Technological Development.

Kaza, S., Yao, L., Bhada-Tata, P., & Van Woerden, F. (2018). What a waste 2.0: A global snapshot of solid waste management to 2050. Urban Development Series. https://openknowledge.worldbank.org/ handle/10986/30317

Khan, M. M., Khan, N. A., & Mahmood, T. (2020). A review on green technologies for sustainable urban planning and management. Journal of Cleaner Production, 256, 120390. https://doi.org/10.1016/j.jclepro.2020.120390

Koch, F., & Krellenberg, K. (2018). How to contextualize SDG. ISPRS International Journal of Geo-Information, 11? Looking at indicators for sustainable urban development in Germany, 7, 464.

Korten, D. (1993). Growth for whom? Rethinking foreign aid, development, and the meaning of human progress. World Business Academy Perspectives, 7(3), 7–18.

Kot, S., Goldbach, I. R., & Ślusarczyk, B. (2018). Supply chain management in SMES—Polish and Romanian approach. Economics and Sociology, 11(4), 142–156. https://doi.org/10.14254/2071-789X.2018/11-4/9

Kwatra, S., Kumar, A., & Sharma, P. (2020). A critical review of studies related to construction and computation of Sustainable Development Indices. Ecological Indicators, 112, 106061. https://doi.org/10.1016/j.ecolind.2019.106061

Luque-Baena, R. M., Gomez-Navarro, T., & Garcia-Sanchez, F. (2019). Renewable energy sources: A review of sustainable policies in Spain. Journal of Cleaner Production, 235, 436–448. https://doi.org/10.1016/j.jclepro.2019.06.241

Meyer, M. A. (2019). Environmental governance. The international encyclopedia of geography: People, the earth, environment and technology, 1–6. https://doi.org/10.1002/9781118786352.wbieg0328

Mirghaderi, S. H. Using an artificial neural network for estimating sustainable development goals index. Manag. Environ. (2020). Qual. International Journal, 31, 1023–1037.

Neofytou, H., Nikas, A., & Doukas, H. (2020). Sustainable energy transition readiness: A multicriteria assessment index. Renewable and Sustainable Energy Reviews, 131, 109988. https://doi.org/10.1016/j.rser.2020.109988

Podesta, J., Stern, T., & Batten, K. (2007). Capturing the energy opportunity: Creating a low-carbon economy. Part of progressive growth, CAP's economic plan for the next administration. Center for American Progress

Preston, F. (2018). Green technology and innovation for sustainable development. Routledge.

Przychodzen, W., Leyva-de la Hiz, D. I., & Przychodzen, J. (2020). First-mover advantages in green innovation—Opportunities and threats for financial performance: A longitudinal analysis. Corporate Social Responsibility and Environmental Management, 27(1), 339–357. https://doi.org/10.1002/csr.1809

Ramdhani, M. A., Aulawi, H., Ikhwana, A., & Mauluddin, Y. (2017). Model of green technology adaptation in small and medium-sized tannery industry. Journal of Engineering and Applied Sciences, 12, 954–962.

Reganold, J. P. (2000). Effects of alternative and conventional farming systems on agricultural sustainability. Washington State University Press.

Renner, M., Sweeney, S., & Kubit, J. (2008). Green jobs: Towards decent work in a sustainable, low carbon world. Worldwatch Institute.

Rosenbaum, E. (2017). Green growth-magic bullet or damp squib? Sustainability, 9(7), 1092. https://doi.org/10.3390/su9071092

Sachs, J., Schmidt-Traub, G., Kroll, C., Lafortune, G., & Fuller, G. (2019). Sustainable development report 2019. Bertelsmann Stiftung and sustainable development solutions network (SDSN); publisher. In New York, NY.

Silander, D. (2019). The European Commission and Europe 2020: Smart, sustainable and inclusive growth. In C. Karlsson, D. Silander & B. Pircher (Eds.), Smart, sustainable and inclusive growth (pp. 2–35). Edward Elgar Publishing.

Ślusarczyk, B., & Kot, S. (2018). Solution for sustainable development: Provisions limiting the consumption of disposable plastic carrier bags in Poland. Journal of Security and Sustainability Issues, 7(3), 449–458. https://doi.org/10.9770/jssi.2018.7.3(7)

UN-Habitat. (2016). Urbanization and development: Emerging futures. United Nations Human Settlements Programme.

United Nations Environment Programme (UNEP). (2019). Global Environment Outlook: Summary for Policymakers. https://www.unenvironment.org/resources/global-environment-outlook-6

United Nations. (2015). Transforming our world: The 2030 agenda for sustainable development. https://sustainabledevelopment.un.org/post2015/transformingourworld

Vargas-Hernández, J. G. (2020). Strategic transformational transition of green economy, green growth and sustainable development: An institutional approach. International Journal of Environmental Sustainability and Green Technologies, 11(1), 34–56. https://doi.org/10.4018/IJESGT.2020010103

Virto, L. R. (2018). A preliminary assessment of the indicators for Sustainable Development Goal (SDG) 14. Conserve and Sustainably Use the Oceans, Seas and Marine Resources for Sustainable Development. Mar. Policy, 98, 47–57.

Walz, R., Pfaff, M., Marscheider-Weidemann, F., & Glöser-Chahoud, S. (2017). Innovations for reaching the green sustainable development goals–where will they come from? International Economics and Economic Policy, 14(3), 449–480. https://doi.org/10.1007/s10368-017-0386-2

Wang, Y., Li, Y., Chen, X., & He, Y. (2020). A review on circular economy-oriented solid waste management in China. Resources, Conservation and Recycling, 162, 105052. https://doi.org/10.1016/j.resconrec.2020.105052

WCED. (1987). Our common future: The Brundtland report. Oxford University Press.

Wicklein, R. C. (1998). Design criteria for sustainable development in appropriate technology: Technology as if people matter. Technology in Society, 20(3), 371–375. https://doi.org/10.1016/S0160-791X(98)00022-0

World Economic Forum. (2019). The Global Risks Report 2019. https://www.weforum.org/reports/the-global-risks-report-2019

World Green Building Council. (2018). Bringing embodied carbon upfront: Tackling the embodied carbon challenge today. https://www.worldgbc.org/news-media/bringing-embodied-carbon-upfront-tackling-embodied-carbon-challenge-today

World Health Organization. (2019). Urban green spaces and health: A review of evidence. https://www.who.int/publications/ i/item/9789241515654

World Wildlife Fund. (2019). Living planet report 2018: Aiming higher. https://www.worldwildlife.org/pages/living-planet-report-2018-aiming-higher

Zhan, Y., Tan, K. H., Ji, G., Chung, L., & Chiu, A. S. F. (2018). Green and lean sustainable development path in China: Guanxi, practices and performance. Resources, Conservation and Recycling, 128, 240–249. https://doi.org/10.1016/j.resconrec.2016.02.006

Zhang, M., Duan, F., & Mao, Z. (2018). Empirical study on the sustainability of China's grain quality improvement: The role of transportation, labor, and agricultural machinery. International Journal of Environmental Research and Public Health, 15(2), 271. https://doi.org/10.3390/ijerph15020271

Zhang, Y., & Mao, G. (2020). Integrating renewable energy into the power grid in China: Status quo and future directions. Renewable and Sustainable Energy Reviews, 117, 109523. https://doi.org/10.1016/j.rser.2019.109523

Legend to Figure – 1

Fig. 1 A-F – (V-viable, NV-non-viable, PT-pollen tube, TR-trichome)

A. Viable and non-viable pollen of long stamen (FCR test). x480
B. In vitro germination of pollen of long stamen by Brewbaker & Kwack's medium. x480
C. Receptive stigma showing pollen grains outside the orific and inside the stylar canal. x230
D. Longitudinal section of hollow style showing germinating pollen. x610
E. Pollen grains with long tubes in the stylar canal. x230
F. Pollen tube penetrating the ovarian surface covered by trichomes. x230

Research Scholar,
School of Statistics,
Gangadhar Meher University, Amruta Vihar,
Sambalpur, Odisha, India
email : dkbehera4@gmail.com

6. Floral Biology and Pollen – Pistil Interaction in Popcorn Cassia *(Cassia Didymobotrya* L.)

Dr. Shashi Bala Sharma

Abstract

Floral biology and pollen-pistil interaction in *Cassia didymobotrya* (Caesalpiniaceae) was studied. Flowers open between 6.00-7.30 am and anthers dehisce between 7.00-9.00 am. There are ten stamens (two long, five medium and three small staminodes). Anthers of long and medium sized stamens dehisce through sub-terminal pores whereas staminodes are non-dehiscent and devoid of pollen grains. There are 220928 pollen/flower. Among them long stamen contributes 67268 pollen/anther whereas medium sized stamen contributes 17278 pollen/anther. Pollen grains are spherical, tricolpate tricolporate with reticulate exine exhibiting 80-98.6% pollen fertility. Pistil is single and sickle shaped. The stigma is non-papillate, dry and become receptive between 9.00-10.00 am. The receptivity is clearly marked by opening of stigma through an orific. Style is hollow up to the ovarian tissue. Pollen grains germinate in the stylar canal as well as on the ovarian surface.

Keywords : Orific, pollen germination, reproductive biology, stylar canal

Introduction

Pollen-pistil interaction is unique to flowering plants. It covers all sequential events that take place in the pistil from pollination until pollen tube entry into the embryo sac. Successful completion of pollen-pistil interaction is an essential pre-requisite for fertilization and seed-set. An understanding of the details of pollen-pistil interaction is, therefore, essential not only for the basic understanding of fertilization in flowering plants, but also in applied aspects of seed and fruit production (Shivanna, 1998).

Genus *Cassia* belongs to family Caesalpiniaceae which is represented by 152 genera and 2800 species (Kumar & Subramanian, 1987). Only 20 members of this family are found growing all over India (Duthie, 1915). Sharma & Dhakere (1995)

have reported 9 species of *Cassia* from Agra, while Bansal & Chauhan (1997 a, b) have reported 10 species of the genus. Present paper deals with the study of floral biology and pollen-pistil interaction in *Cassia didymobotrya*.

Material and Methods

Ten plants each growing at ten different localities of Agra city were marked and observations were recorded from them.

Different aspects of floral morphology and floral biology were studied by various methods given by Kearns & Inouye (1993). Pollen viability was checked by FCR test using fluorescein diacetate solution in acetone (2 mg/ ml) and in vitro pollen germination by Brewbaker & Kwack's (1963) medium. In vivo pollen germination was studied by aniline blue fluorescence microscopic method (Shivanna & Rangaswamy, 1992).

For light microscopic studies, floral buds were collected and fixed in FAA. They were dehydrated and infiltrated by customary schedule using tertiary butyl alcohol series and embedded in paraffin wax. The sections were cut, stained in Delafield's Haematoxylin.

Observations and Discussion

Cassia didymobotrya, also known as Popcorn Cassia, is an evergreen spreading shrub with compound leaves. It flowers throughout the year with optimum flowering during December-March.

Flowers are semi-open, yellow, hermaphrodite and helmet shaped arranged in spikes of axillary racemes. They are protandrous in nature. They open between 6.00-7.30 am followed by anther dehiscence taking place between 7.00-9.00 am. The stigma becomes receptive between 9.00-10.00 am. Similar observations have also been recorded by Bansal & Chauhan (1997 a, b) and Chauhan et al. (2003) in some *Cassia* species.

Flower bears ten stamens of unequal size arranged in two whorls of 5 each. Out of the 5 stamens of outer whorl, 2 are long, 1 is medium and 2 are small. However, in inner whorl 4 are medium and 1 is small. Thus, out of the total ten stamens, there are 2 long, 5 medium and 3 small stamens which are reduced to staminodes. Heterostameny in some *Cassia* species have also been recorded by

Bansal & Chauhan (1997 a, b), Chauhan et al. (2003), Sharma et al. (2005) and Marazzi et al. (2007). Anthers of both long and medium sized stamens dehisce through sub-terminal pores with a false longitudinal slit on the lateral side while staminodes fail to dehisce.

Number of pollen/flower is 220928 (187932-250624). Among them long stamen contributes 67268 pollen/anther whereas medium sized stamen contributes 17278 pollen/anther. Staminodes are sterile and devoid of pollen grains (Table 1). Pollen grains are spherical, tricolpate and tricolporate with reticulate exine. The pollen grains in long stamen are 53μm in diameter and those in medium sized stamens are 45μm in diameter. According to Nair & Sharma (1962), the size of pollen in *Cassia* species ranges between 28-55 μm.

FCR test shows 98.6% pollen viability in long (Fig. 1A) and 80% in medium sized stamens. However, in vitro germination in Brewbaker & Kwack's (1963) medium shows 98% and 82 % pollen germination with 282 and 168 μm long pollen tubes in long (Fig. 1B) and medium sized stamens respectively (Table 1).

Pistil is sickle shaped and consists of a short, curved style with an unifid, non-papillate and dry stigma. Ovary is superior and unilocular having campylotropous ovules lying on marginal placenta.

The mature pistil measures 2.7 cm in length and 2 mm in diameter (across the ovary). The ontogeny of style shows a transition from solid to hollow condition. The style is solid in early bud stages (0.9 ± 1.3 cm). There is a strand of elongated, specialized cells that constitute the "conducting tissue" or the "transmitting tissue." With age, a canal develops gradually by the dissolution of transmitting tissue, making the style hollow which continues up to the ovarian tissue.

At the time of receptivity of stigma, the transmitting tissue surrounding the hollow cavity is completely dissolved and the stylar canal is filled with a large quantity of fluid. This enforces the stigma to open through an orific. During pollination, a considerable amount of pollen grains carried by insects enter the canal fluid through orific (Fig.1 C). Pollen grains inside the canal germinate (Fig. 1D, E).

These observations are supported by those of Saradhi & Mohan Ram (1981) and Shivanna & Mohan Ram (1993) in *Cassia fistula*. There is 92% in vivo pollen germination (inside the stylar canal) with 286 μm long pollen tubes. Pollen tubes travel across the entire style and reach up to the ovarian tissue and fertilize the ovules. Another interesting observation is the presence of a large number of densely dispersed secretory trichomes on the outer surface of ovary (Fig. 1F). Numerous pollen grains are observed entangled between the trichomes. Similar features have also been observed by Sharangpani & Shirke (1996) in *Cassia occidentalis*. They germinate and pollen tubes penetrate through the ovary wall (Fig. 1F) to fertilize the ovules. Sharma et al. (2001) have also observed pollen germination on the ovary wall in *Thalaspi arvense* L., a Crucifer.

It is evident from the present investigation that the large numbers of insects carry pollen grains which are forced into the stylar canal through an orific. Inside the stylar canal, they germinate and pollen tubes reach up to the ovarian tissue and fertilize the ovules to form seeds. On the other hand, pollen grains are also seen germinating on the ovarian surface. The pollen tubes penetrate through the ovarian surface to facilitate fertilization.

References
Bansal S. & Chauhan S.V.S. (1997 a). Biodiversity in the genus *Cassia. J. Mendal,* 14, 13-14.
Bansal S. & Chauhan S.V.S. (1997 b). Reproductive biology of some *Cassia* species. *Uni. J. Res.* (Sci.), 1, 49-56.
Brewbaker J.L. & Kwack B.H. (1963). The essential role of calcium ion in pollen germination and pollen tube growth. *Am. J. Bot.,* 50, 859-865.
Chauhan S.V.S, Anuradha & Singh J. (2003). Stamen dimorphism in three *Cassia* species. *Phytomorphology.* 53, 173-178.
Duthie J. F. (1915). *Flora of Upper Gangetic Plain* (Government of India Press: Calcutta, India)

Kearns C. A. & Inouye D. W. (1993). *Technique for Pollination Biologist* (University Press of Colorado City, Niwot Co.: Colorado, USA).

Kumar V. & Subramanian B. (1987). *Chromosome Atlas of Flowering Plants of the Indian Sub Continent.* Vol. 1 (1-464), Dicotyledons; Vol. 2 (465-1095), Monocotyledons, *Bot. Surv. India* (Calcutta).

Marazzi B, Conti E.& Endress P. K. (2007). Diversity in Anthers and Stigmas in the Buzz- Pollinated Genus *Senna* (Leguminosae, Cassinae). *Int. J. Plant Sci.,* 168 (4): 371-391.

Nair P. K. & Sharma M. (1962). *Pollen grains of Indian Plants – IV. Leguminosae,* Part 1 (National Botanical Garden: Lucknow, India).

Saradhi P. P. & Mohan Ram H.Y. (1981). Some aspects of floral biology of *Cassia fistula* (The Indian Laburnum), *Curr. Sci.,* 50 802-805.

Sharangpani P. R. & Shirke D.R. (1996). Scanning Electron Microscopic Studies on Ovarian Nectaries of *Cassia occidentalis* L. *Phytomorphology,* 46 277-281.

Sharma A.K. & Dhakere J. S. (1995). *Flora of Agra District. Bot. Surv. India* (Calcutta).

Sharma S, Kaul V., Magotro R. & Koul A.K. (2001). Pollen germination on ovary wall and consequences thereof, *Curr. Sci.* 80 824-826.

Sharma S. B., Rana A. & Chauhan S.V.S. (2005). Reproductive Biology of *Cassia tora* L. *Ann. For.,* 13(63-66).

Shivanna K.R. 1998 *Pollen-Pistil Interaction and Fertilization in Plant Reproduction* pp. 93-94 (Scientific Publishers, Jodhpur).

Shivanna K.R. & Mohan Ram H.Y. (1993). Pollination biology: Contribution to fundamental and applied aspects. *Curr. Sci,* 65 (226-233).

Shivanna K.R. & Rangaswamy N.S. (1992). *Pollen Biology: A Laboratory Manual* (Narosa Publishing House: New Delhi, India).

Table 1-Number of Stamens, Size, Mode of anther Dehiscence, No. of Pollen/ Anther, No. of Pollen/Flower, Pollen

No. of Stamens	Stamen Size (Cm)	Anther Dehiscence		No. Of Pollen/ Anther	No. Of Pollen/ Flower	Pollen Viability (%)	In Vivo Pollen Germination (%)	Pollen Tube Length (μm)
		Mode	Time					
10	L – 1.2 ±	L – STP	7.00-9.00	L –67268	220928	FCR		In vitro
2 L	0.3	M – STP	am	M –17278	(187932-	L – 98.6 ±	92 ± 2.06	L – 282 ±
5M	M – 0.4 ±	S – ND			250624)	3.02		2.22
3S	0.2					M - 80 ± 3.82		M = 168 ±
	S – 0.2 ±					In vitro		1.12
	0.01					L – 98 ± 2.33		In vivo
						M – 82 ± 2.42		286 ± 2.0

L=long , M =medium, S =small, STP=sub-terminal pore, ND=non-dehiscent, ±=standard deviation

Viability and in Vivo Pollen Germination in *Cassia Didymobotrya*

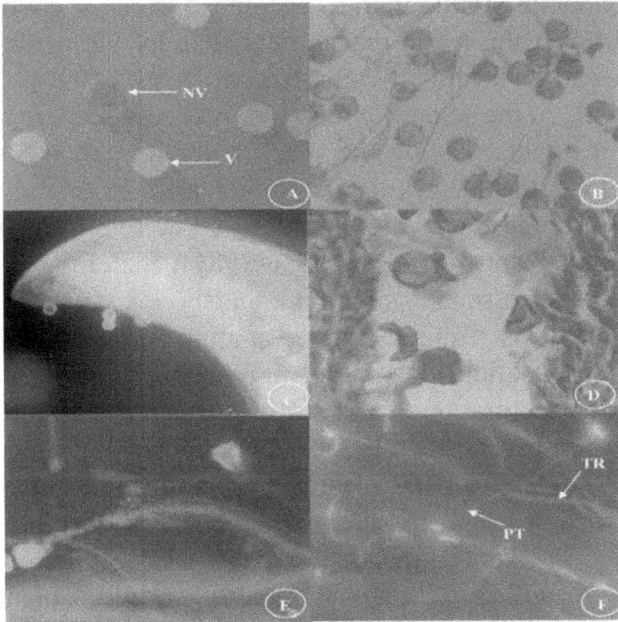

Assistant Professor
Department of Botany,
BBN College, Chakmoh, Hamirpur, (H.P.) India
e-mail: dr.vshashi@gmail.com

7. Impact of Nickel (Ni) Stress on Mustard plants

Barket Ali

Abstract

Indian mustard (*Brassica juncea*) plants exposed to 50 and 100 μM Ni stress were assessed for dry matter accumulation, chlorophyll content, net photosynthetic rate, carbonic anhydrase, nitrated reductase, and proline concentration. The metal decreased all the parameters except the proline concentration. The decrease in the parameters was proportionate to the concentration of the metal. However, the proline content increased in response to the treatment.

Introduction

The heavy metal pollution has become a serious environmental problem all over the world that inflicts huge loss in agriculture and triggers negative health effects (Naeem et al., 2020). The term "heavy metal" in the scientific literature is used to denote toxicity or pollution of a metal having the specific gravity above 5 (Li et al., 2014). Among the heavy metals Nickel (Ni) is an indispensable component of urease enzyme that plays a key role in urea/nitrogen metabolism in plants (Brown et al., 1987) Therefore, it has been designated as an essential micronutrient, the latest one included in the list of elements required in trace amount (Ali et al 2008) Plants rarely face the deficiency of this micronutrient because the seed possesses a concentration that is sufficient for the entire life span of the plant. However, its absence or deficient concentration is manifested in characteristic disorders or deficiency diseases called leaf-burn disease, leaf-tip necrosis and mouse-ear disease (Ali, 2022). Excess concentrations of Ni also inflicts different physiological and metabolic alterations such as plant growth inhibition, disturbed uptake and translocation of water and mineral nutrients, slowing of the attributes related to photosynthesis including stomatal functioning, and enzyme inhibition (Ali, 2022). Ni also generates oxidative stress and stimulates both the enzymatic and non-enzymatic antioxidant system. To cope with the stress generated by excess Ni, plants have evolved some peculiar strategies such as the prevention of influx or exclusion by the plasma membrane, chelation by phytochelatins, metalothionines and nicotinamine. The complexed Ni is subsequently compartmentalized into the vacuole. These tolerance strategies help in the accumulation of large amount Ni in plants by the process called hyperaccumulation and subsequently in the management of the Ni polluted soil (Ali et al., 2008). Present study was taken up with an objective to investigate the impact of different concentrations of Ni on some physiological attributes in mustard plants.

Materials and Methods

The seeds of mustard plants were purchased from the local market. The seeds were surface sterilised with mercuric chloride and were repeatedly washed with distilled water to remove any adhered mercuric chloride. The seeds were sown in earthen posts with soli and manure in an appropriate ratio. The pots were supplemented with 50 and 100 µM at one week stage. The pots were kept under natural conditions. The samples were collected at one month stage of growth to assess different parameters. Some plants were uprooted along with the roots and were washed with running tap water and placed in an oven dryer. These dried plants were weighed to record their dry weight. The carbonic anhydrase activity was measured by the method proposed by Dwivedi and Randhawa (1974) and nitrate reductase was assessed by the method of Jaworski (1971). However, the proline concentration was measured by the method suggested by Bates et al. (1973).

Results and Discussion

The data presented in figure 1 depicts that the exposure of the mustard plants significantly declined the plant dry weight, photosynthesis and chlorophyll concentration. The higher concentration of the metal was the most deleterious concentration that decreased these parameters by 34, 36 and 53%, respectively. The activities of the enzymes carbonic anhydrase and nitrate reductase also exhibited a decline that was proportionate to the metal concentration. The lower concentration was lesser toxic compared to the higher one. Unlike these parameters, the proline concentration in the stressed plants increased proportionate to the metal concentration. The plants subjected to the stress of the higher concentration of the metal possessed the maximum level of proline.

The deterioration in different processes depicted above is in conformity with the impact of heavy metal stress on diverse plant species. It is one of the major environmental problems that affect diverse physiological processes including mineral uptake/nutrition, water relations (Barcelo and Poschenrieder, 2002), photosynthesis, hormonal balance (Ali 2022). The altered metabolism leads to a sharp decline in the dry matter accumulation (Fig. 1A). The decrease in plant dry weight can also be attributed to the decrease in the photosynthetic rate and declined enzyme activities (Fig. 1CE). Heavy metals are known to activate the chlorophyllase enzyme that degrades the chlorophyll pigment (Abdel-Basset et al 1995) consequently leading to a decrease in the chlorophyll pigment in mustard plants (Ali 2022).

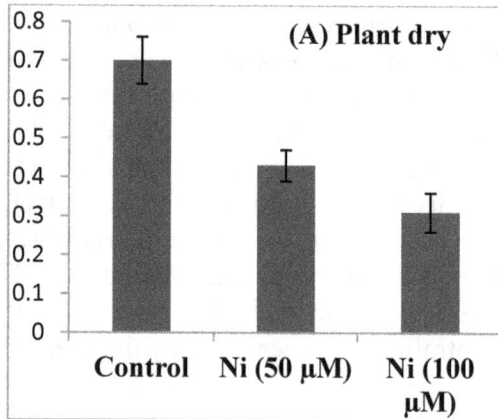

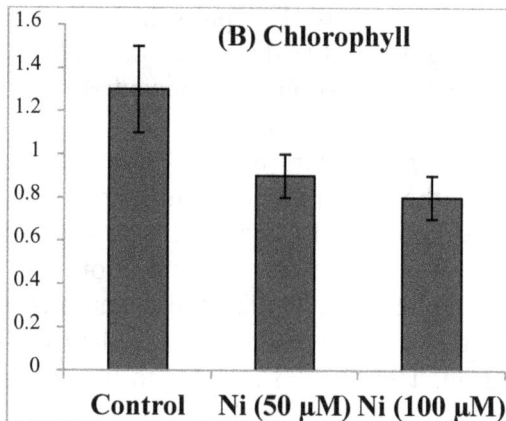

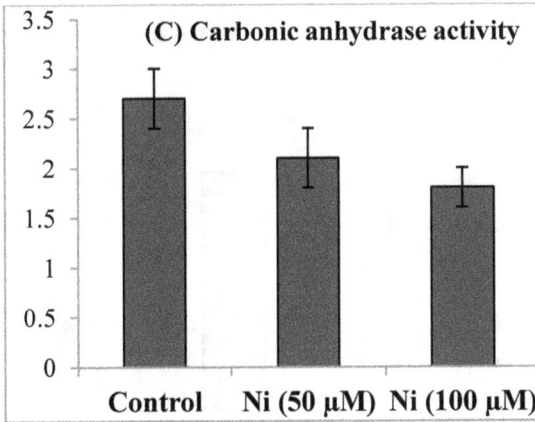

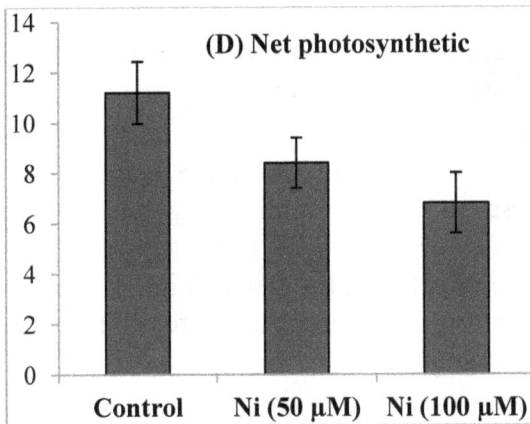

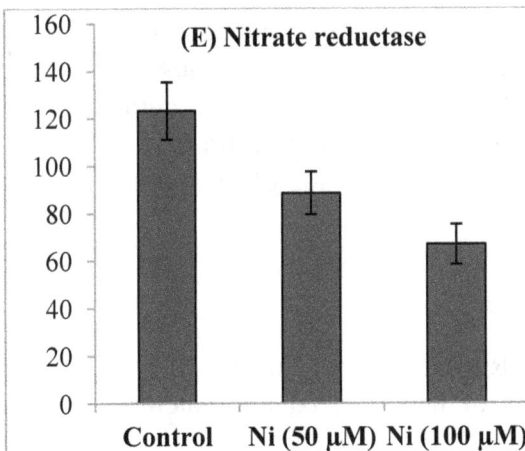

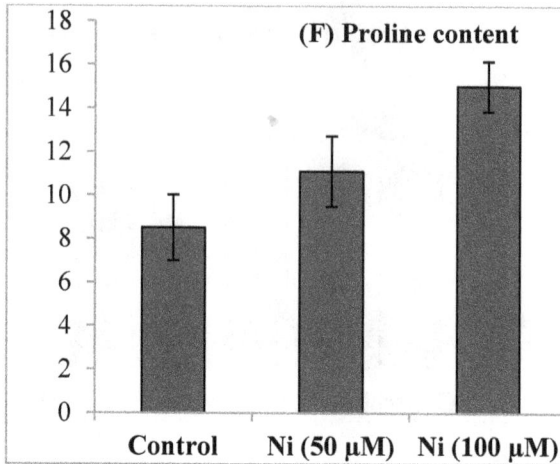

Figure 1. Impact of 50 and 100 μM of Ni on different growth and metabolic attributes in Indian mustard.

One of the most important impacts of the heavy metal stress in plants is the oxidative radicals or reactive oxygen species ROS. The toxicity of these ROS is neutralised by the involvement of the antioxidant system comprised of many enzymes and metabolites including proline (Apel and Hirt, 2004; (Fig. 1F). In conformity with this Ni stress also triggered more and more proline in mustard plants in the present investigation.

Conclusion

It is concluded from this study that Ni exerts deleterious impact on physiological and metabolic attributes in plants including chlorophyll content and enzyme activities. The altered metabolism leads to a decline in the dry matter accumulation. However, the plants respond to the stress in the form of elevated level of proline, which helps in the detoxification of the oxidative stress triggered by the metal.

References

Abdel-Basset, R., Issa, A.A., Adam, M.S. 1995. Chlorophyllase activity: effects of heavy metal and calcium. Photosynthetica 31, 421–425.

Ali, B., Hayat, S., Fariduddin, Q. Ahmad, A. 2008. Nickel: Essentiality, toxicity and tolerance in plants. In: B.Ali, S.Hayat and A.Ahmad (Eds) Nickel in relation to plants. Narosa Publishing House Pvt. Ltd., New Delhi. Pp. 70-88.

Ali, B. 2022. Physiological role, toxicity, hyperaccumulation and tolerance of nickel in plants. In: V. Kumar, A. Sharma and R. Setia (Eds.), Appraisal of Metal(oids) in the ecosystem. pp 105-133. DOI: 10.1016/B978-0-323-85621-8.00001-7

Apel, K., Hirt, H. 2004. Reactive oxygen species: metabolism, oxidative stress, and signal transduction. Annual Review of Plant Biology 55, 373–399.

Barcelo, J., Poschenrieder, C. 2002. Fast root growth responses, root exudates and internal detoxification as clues to the mechanisms of aluminium toxicity and resistance: a review. Environmental and Experimental Botany 48, 75–92.

Bates, L.S., Waldeen, R.P., Teare, I.D. 1973. Rapid determination of free proline for water stress studies. Plant and Soil 39, 205-207.

Brown, P.H., Welch, R.M., Cary, E.E. 1987. Nickel: a micronutrient essential for higher plants. Plant Physiology 85, 801–803.

Li, C., Jiang, W., Ma, N., Zhu, Y., Dong, X., Wang, D., Meng, X., Xu, Y. 2014. Bioaccumulation of cadmium by growing *Zygosaccharomyces rouxii* and *Saccharomyces cerevisiae*. Bioresource Technology 155, 116–121.

Naeem, N., Tabassum, I., Majeed, A., Khan, M.A., Shahbaz, S. 2020. Review article on phytoremediation and other remediation, technologies of soil contaminated with heavy metals. ASAG 4 (3), 01–05.

**Department of Botany,
Government Degree College Kilhotran, Doda, J&K, India
email : barketali1@gmail.com
ORCID: https://orcid.org/0000-0001-9523-5889**

8. Environment and Sustainable Development in India

Vishnu Kumar Khandelwal

Abstract

Environment is a broad concept encompassing the whole range of diverse surroundings in which one perceives experience and react to events and changes. It includes the land, water, vegetation, air and the whole gamut of the social order. It also includes the physical and ecological environment. It concerns people's ability to adapt both physically and mentally to the continuing changes in environment.

Keywords : Environment, Sustainable Development

Introduction

The concept of sustainability has been more commonly linked back to human sustainability on planet earth Since 1970s, and this has resulted in the most widely quoted definition of sustainability and sustainable development. World Commission on Environment and Development of the United Nations[1] defined sustainability development as "development that meets the needs of the present without compromising the ability of future generations to meet their own needs." The definition of sustainability development relates to three interlocking goals: environmental, economic, and social.[2]

The growth of the sustainability development concept that was integrated into various disciplines has increased significantly since 1987. This phenomenon is proven by a rise in both the number of sustainability articles and the number of dedicated engineering environmental journals.[3]

Academicians from every field are contributing their empirical research to better understand issues such as the use of materials and technologies, green engineering/manufacture, pollution control and prevention, energy management, and water research. This study attempts to provide a comprehensive assessment of environmental sustainability research based on historical analysis.It begins by reviewing the articles that similar to this document and describing the approach in comparison to previous works.

The results represent the historical trends of sustainability research particularly, in the last 24 years of sampling period, as well as the research area that different journals have focused on developing and promoting with regards to sustainability research. Finally, this paper ends with general discussion, implications for future research, and conclusions. A number of studies have used bibliographic research methods in order to analyze the growth of sustainability researches. For instance Melville and Ross[4] focused on developing a research agenda on information systems innovation for environmental sustainability. They began by summarizing the results of a literature search for environmental sustainability articles published in five information system top journals and five operations research top journals for the entire 8-year period. The potential research issues that information system scholars might analyze were derived from the results of their analysis. As a result, information scholarship is needed to contribute the body of knowledge about environmental sustainability that leads to improvement of the natural environment. In addition, Seuring and Muller[5] adopted content analysis to focus specifically on sustainable supply chain management research. They have taken a broad look at sustainable supply chain management and the issues emerging in this field. They examined 191 papers published from 1994 to 2007 and offered a literature review and a conceptual framework for sustainable supply chain management. Discussions of specific features of sustainable supply chains as well as limitations of existing research were presented to stimulate further research in this field. Rungtusanatham, et al.[6] sought to provide an assessment of 285 survey research articles from six journals in the Operation Management (OM) discipline, published between 1980 and 2000. They used a historical perspective by addressing the issues of time horizon, journal selection, article selection, coding, and analysis. In their study, they presented the analytical results of operation Management survey research growth, operation Management research focus, purpose, sampling strategies, and methodology. These results indicated that there was an increasing operation Management survey research since 1980 and their assessment could be used in the boundaries of the operation Management discipline. In this study, the fundamental objective is similar to those of previously published articles. For instance, Melville and Ross[4] adapted Coleman's model in their study and focused on five information systems top journals and five operations research top journals for the entire 8-year period. Seuring and Muller[5] used content analysis and focused on 191 papers published from 1994 to 2007. Finally, Rungtusanatham, et al.[6] used historical perspective to assess 285 articles from six journals published between 1980 and 2000, in the operation Management research area.

A historical perspective is adopted to analyze 29, 616 articles in sustainability discipline that were published in top five ISI journals. The time horizon of the assessment has expanded from 1987 to 2010. The research growth in the field of sustainability is analyzed and compared to published articles, the sustainability research category and the focus. In addition, the different contributions in the development of sustainability research are highlighted

Environment is a broad concept encompassing the whole range of diverse surroundings in which one perceives experience and react to events and changes. It includes the land, water, vegetation, air and the whole gamut of the social order. It also includes the physical and ecological environment. It concerns people's ability to adapt both physically and mentally to the continuing changes in environment. In its natural condition, the environment of any region is in a state of dynamic equilibrium. This is what is called the balance of nature. But when people try to exploit and interfere with nature, this equilibrium is disturbed, in many cases to the detriment of all forms of life. Ultimately, it is condition of land and water resources and the quality of the air, which one breathes that determine the health and wealth of a nation.

The Greek philosopher Aristotle used the spirit of sustainability in defining the term "Oikonomia" the root of the current term economics and contrasting it with an alternate form of development, 'Chrematistics'. Oikonomia is defined by Daly and Coob as "The Management of Household" so as to increase it value to all members of the household over the long run. Much as in the case of sustainable development, Oikonomia takes a long run perspective, considers the welfare of the household (or community) as a whole and recognizes the necessity of limited accumulation of suppliers if the needs of every one are to be satisfied over the flong term. Unfortunately, most of the current economic activities are far from being characterized by the oikonomia. Human kind seems to be much more fascinated by chrematistics. The manipulation of property and wealth so as to maximize short-term monetary exchange value to the owner (taken from XIth Annual International Conference of National Environmental Science Academy Proceeding 1996).

The United Nations (UN) Decade of Education for Sustainable Development (DESD) 2005-2014 states that 'Universities must function as places of research and learning for sustainable development. The government of the United Kingdom has answered in the affirmative. It's Department for Education and Skills "shares responsibility for learning about sustainable development". Sustainable development has become an important issue on international, regional and national agendas concerning, education policy over the past few years, Articulating the goals of Higher Education Radhakrishan Commission on University Education, 1948-49 put it in following words: "The most important and urgent reform needs in education is to transform it, to endeavour to relate it to the life, needs and aspirations of the people and thereby make it the powerful instrument of social, economic and cultural transformation necessary for the realization of the national goals. For this purpose, education should be developed so as to increase productivity, achieve social and national integration, accelerate the process of modernization and cultivate social, moral and spiritual values".

Methodology

This study adopted time horizon analysis as used by Rungtu - sanatham, et al.[6] There are four phases of methodology: estimation of the time, determination of the scope of the journal, article selection, and analysis. Estimation of the time—A 24-year time horizon is chose for the evaluation between 1987 and 2010.

Determination of the scope of journal—The JCR's database of the ISI is used to select the journals. Top five high impact factor

67

journals are selected from the engineering environmental category. These journals are Energy Education Science and Technology, Environmental Science and Technology, Applied Catalysis B-environmental, Water Research, International Journal of Greenhouse Gas Control. Article selection—Two criteria are applied to select articles from all potential articles published in the five journals noted above. First, the selected articles should address an issue that falls under the sustainability development research concept. Second, the selected articles should have a data collection approach.

Analysis—All articles are analyzed in order to obtain the information regarding several evaluation dimensions: research growth in sustainability and research focus in the sustainability development concept. This study engages in trend and pattern analysis in order to contribute in a greater understanding on the development and evolution of sustainability research and to identify potential areas for improvement. The analytical results are presented in the form of tables and graph

Analysis

Research Trend in Sustainability Research

The environmental sustainability articles published in the five selected journals since 1987 has been counted and they are shown in Table I.

Table I. Sustainability articles published.						
Year Journals Total						
1 2 3 4 5 by year						
1987	NA	169	NA	199	NA	368
1988	NA	218	NA	204	NA	422
1989	NA	220	NA	203	NA	423
1990	NA	260	NA	209	NA	469
1991	NA	273	NA	191	NA	464
1992	NA	341	18	198	NA	557
1993	NA	366	27	221	NA	614
1994	NA	338	31	300	NA	669
1995	NA	461	50	364	NA	875
1996	NA	489	91	387	NA	967

1997	NA	505	89	383	NA	977
1998	23	536	119	439	NA	1117
1999	25	628	92	397	NA	1142
2000	15	791	108	527	NA	1441
2001	20	691	185	534	NA	1430
2002	17	737	126	571	NA	1451
2003	24	782	243	537	NA	1586
2004	21	877	225	468	NA	1591
2005	15	1238	229	506	NA	1988
2006	11	1082	252	431	NA	1776
2007	16	1175	360	497	49	2097
2008	19	1365	358	515	56	2313
2009	25	1360	469	530	79	2463
2010	21	1390	394	498	113	2416
Total by journal	252	16292	3466	9309	297	29616

Notes: 1: Energy education science and technology; 2: Environmental science and tech- nology; 3: Applied catalysis B-environmental; 4: Water research; 5: International journal of greenhouse gas control; NA: Not available.

Table I. Sustainability articles published.

Based on the total number of environmental engineering sustainability articles year-by-year, it can infer that there has been an increase in the quantity of this research discipline since 1987. Comparing the total number of articles published in each journal, Environmental Science and Technology at 16,292 appears as the journal that published the highest number of articles in sustainability research. In the next tier, the Water Research Journal published 9,309 research articles. These two journals then become the gatekeeper of publishing articles in sustainability because they existed since 1967.

Literature Categorization of Sustainability Research

In order to analyze the primary research focus of published sustainability articles, the literature categorization of sustainability research based on reviewed articles is identified. The sustainability development research in this framework consists of three main categories. They are sustainability in the built environment, sustainability in industry and energy sustainability. These categories consist of 21 detail research focuses that can be evidenced in Figure 1.

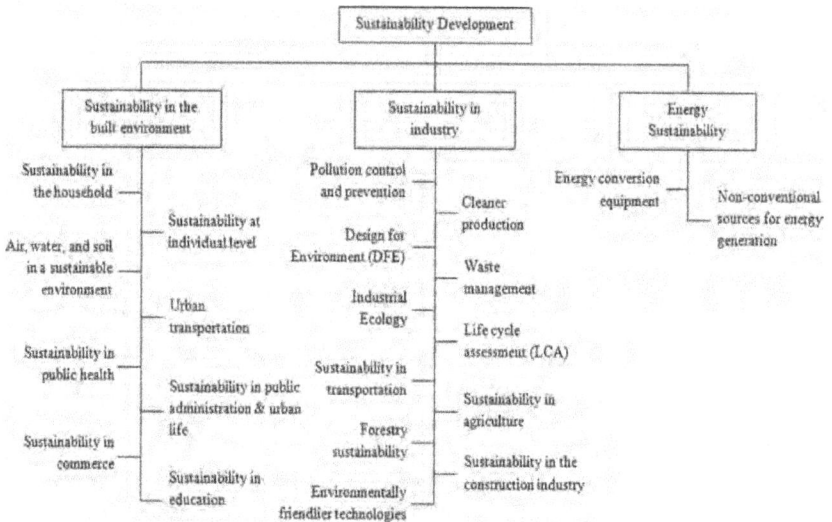

Sustainability Research Focus

The authors classified 29,616 sustainability articles into 21 detailed research focuses, where one published article can be classified into one or more research focus. For example, Wiedinmyer and Hurteau[7] assigned one to forestry sustainability and one to pollution control and prevention whereas the research article from Hu, Martinez, and Hornbuckle[8] is assigned one to water, air and soil in a sustainable environment and one to pollution control and prevention. After knowing the number of articles from each research focus, five primary research focuses with the highest number of published articles are identified. These research focuses are use of materials and technologies, green engineering/manufacture, pollution control and prevention, sustainable energy/energy management, and water research. The classification of sustainability articles by research focuses is portrayed in Table II.

Table II. Sustainability research articles by research focus.

Research focus	Sustainability articles across five journals
Use of materials and technologies (waste minimization)	46.7
Green engineering/manufacture	30.8
Pollution control and prevention	59.1
Sustainable energy/energy management	49.7
Water research	62.7
Total sustainability articles classified	249
All sustainability articles published	29616

As indicated in Table II, water research shows the highest count with 62.7 followed by, pollution control and prevention at 59.1. Green engineering/manufacture shows the lowest at 30.8. The cumulative counts of each research focus as per Table II are then plotted into a curve in Figure 2 to comparatively indicate sustainability research growth over a 24-year period.

As shown in Figure 2, the sustainability research focused constantly on water research growth. This is in contrast to pollution control and prevention. The growth of this research focus was faster than water research especially, in 2000 to 2003 showing the steepest sloped curve that serves as an indication of the quick growth of publications. Green engineering/manufacture showed the smallest slope, indicating a deteriorating growth of publications.

Discussion

This study takes a more comprehensive assessment in sustain- ability survey research although, there have been other articles published with a similar objective. About 29,616 survey articles that have impact factor journals of more than four in sustain- ability, spanning a 24-year time period from 1987 to 2001 has been evaluated. The authors believed that this working paper is necessary for a historical overview of sustainability research and to direct future sustainability research.

The results of analysis depicted in Table I show that the total number of articles from all of the journals consistently increases over the years. This indicates the expeditious growth of   sustainability research published across a 24-year time span. With regards to the research focus, Environmental Science and Technology and Applied Catalysis B-environmental have more   varieties of research focus whereas Energy Education Science and Technology, Water Research and the International Journal of Greenhouse Gas Control is more specifically focused on one area of research. The authors firmly believe that these results can direct researchers for selecting and evaluating their citation in thejournals.

This study proposed a literature categorization that could be helpful to researchers in categorizing their citation based on research focus. The three main categories, including sustain- ability in the built environment, sustainability in industry, and energy sustainability, consist of several research focuses deter- mined based on articles reviewed. The conclusion from these results is that over the years, the majority of sustainability articles are largely focused on water research/pollution control and prevention. The least number of researches focused on green engineering/manufacture. In spite of the fact that this research focus has a limited amount of published articles, the trend of the sustainability research continues to be on the rise.

Furthermore, as given in Figure 2, research in pollution control and prevention grows faster than water research, especially between the years 2000 to 2003. In contrast, research focused on green engineering/manufacture has indolent growth. Indeed, water research as well as pollution control and prevention as a research focus has been the most dominant throughout the history of sustainability research. Hopefully the research topic of green engineering/manufacture will increase considering the important role of industries especially, manufacturers, to apply sustainability concept for designing and producing their products including the integration between sustainability and supply chain management perspective.

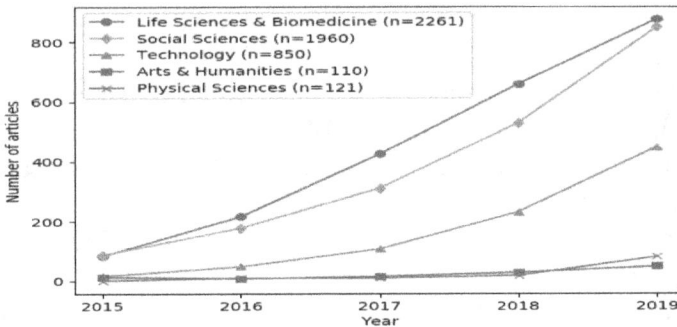

FIG. 2. TOTAL NUMBER OF SUSTAINABILITY ARTICLES BY FIVE PRIMARY RESEARCH FOCUSES OVER THE YEAR

Conclusion

Over the past couple of decades, the research in sustainability has progressed significantly. It has been proven in Figure 2, which shows the total number of sustainability articles since 1989 until 2010. In addition, the sustainability research focused constantly on water research; however, the growth of research focus on green engineering/manufacture is slow.

Therefore, there is a need for academic researchers to focus their study more on green engineering/manufacture as this area has significant impaction sustainable development. Survey research in sustainability is able to furnish a deeper understand- ing about the core issues and problems that researchers face. The authors believe that this study can direct researchers in selecting their research focus because the results in this study show actual information about the growth of sustainability research. Be that as it may, the authors acknowledge that opportunities for improvements still exist in order to encourage this study to advance into a greater arena of acceptance in sustainability research.

References

G. H. Brundtland, World commission on environment and development, Our Common Future, Oxford University Press, UK **(1987)**.

M. Redclift, Sustainable development and global environmental change: Impli- cations of a changing agenda, Global Environmental Change, 2, 32 **(1992)**.

A. G. Chofreh, F. A. Goni, A. M. Shaharoun, S. Ismail, and J. J. Klemeš, J. Clean. Prod. 71, 139 **(2014)**.

S. Paramanathan, C. Farrukh, R. Phaal, and D. Probert, Research and Devel- opment Management 34, 527 **(2004)**.

J. Pitt and F. Lubben, Int. J. Technol. Des. Ed. 19, 167 **(2009)**.

J. Elkington, Cannibals with Forks: The Triple Bottom Line of Twenty First Century Business, Oxford, Capstone Publishing, UK **(1997)**.

N. P. Melville and S. M. Ross, MIS Quarterly 34, 1 **(2010)**

S. Seuring and M. Müller, J. Clean. Prod. 16, 1699 **(2008)**.

M. J. Rungtusanatham, T. Y. Choi, D. G. Hollingworth, Z. Wu, and C. Forza, J. Oper. Manag. 21, 427 **(2003)**.

C. Wiedinmyer and M. D. Hurteau, Envir. Sci. Technol. 44, 1926 **(2010)**.

D. Hu, A. Martinez, A., and K. C. Hornbuckle, Envir. Sci. Technol. 42, 7873 **(2008)**.

Department of Chemistry
JECRC University Jaipur (Rajasthan) India
email : vishnukumar.khandelwal@jecrcu.edu.in

9. India's Progress towards Achieving Global Goals on Family Planning

Ms. Margi K. Joshi[1]
Dr. Sushman Sharma[2]

Abstract

Population explosion is a major threat to human existence and resources. Unintended and unwanted pregnancies can lead to abortion, an adverse impact on maternal reproductive health. To combat these consequences we need to accept various contraceptives and reduce the risk of unintended pregnancies. Delay the first, Postpone the second and prevent the third use this formula for the reduction of high decadal growth. The government of India also started various programs to achieve the global target of Family Planning like the National Family Planning Program, Mission Parivar Vikas, and National Family Health Survey (NFHS). To achieve target 2030 Sustainable Development Goals there is a requirement for support from end users.

Keywords : Contraceptives, SDGs, NFHS, Unintended Pregnancy

Introduction

The greatest threat to human existence is our lack of ability to control our growth this will also be burdened on resources with high decadal growth. The single most important recognized impediment to national development is uncontrolled population growth, which is the single greatest threat to the country's Economic, Social, and Political Development. India was the first country in the world which had implemented a national population control program in 1952 to reduce the birth rate to stabilize the population but still cannot control population growth to the desired level. Many efforts and resources have gone into the program but still desired results we cannot get(Ministry of Health & Family Welfare, 2016).

The challenges now have extended beyond population stabilization to addressing sustainable development goals for maternal and child health. As maternal mortality in India is very high, the focus of the national family program has shifted from population control to saving lives and improving the health of mothers and children. Now importance is also given to the use of various reversible spacing methods thus reducing unwanted, closely spaced, and mistimed pregnancies.

Objectives Method and Material of the Study

- To study the global target to reduce the burden of population explosion.
- To study various government programs regarding family planning in India.
- Secondary data was collected for this paper from the web, guidelines of health and family welfare, the press information bureau, the national family health survey, United Nations SDGs.

World's Population – Current Scenario :

The world is going through a period of unprecedentedly rapid demographic change. The current world's population is 7.9 billion, which is a most obvious example of this change as a result of a huge expansion of human numbers(*World Population Clock: 7.9 Billion People (2022) - Worldometer*, n.d.). According to United Nations (UN), a report launched in 2017, by 2030 - 8.5 billion, by 2050 – 9.7 billion, and by 2100 – 11.2 billion. Every year people have added to the world's population showing an upward trend in size which assumes that the fertility level will decline continuously(*World Population Prospects: The 2017 Revision | Multimedia Library - United Nations Department of Economic and Social Affairs*, n.d.).

The gap in population between India and China is narrowing down year by year as it was 238 million in 2001 and nearly 131 million in 2011. While the gap in population between India and the USA, the world's third populous country widened day by day as it was around 742 million in 2001, and in 2011 it was 902 million(Government of India. Ministry of Home Affairs, 2011).

Fertility Trends in India :

Fertility is meant the actual bearing of children. Natality word preferred by some demographers instead of fertility. From 15 to 45 years (~ 30 years period) is the reproductive period of a woman where she married at 15 years and expected risk of pregnancy till 45 years during her married life. During this period 15 children might be given birth by her which is rarely achieved. Fertility depends upon several factors. The higher fertility in India is attributed to the universality of marriage, lower age at marriage, low level of literacy, poor level of living, limited use of contraceptives, and traditional ways of life(Park, 2019).

Research indicates that the level of fertility in India is beginning to decline. The crude birth rate which was about 49 per thousand population during 1901 – 11 declined to about 25.0 per thousand population in 2002 and was 20.4 per thousand population in 2016 and 19.7 per thousand population as per Sample Registration System (SRS) report 2019. The rural-urban differential has narrowed. However, in the last 3 decades, rural areas witnessing a continuous rise in crude birth rate compared to urban areas. The total fertility rate (TFR) has declined from 3.6 in 1991 to 2.1 in 2019(*India - SAMPLE REGISTRATION SYSTEM (SRS)-STATISTICAL REPORT 2019*, n.d.).

Family planning refers to the planning of the timing of birth, the number of children, and a healthy spacing between consecutive births with the help of contraceptive methods. With 31% of unintended pregnancies, family planning is a matter of prior consideration.

The international conference on population and development (IPCD) defined voluntary family planning services as a fundamental human right as well as a couples' right.

The report of the Economic and Social Council, under resolution 1975, UN seminar on 'Status of Women and Family Planning says that, " the term family planning is difficult to define precisely, especially because the phrase means very difficult things to different people depending upon their social or political perspectives."

Women with unmet needs are those who are fecund and sexually active but are not using any method of contraception, and report not wanting any children or wanting to delay the next child. The concept of unmet need points to the gap between women's reproductive intentions and their contraceptive behavior(*Unmet Need for Family Planning (%)*, n.d.). It applies only to married women and indicates those women who say they prefer to avoid a pregnancy but are not using any methods of contraception. The most common reason for the unmet need for family planning is inconvenient and unsatisfactory services, lack of information, fears about the side effects of contraceptives, and opposition from husband or relatives(Park, 2019).

In India total unmet need for family planning was 9.4% in NFHS – 5 (2019 – 2021) which decreased from 12.9% in NFHS – 4 (2015 – 2016). Which were 8.4% for urban areas and 9.9% for rural areas as per NFHS – 5 (2019 – 2021). The unmet need for spacing was 4% in NFHS – 5 (2019 – 2021) which was lower and also decreased from 5.7% in NFHS – 4 (2015-2016). Which were 3.6% for urban areas and 4.3% for rural areas as per NFHS – 5 (2019 – 2021)(IIPS & ICF, 2016).

Unintended pregnancies consist of unplanned births, induced abortions, and miscarriages resulting from unintended pregnancies each year one-third of unintended pregnancies resulted from failure or improper use of contraceptives. In developing countries, major roadblocks were a lack of knowledge of contraceptive methods, source of supply, cost, or poor accessibility(Gothwal et al., 2020). Each year, approximately 85 million women in the world face an unintended pregnancy among them one in seven cases evident from India(Gilda Sedgh, Susheela Singh, n.d.)(Dehingia et al., 2020). From global evidence, These can lead to the risk of maternal morbidity and mortality. It is associated with poorer infant health outcomes and lower maternal healthcare utilization which is indicated by studies in India(*UNFPA India | State of the World Population Report 2022: Seeing the Unseen*, n.d.).

Unplanned or unintended pregnancies are causing major health hazards in young adults. As the age of menarche is decreasing more girls are exposed to unplanned and unprotected sexual intercourse. This is increasing the number of unwanted pregnancies and unsafe abortions. Again, abortion outside the medical setup leads to very dangerous consequences of unwanted pregnancy(Barman et al., n.d.).

Family Planning Program In India :

In 1952, a national family planning program was launched by India in the world. Over the decades, these have transformed in terms of policy and actual program implementation and are currently being repositioned to not only achieve population stabilization goals but also promote reproductive health and reduce maternal, infant, and child mortality and morbidity(*Family Planning :: National Health Mission*, n.d.)'(D. of H. & F. Welfare, n.d.)'(F. Welfare, 2021).

Over the years, the program has been expanded to reach every nook and corner of the country and has penetrated Public Health Centres (PHCs) and Sub Centres (SCs) in rural areas, Urban Family Welfare Centres in urban areas. Technological advances, improved quality, and coverage for health care have resulted in a fall in the total fertility rate and growth rate (the 2011 Census showed the steepest decline in the decadal growth rate)(F. Welfare, 2021).

In FY 2019-20, 19.53 lakh doses of Injectable MPA (Medroxypro-gesterone acetate) had been administered and 34.50 lakh Centchroman tablets had been distributed all over the country. In FY 2020-2021 (up to December 2020), 9.97 lakh doses of injectable contraceptives and 32.31 lakh Centchroman tablets were distributed. All over India, 15,435 Medical, and 44,409 Nursing Personnel (Staff Nurses/LHV/ANM) have received training on Injectable contraceptives(F. Welfare, 2021).

Mission Parivar Vikas (MPV) was launched in 2016 to substantially increase access to contraceptives and family planning services in 146 high-fertility districts of seven high-focus states (Uttar Pradesh, Bihar, Rajasthan, Madhya Pradesh, Chhattisgarh, Jharkhand, and Assam) having TFR of 3 and above(D. of H. & F. Welfare, n.d.)'(F. Welfare, 2021).

Millennium Development Goals to Sustainable Development Goals (MDGS TO SDGs) - MDG 5 is related to Improve Maternal health Universal access to reproductive health, including family planning, is designated in MDG 5B. Also, if a woman seeks to terminate an unintended pregnancy, the risks associated with unsafe abortion are among the main causes of maternal death, especially in young women. If she wishes to continue the pregnancy, in low-resource settings without safe delivery services, the risks of maternal mortality and serious complications are also high. After the success of MDGs, the world accepted 17 SDGs among them SDG 3 is related to ensuring healthy lives and promoting well-being for all at all ages. Target 3.7 indicate ensuring universal access to sexual and reproductive healthcare services, including family planning, information and education, and the integration of reproductive health into national strategies and programs by 2030. SDG indicator 3.7.1 is related to the " use of contraceptives" which is translated as the percentage of married women ages 15-49 years whose need for family planning is satisfied with modern methods of contraception. It will be helpful for coverage of family planning programs and services, access, and use of contraceptives(*SDG Indicator 3.7.1 on Contraceptive Use | Population Division*, n.d.)'(*#Envision2030 Goal 3: Good Health and Well-Being | United Nations Enable*, n.d.).

Recently at International Conference on Family Planning India was the only country in the country category that wins the **"Excellence in Leadership in Family Planning (EXCELL) Awards" – 2022.** This award applauds and recognizes India's achievements in ensuring access and adoption of modern contraceptive methods and continuously reducing unmet needs for family planning according to NFHS – 5 data stated by the ministry of health and family welfare(*India: India Wins Excellence in Leadership in Family Planning Awards, Health News, ET HealthWorld*, n.d.).

Current Use of Family Planning Methods (currently married women aged 15–49 years) in India(*National Family Health Survey (NFHS-5)*, n.d.)'(IIPS & ICF, 2016).

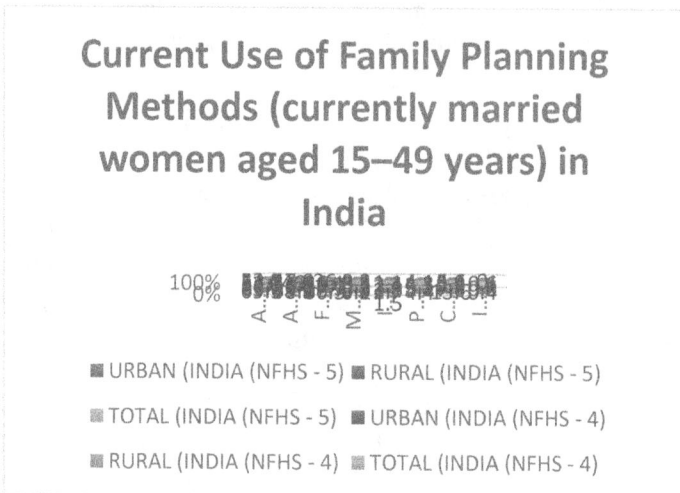

Current Use of Family Planning Methods (currently married women aged 15–49 years) in India

100%
0%

■ URBAN (INDIA (NFHS - 5) ■ RURAL (INDIA (NFHS - 5)
■ TOTAL (INDIA (NFHS - 5) ■ URBAN (INDIA (NFHS - 4)
■ RURAL (INDIA (NFHS - 4) ■ TOTAL (INDIA (NFHS - 4)

Note: Any method and Any modern method include other methods that are not shown separately.

Challenges

Although various contraceptives are available at public hospitals, and sub-centers, there is a lack of awareness regarding the same in most of the population. Many women were not aware of how and where to purchase. This is also because of inconvenient and unsatisfactory services, lack of information, fears about the side effects of contraceptives, and opposition from husbands or relatives, preference for a male child, religious beliefs.

Conclusion

Despite having the services available in India, there is a requirement for public awareness of the use of contraceptives for, reduction in unprotected intercourse and unintended pregnancies. For the same, we need to increase the use of Information and communication technology, Delay the first, Postpone the second and prevent the third child formula else very soon India will surpass china in the population.

References

#Envision2030 Goal 3: Good Health and Well-being | United Nations Enable. (n.d.). Retrieved December 3, 2022, from https://www.un.org/development/desa/disabilities/envision2030-goal3.html

Barman, K., Roy, M., Choudhary, S., & Naznin, W. (n.d.). *Knowledge, attitude and practices of contraception among the married women of reproductive age Distributed under Attribution-Non Commercial-Share Alike 4.0 International (CC BY-NC-SA 4.0).* https://doi.org/10.21276/obgyn.2021.7.2.22

Dehingia, N., Dixit, A., Atmavilas, Y., Chandurkar, D., Singh, K., Silverman, J., & Raj, A. (2020). Unintended pregnancy and maternal health complications: Cross-sectional analysis of data from rural Uttar Pradesh, India. *BMC Pregnancy and Childbirth, 20*(1), 1–11. https://doi.org/10.1186/S12884-020-2848-8/TABLES/3

Family Planning :: National Health Mission. (n.d.). Retrieved May 17, 2022, from https://nhm.gov.in/index1.php?lang=1&level=2&sublinkid=821&lid=222

Gilda Sedgh, Susheela Singh, and R. H. (n.d.). *Intended and Unintended Pregnancies Worldwide in 2012 and Recent Trends | Enhanced Reader.* Retrieved May 17, 2022, from https://pubmed.ncbi.nlm.nih.gov/25207494/

Gothwal, M., Tak, A., Aggarwal, L., Rathore, A. S., Singh, P., Yadav, G., & Sharma, C. (2020). A study of knowledge, attitude, and practice of contraception among nursing staff in All India Institute of Medical Sciences, Jodhpur, Rajasthan. *Journal of Family Medicine and Primary Care, 9*(2), 706. https://doi.org/10.4103/ JFMPC.JFMPC_1012_19

Government of India. Ministry of Home Affairs. (2011). Size, Growth Rate and Distribution of Population. *Chemistry &,* 35– 60. http://www.censusindia.gov.in/2011-prov-results/data_files/ india/Final PPT 2011chapter7.pdf%5Cnhttp://www.censusindia.gov.in/2011-prov-results/data_files/india/Final PPT 2011_chapter3.pdf

IIPS, & ICF. (2016). *National Family Health Survey - 4 201-21 (India fact).* http://rchiips.org/nfhs/pdf/NFHS4/India.pdf

India: India wins excellence in leadership in family planning awards, Health News, ET HealthWorld. (n.d.). Retrieved December 3, 2022, from https://health.economictimes.indiatimes.com/ news/policy/india-wins-excellence-in-leadership-in-family-planning-awards/95603204

India - Sample Registration System (Srs)-Statistical Report 2019. (n.d.). Retrieved May 31, 2022, from https://censusindia.gov.in nada/index.php/catalog/40526

Ministry of Health & Family Welfare. (2016). *Reference Manual For Injectable Contraceptive (DMPA). March.* https://nhm.gov.in/ images/pdf/programmes/family-planing/guidelines/ Reference_Manual_Injectable_ Contraceptives. pdf

National Family Health Survey (NFHS-5). (n.d.). Retrieved January 8, 2022, from http://rchiips.org/nfhs/factsheet_NFHS-5.shtml

Park, K. (2019). *Park's Textbook of Preventive and Social Medicine M/S Banarsidass Bhanot Publishers Edition* (26th ed.).

SDG Indicator 3.7.1 on Contraceptive Use | Population Division. (n.d.). Retrieved December 3, 2022, from https://www.un.org/development/desa/pd/data/sdg-indicator-371-

contraceptive-use

UNFPA India | State of the World Population Report 2022: Seeing the unseen. (n.d.). Retrieved November 29, 2022, from https://india.unfpa.org/en/seeing-unseen

Unmet need for family planning (%). (n.d.). Retrieved January 8, 2022, from https://www.who.int/data/gho/indicator-metadata-registry/imr-details/3414

Welfare, D. of H. & F. (n.d.). *National Programme for Family Planning | National Health Portal Of India.* Ministry of Health & Family Welfare, Government of India of Health & Family Welfare. Retrieved June 15, 2022, from https://www.nhp.gov.in/national-programme-for-family-planning_pg

Welfare, F. (2021). Annual Report MoHFW 2020-21 English. *MoHFW.*

World Population Clock: 7.9 Billion People (2022) - Worldometer. (n.d.). Retrieved May 27, 2022, from https://www.worldometers.info/world-population/

World Population Prospects: The 2017 Revision | Multimedia Library - United Nations Department of Economic and Social Affairs. (n.d.). Retrieved January 8, 2022, from https://www.un.org/development/desa/publications/world-population-prospects-the-2017-revision.html

[1]**Research Scholar,**
Department Of Hospital Management, Hngu, Patan
email : margijoshi153@gmail.com
[2]**Assistant Professor,**
Department of Hospital Management, Hngu, Patan
email : godiihmr@gmail.com

10. वेदों में सूर्यरश्मि–चिकित्सा : एक पर्यावरणीय अध्ययन

डॉ. मधु बाला मीना

**प्राची के भाल पर, तुम्हारा चमकता कितना मोहक है।
ओ आदि प्राण! जीवित अतून
जब तुम पूर्वीय आकाश में उदित होते हो,
समग्र विश्व सौन्दर्य से उद्भसित हो उठना है।
तुम सुन्दर तथा महान हो, भास्वान् हो,
और हो, समग्र पृथ्वी से ऊपर, तुम्हारी यह सम्पूर्ण सृष्टि,
तुम्हारी ही प्रभा से परिव्याप्त है।**

मिस्र के सम्राट अखनातून की (1375–1358 ई.पू.) की है यह सूर्य स्तुति। सूर्य है उष्मा एवं शक्ति का अजस्र स्रोत, उसके बिना 'संसार' की कल्पना भी नहीं की जा सकती है। प्रातः प्राची में उदित होता हुआ, अन्धकार को चीरता हुआ, विश्व के कण–कण को प्रकाशित करता हुआ, शीत को भगाता हुआ सूर्य मानव के दृष्टिपथ में सर्वप्रथम आया होगा। उसके प्रकाश व उष्मा ने मानव–मन को प्रभावित किया होगा, सम्भवतः सूर्य के प्रति इसी सम्मान तथा कुछ–कुछ भय की भावना के कारण भिन्न–भिन्न रूपों में सूर्य की स्तुति एवं प्रशंसा की गई होगी। यही कारण है कि सूर्योपासना प्रत्येक प्राचीन धर्म एवं संस्कृति का भाग है, चाहे वह मिस्र हो, ग्रीक हो, रोमन सभ्यता हो, ईरानी हो या भारतीय सभ्यता।[1] भारत में प्राचीन काल से सूर्योपासना किसी न किसी रूप में प्रचलित रही है।

वैदिक वाङ्मय हमारी सभ्यता, संस्कृति, धर्म, दर्शन, कला, स्थापत्य आदि से सम्बद्ध तत्वों को अपने दामन में समेटे हुए हैं। वेदों में मानव जीवन के वे समस्त पक्ष समाहित हैं जो जीवनचर्या के आधारभूत तत्व हैं। वेद के मन्त्रद्रष्टा ऋषि जीवन के प्रति आस्थावान रहे हैं। वैदिक उपदेश समाज का सुख–शान्ति, उत्साहयुक्त और प्रसन्नतापूर्वक जीवन जीने के लिए उत्प्रेरित करते हैं और प्रसन्नता के साथ चरम उन्नति को प्राप्त करना ही मनुष्य का ध्येय रहा है। इसी ध्येय की पूर्णता के लिए ऋषियों में उदीयमान सूर्य की स्तुतियाँ उपदिष्ट की हैं। संस्कृत साहित्य के प्रसिद्ध आख्यान के अनुसार "मयूर भट्ट" ने भी सूर्य की उपासना से कुष्ठ रोग से निवृत्ति प्राप्त की थी। प्रस्तुत उदाहरण आचार्य मम्मट ने काव्य प्रकाश में काव्य प्रयोजन को स्पष्ट करने के सम्बन्ध में कहा–

---

[1] वेदों में पर्यावरण संरक्षण, डॉ. प्रवेश सक्सेना, प्रथम संस्करण 2004, पृ.सं. 177

'आदित्यादेर्मयूरादीनामिव अनर्थनिवारणम्'[2]

वेदों में सूर्य को समस्त जड़ चेतन प्रकृति की आत्मा कहा है, सूर्य शब्द का अर्थ है–उत्पन्न करने वाला। सूर्य सर्वाधिक प्रत्यक्ष देवता है, भौतिक सूर्य के साथ इनका घनिष्ठ सम्बन्ध है। आकाश में सूर्य प्रकाशमान होकर अग्नि के मुख हैं, सूर्य दूरद्रष्टा, सर्वद्रष्टा और सम्पूर्ण पृथ्वी–मण्डल के सर्वेक्षक हैं। सूर्य के रथ में सप्त घोड़े हैं जो इनके रथ को खीचतें हैं, सूर्य के रथ को वरुण देवता ने किया है। सूर्य का रक्त वर्ण है, इनके रथ में एक ही चक्र है जो संवत्सर कहलाता है। इस रथ में मासस्वरूप बारह अरे हैं, ऋतुरूप छःनेमियां और तीन चौमासें रूप तीन नाभियां है। इनके साथ साठ हजार बालखिल्य स्वस्तिवाचन और स्तुति करते हुए चलते हैं। सूर्य को आदित्य या आदितेय नाम से भी पुकारा जाता है क्योंकि देवमाता अदिति ने सूर्य देव की तपस्या की और उन्हें पुत्र रूप में प्राप्त किया और अदिति को मारिचम अण्डम् कहा जाने के कारण सूर्य देव मार्तण्ड नाम से प्रसिद्ध हुए। ब्रह्म पुराण में अदिति के गर्भ से जन्में सूर्य के अंश को विवस्वान कहा गया है। ये अन्धकार, दुःस्वप्न व बीमारी के नाशक हैं, आकाशमण्डल में सूर्य के उदित हो जाने पर सभी वनस्पतियाँ एवं पशु–पक्षी सुख व प्रसन्नता का अनुभव करते हैं। सूर्य शब्द की उत्पत्ति स्वः से हुई है जिसका अर्थ है–प्रकाश। सूर्य को सम्पूर्ण संसार का नेत्र कहा गया है। ऋग्वेद में उदीयमान सूर्य से ऋषियों ने प्रार्थनाएँ अर्पित की हैं–

आ कृष्णेन रजसा वर्तमानो निपेशयन्नमृतं मर्त्यं च।
हिरण्ययेन सविता रथेना देवों याति भुवनानि पश्यन्।।[3]

अर्थात् अमर और मर्त्य ऐसे दो पदार्थ इस विश्व में हैं, इनका निवास स्थान सदैव सूर्य की किरणों में है। अतः सर्वप्रेरक सूर्यदेव स्वर्णिम रथ पर विराजमान होकर अन्धकार पूर्ण अन्तरिक्ष–पक्ष में विचरण करते हुए देवों और मानवों को उनके कार्यों में संलग्न करते हुए, लोगों को देखते हुए चले आ रहे हैं, ऋग्वेद में अन्यत्र कहा है–

ऊर्ध्वो नः पाहयंहसो.........................नो दुवः।।[4]

अर्थात् हे सूर्य! तुम हमें ज्ञान के द्वारा पाप से बचाओ, सब पदार्थ भक्षण करने वाले असुरों को जलाकर नष्ट करो, प्रगति और दीर्घ जीवन के लिए हमें श्रेष्ठ और उच्च बनाओ, हमारी प्रार्थना को देवों तक पहँचाओ। सूर्य किरणें अग्नि की तरह जाज्ज्वल्यमान जगमगाती हैं, जो सूर्य के आगमन की सूचना देती हैं, ये किरणें सप्तवर्णी हैं, इनमें रोगनाशन की क्षमता है, ये पवित्र करती हैं। सूर्य की किरणें जिस स्थान पर पड़ती है, उस स्थान के रोगजन्य कीटाणु

---

[2] आचार्य मम्मट, काव्यप्रकाश, प्रथम उल्लास, वृत्ति 3
[3] ऋग्वेद 1.35.2
[4] ऋग्वेद 1.36.14

नष्ट हो जाते हैं। शुक्ल यजुर्वेद में सूर्य रश्मि से पवित्रता के सम्बन्ध में कहा है—

सवितुर्वः प्रसव उत्पुनाभ्यच्छिद्रेण पवित्रेण सूर्यस्य रश्मिभिः।।[5]

अर्थात् सृजनकर्ता परमात्मा की इस सृष्टि में छिद्ररहित पवित्रता करने के माध्यम से और सूर्य किरणों से मैं तुम सबको शुद्ध करता हूँ। सूर्य किरण अत्यन्त प्रबल एवं प्रभावशाली है विश्व में सूर्य किरणों द्वारा पवित्रता का सृजन होता है। गृह आँगन में जो लोग सूर्य की किरणों को प्रवेश कराते हैं उन्हें रोगों का भय नहीं होता हैं, जो अपने शरीर पर सूर्य–प्रकाश का उपयोग करते हैं वे स्वयं आरोग्य सम्पन्न बनते हैं, इस तरह सूर्य किरणों में शुद्धता करने का धर्म है। अनेक अदृश्य जन्तुओं को विनष्ट करते हुए सूर्य देव ऊपर उठते हैं और सूर्य के उदित होते ही अनेक अनिष्टकारी जीव छिप जाते हैं।[6] आसव को जिस प्रकार पात्र में रखते हैं, उसी प्रकार हम सूर्य किरणों में विष को रखते हैं, इस विष सूर्यदेव प्रभावित नहीं होते तथा हमारे लिए विष निवारक सिद्ध होते हैं। अश्वारुढ़ सूर्यदेव इस विष का निवारण करते हैं तथा मधुला–विद्या इस विष को मृत्यु निवारक अमृत बनाती है। अथर्ववेद के प्रथम काण्ड में भी सूर्य–चिकित्सा के दर्शन होते हैं, वहाँ हृदयरोग, कामला–नाशन के लिए प्रातःकालीन सूर्य की किरणों के सेवन का विधान है तथा उगते हुए सूर्य की प्रातःकालीन लाल रंग की किरणों से रोग का उपचार माना गया है—

अनु सूर्यमुदयतां हृद्योतो हरिमा च ते।
गो रोहितस्य वर्णेन तेन त्वा परिदध्मसि।।[7]

अथर्ववेद के द्वितीय काण्ड में सूर्य की प्रातःकालीन किरणों को कृमियों का नाशक कहा गया है—

उद्यन्नादित्यः क्रिमीन् हन्तु निम्रोचन् हन्तु रश्मिभिः।
ये अन्तः कृमयो गवि।।[8]

ऋग्वेद में एक सम्पूर्ण सूक्त विषशंकायुक्त मैत्रावरुणि अगस्त्य ऋषि द्वारा विषनाश के लिए सूर्य की स्तुति में है।[9] इस सूक्त को विषघ्नोपनिषद भी कहते हैं। सूर्य एवं सूर्य किरणों के चिकित्सकीय गुणों का उल्लेख हमें अथर्ववेद के छठवें काण्ड में भी प्राप्त होता है। तीन मन्त्रों वाले इस सूक्त के ऋषि भागलि तथा देवता क्रमशः सूर्य, गौएँ और वीरुध् हैं। इन मन्त्रों में अदृष्ट रोगाणुओं के

---

5 शुक्ल यजुर्वेद 1.12
6 ऋग्वेद 1.191.8
7 अथर्ववेद 1.22.1
8 अथर्ववेद 1.31.1
9 ऋग्वेद 1.191

शमन का वर्णन है, प्रथम मन्त्र में जहाँ सूर्य की किरणों को रोगाणु नाशक बताया गया है, वहीं तृतीय मन्त्र में किसी वनस्पति विशेष को भी रोगाणु नाशकबताया गया है। वैदिक साहित्य के उपरान्त भी सूर्य का रोग निवारक रूप प्राप्त होता है, पुराणों में भी सूर्य आयु और आरोग्य के स्वामी हैं। स्तोत्रों में भी रोगनाशक सूर्यदेव का कुछ विशेष रोगों को दूर करने के लिए आवाह्न किया गया है जिसमें 'चर्मरोग' महत्वपूर्ण है। अपचित (गण्डमाला) को दूर करने की प्रार्थना भी ऋग्वेद में की गई है[10], वह विष दूर करने में सहायक है।

सूर्य लोक को अमृत लोक भी कहते है, आशीर्वाद के रूप में दीर्घकाल तक सूर्य को देखने की माँग अनेक सूत्रों में मिलती है।[11] सूर्य लोक में सूर्य सदा उदित होने के कारण वहाँ नित्य आनन्द प्रसृत रहता है, अबाधित रूप से इडा (अन्नादि) का सुख भोग प्राप्त होता है। इसीलिए वहाँ रहकर चिरकाल तक उदित होते हुए सूर्य को देखने अर्थात् दीर्घजीवी होने की कामना स्वाभाविक है–

इहेऽया सघमादं मदन्तो ज्योक् पश्येम सूर्यमुच्चरन्तम्।[12]

सूर्य हमारे चक्षु को नष्ट न होने दे, उदित होते हुए सूर्य हमारे शत्रूओं को नष्ट कर डाले और सबके मन में मेरे लिए सदभाव हो। शत्रू को मेरे वश में ला दे, मुझे शत्रू के वश में न जाने दे। सूर्य की किरणों में हृदय सम्बन्धी तथा हरिमा (पीलिया) जैसे रोगों को दूर करने की शक्ति है–

हृदयरोगं मम सूर्य हरिमाणं च नाशय।[13]

वह वृहत् विश्व के ऊपर चढ़कर मनुष्यों के सत्कर्मों और दुराचरणों को देखता है। काले रंग के आवरण को चीरता हुआ वह शक्तिशाली अश्वों पर आता है और उसकी दीप्तिमान रश्मियाँ चर्म के समान फैले हुए तमों को जल में डुबों देती है। द्यौ का आधार–स्तम्भ यह सूर्य नाक की रक्षा करता है। 'सायण' ने सूर्य का अर्थ उसके धाता, अर्यमा आदि सप्त रूप किया है।[14] वह विश्वदर्शन ज्योतिष्कृत है, प्रजा, मनुष्य, सारा विश्व और स्वर्गलोक उसे देख सके, यही सूर्य के उदय का उद्देश्य है।

अपने उदय के अन्तर ही सूर्य पदार्थों को उदभाषित कर देते है, सूर्य को प्राणियों का एकमात्र चक्षु कहा गया है क्योंकि सूर्योदय से ही मनुष्य के नेत्र सांसारिक विषयों को देख पाते हैं–

---

10 ग्वेद 6.83.1
11 ऋग्वेद 2.29.1
12 ऋग्वेद 6.62.3
13 ऋग्वेद 1.50.11
14 ऋग्वेद 20.20.2

सूर्यो भूतेस्यैकं चक्षुः।[15]

प्रकृति के कोने–कोने में सूर्य की रश्मियों के प्रवेश के कारण सूर्य को 'उरुचक्षा'[16] तथा 'विश्वचक्षा'[17] कहा गया है। संसार को स्थिर रखने वाले एवं जगत् के रक्षक है–

विश्वस्य स्थातुर्जगतश्च गोपा।[18]

वेद का सबसे अधिक महत्वपूर्ण मन्त्र गायत्री है, जिसे वेदों की माता भी कहा जाता है। यह मन्त्र भी सविता अथवा सूर्य के महत्व को ही दर्शाता है, मानवता का उद्बोधक है सूर्य। जागरण तथा कर्म का सन्देश देने वाले सूर्य देव से बुद्धि को शुभ कर्मों में प्रेरित करने की प्रार्थना है गायत्री मन्त्र। सूर्य अकेला चलता है, सूर्य के प्रकाश से ही चन्द्रमा व नक्षत्र प्रकाशित होते है। सूर्य उदय और अस्त से दिन और रात्रि को ही नहीं बनाता अपितु पूरा काल चक्र ही सूर्य से चलता है यथा–

वेद मासो धृतव्रतो द्वादश प्रजावतः वेदा य उपजायते।

वैदिक ऋषियों ने भविष्य में पर्यावरण की प्रदूषण की समस्या को ध्यान में रखते हुए ही अनेकों निर्देश जन–साधारण को दिये थे, सूर्य ही पृथिवी सहित सभी लोकों को ताप उष्मा देता है यह तथ्य बार–बार वेदों में बताया है–

तपन्ति शत्रू स्वर्णभूम।[19]

धृणा तपन्तमति सूर्य।[20]

सूर्य की किरणों की शक्ति को वज्र की शक्ति कहा गया है, शतपथ ब्राह्मण में–

ते एतं वज्रमापश्यन्–अमुमेवादित्यम्।

इन वज्रमय किरणों से सूर्य राक्षसों को नष्ट कर मनुष्यों को अभय प्रदान करता है–

एतेन वज्रेण पुरस्ताद रक्षांसि नाष्ट्रं अपहत्य अभये अनाष्ट्रे स्वस्ति समश्नुते।[21]

सौर ऊर्जा से यन्त्रों के संचालन का तथ्य ऋग्वेद में वर्णित है।[22] सौर ऊर्जा के यन्त्र द्वारा अन्न परिष्कार[23] और जलपोत[24] तथा सौर ऊर्जा से चलने

---

[15] ऋग्वेद 10.158.4

[16] ऋग्वेद 7.35.8

[17] ऋग्वेद 1.50.2

[18] ऋग्वेद 7.60.2

[19] ऋग्वेद 7.34.19

[20] ऋग्वेद 9.107.20

[21] शतपथ ब्राह्मण 7.3.2.10

[22] ऋग्वेद 6.54.3, 10.149.1

वाले विमानों का भी उल्लेख ऋग्वेद[25] तथा यजुर्वेद[26] में मिलता है। सूर्य–रश्मि चिकित्सा अथर्ववेद का एक महत्वपूर्ण विषय है।

सूर्योपासना से शारीरिक के साथ मानसिक रोग भी विनष्ट हो जाते हैं, सायण के अनुसार इन्हीं मन्त्रों का जप करने से प्रस्कण्व ऋषि का चर्म रोग विनष्ट हो गया था। कुष्ठ रोग का निवारण भी सूर्य की उपासना से हो जाता है। यह धारणा न केवल भारतीयों में प्रचलित थी अपितु प्राचीन काल से ही पारसियों में भी प्रसिद्ध थी। "हेरोडोरस" के अनुसार कुष्ठ रोग का कारण सूर्य भगवान के प्रति पाप करना था, वर्तमान में भी यही धारणा प्रचलित है कि आदित्योपासना से सभी रोग दूर हो जाते हैं। अयोध्या के निकट 'सूर्यकुण्ड' नामक एक जलाशय है, जनश्रुति है कि उसमें स्नान करने से सभी चर्म रोगों का विनाश हो जाता है। आज वैज्ञानिक भी इस तथ्य को स्वीकारतें हैं कि चर्म रोगों के विनाश के लिए सूर्य किरणें बहुत लाभदायक हैं। सूर्य स्नान करना भी संभवतः शरीर को स्वस्थ रखने के लिए ही किया जाता है, क्योंकि सूर्य के प्रकाश से हमें सीधे ही विटामिन 'डी' मिलता है। इन्हीं विशेषताओं के कारण ही सूत्र–साहित्य में भी अधिकतर संस्कारों में सूर्योपासना का अपना महत्व है। सूर्य को अर्घ्य देने का भी वैज्ञानिक सत्य है, सूर्य को ताँबे के पात्र से जल चढ़ाया जाता है। जल चढ़ाते समय दृष्टि किनारे पर चमकते हुए सूर्य बिम्ब पर स्थिर करनी चाहिए, इस क्रिया से आँखों की ज्योति में वृद्धि होती है। 'कुमारसम्भव' महाकाव्य में भी पार्वती ने शिव को प्राप्त करने के लिए पञ्चाग्नि तप किया था अर्थात् सिर पर चमकने वाले सूर्य के ताप के साथ ही अग्नियों का ताप भी था।

वैदिकयुगीन लोगों को यह विदित था कि सूर्य की किरणों की उष्णता से बादल बनते है, जो पृथ्वी पर वर्षा कर अन्न उत्पन्न करते हैं तथा औषधियों और वनस्पतियों को पुष्ट करते हैं। अन्न से मानव शरीर का पोषण तथा औषधियों से शरीर पुष्ट होता है, ऋषि सूर्य को प्रसन्न करने के लिए लिखी गई ऋचाओं से मानव को सूर्य का प्राणी तथा वनस्पति जगत पर पड़ने वाले प्रभावों का ज्ञान कराता हैं। ऋग्वेद में वर्णित है–द्युलोक मं विद्यमान रहने वाले, उत्तम गति वाले, महिमाशाली जल के केन्द्र, औषधियों को पुष्ट बनाने वाले, जलवृष्टि द्वारा भूमि को तृप्त करने वाले सूर्यदेव का हम संरक्षण के लिए आवाहन करते है।[27] अथर्ववेद में सूर्य को हृदय रोग एवं प्रदूषण का नाशक कहा गया है–

---

23 अथर्ववेद 6.116.1
24 अथर्ववेद 17.1.25, 26
25 ऋग्वेद 4.36.1
26 यजुर्वेद 17.59
27 ऋग्वेद 11.164.52

अद्यन्नद्य मित्रमह आरोहन्नुतरां दिवस।
हृद्रोग मनः सूर्य हरिमाणं च नाशय।।[28]

वैदिक वाङ्मय में सूर्य को पर्यावरण–प्रदूषण को नष्ट करने वाला कहा गया है, दृष्ट व अदृष्ट सभी प्रकार के प्रदूषण को सूर्य नष्ट करता है। यजुर्वेद में भी कहा है कि सूर्य अपनी पवित्र किरणों द्वारा वायुमण्डल को प्रदूषण से मुक्त कर वातावरण को शुद्ध कर देता है–

सविता पुनातु आछिद्रेण पवित्रेण सूर्यस्य रश्मिभिः।[29]

सूर्य किरणें रोगों के तत्वों को विनष्ट कर मनुष्य को आरोग्यता प्रदान करती हैं।

भद्रा अश्वा हरितः सूर्यस्य चित्रा एतग्वा अनुमाद्यासः।।[30]

प्रश्नोपनिषद् में सूर्य को जगत् की प्राणशक्ति के रूप में माना गया है–

प्राणः प्रजानामुदयत्येष सूर्यः।[31]

प्राणशक्ति और आत्मशक्ति के रूप में सूर्य चिकित्सक हैं। सूर्य किरणों से हृद्रोगी, हलीमक, कामला, पाण्डुरोग इत्यादि नष्ट हो जाते है। सूर्य ताप में जल, दूध और अन्य भोजन रखकर खाना, पीना व सेवन करना चाहिए, इससे रक्त शुद्धि होती है। इनके अतिरिक्त सूर्य किरणें अन्य कई प्रकार के रोगों को नष्ट करती हैं यथा– शीर्षक्ति, शीर्षामय, कर्णशूल, विलोहित विसल्पक, अंगभेद, अंगज्वर, तक्मन (ज्वर) उरु एवं गवीनिकाओं में उत्पन्न होने वाले रोगों की, बलास की, हरिमा, मूत्ररोग, पार्श्वशूल, गुदारोग, आन्त्ररोग, विद्रधि, अलाजी, पैर के रोग आदि प्रमुख रोगों को सूर्य–किरणें नष्ट करती हैं।[32]

सूर्य भेषज है,चिकित्सक है, ये रोगी या रुग्णावयव को सूर्य की स्वाभाविक किरणों के प्रकाश में या विशेष प्रकार के काँच या शल्यविधान सम्पादित करते हैं। इस सम्पूर्ण विवरण से निष्कर्ष निकलता है कि प्राचीनकाल में सूर्य–रश्मियों से रोगों का उपशमन कर रोगजन्य कीटाणुओं को नष्ट किया जाता है। अतः मनुष्य को प्रतिदिन सूर्य–रश्मियों से प्रकाश ग्रहण कर आरोग्य प्राप्त करना चाहिए, यही सूर्यरश्मि–चिकित्सा है। सूर्य के एक चक्रीय रथ में अश्वों को नियन्त्रित करने में जो वल्गाएँ सौर–रश्मियाँ परिलक्षित होती है, वही सात प्रकार की किरणें हैं। वर्तमान में विज्ञान ने भी इन सात किरणों के अस्तित्व को मान लिया है और इनके पृथक–पृथक महत्व को भी समझा है, अभी तक के

---

28 अथर्ववेद 1.50.11
29 यजुर्वेद 44.10.6
30 ऋग्वेद 1.115.3
31 प्रश्नोपनिषद् 1.8
32 अथर्ववेद 9.8.1–22

शोधों से ज्ञात हुआ है कि सूर्य किरणों के अदृश्य हिस्से में अवरक्त और पराबैंगनी किरणें होती हैं। भूमंडल को गर्म रखने और जैव रासायनिक क्रियाओं को तेज बनाए रखने का काम अवरक्त किरणें और जीवधारियों के शरीर में रोगप्रतिरोधात्मक क्षमता बढ़ाने का काम पराबैंगनी किरणें करती हैं। धातक पराबैंगनी–सी किरणों से बचने के लिए उदित होते हुए सूर्य को अर्ध्य देने का विधान है, ओजोन परत भी इन किरणों को अवरुद्ध करती है, इस तरह सूर्य का एकचक्रीय होना गतिशील बने रहने का द्योतक है।

प्रत्यक्ष ज्योतिर्मय विश्वात्मा सूर्य देवता को समस्त धर्म किसी न किसी रूप में आराधना करते है, ज्योतिष शास्त्र में सूर्य को सात घोड़ों पर सवार प्रातःकाल रोजगार बढ़ाने वाला, दोपहर में भोजन दने वाला और सांयकाल के बाद विश्राम देने वाला कहा गया है। सनातन संस्कृति में सूर्य की आराधना की जाती है। वारों में रविवार, तिथियों में भानु सप्तमी और सूर्य षष्ठी, वर्ष में मकर सक्रान्ति पर विशेष पूजन और दान किया जाता है। क्योंकि मकर सक्रान्ति पर्व पर सूर्य की आराधना से पाण्डु रोग का विनाश, कान्ति, आयु बल में वृद्धि, नेत्र रोग और चर्म रोग में लाभ मिलता है साथ ही इस तिथि पर दान करने से सभी तरह के लाभों की प्राप्ति होती है। मकर सक्रान्ति से पूर्व सूर्य दक्षिणी गोलार्ध पर होता है अर्थात् सर्दी प्रारम्भ होती है और सूर्य के भारत से दूर होने के कारण रात बड़ी व दिन छोटे होते है और सक्रान्ति से सूर्य उत्तरार्ध में आते ही धीरे–धीरे रातें छोटी व दिन बड़े और गर्मी का मौसम प्रारम्भ हो जाता है।[33] सूर्य का यह संक्रमण छह–छह माह का होता है इसे उत्तरायण और दक्षिणायन कहते है।

भारतीय संस्कृति सूर्योपासना का सर्वाधिक महत्व है, संस्कृति के प्रसिद्ध चिन्ह स्वास्तिक, वृत, चक्र इत्यादि सभी सूर्य के प्राचीन प्रतीक रहे है। ┐ भी मण्डलाकार में इस प्रकार लिखा जाता है कि वह भी सूर्य का ही प्रतीक माना जाता है। यज्ञों के समय या काल–निर्धारण में सूर्य का बहुत महत्व रहा है। तैत्रिरीय संहिता में बारह महिनों के बारह आदित्य कहे गये है–

द्वादशादित्याः द्वादशमासाः।[34]

अथर्ववेद में सूर्य की किरणों से रोगी का रोग दूर करने की प्रार्थना की गई है– हे रोगी, सूर्य चिकित्सा के अनुसार तेरे हृदय की जलन और तेरा हरापन उठ जाए, समाप्त हो जाए। इस निमित लाल सूर्य की उन लाल रंग की रश्मियों की परिधि बना देते है। सूर्य का ताप इतना रहे कि रक्त की कमी से होने वाला हरित–रोग दूर हो जाए। इस प्रकार मनुष्य को प्रतिदिन सूर्य रश्मियों से प्रकाश ग्रहण कर आरोग्य प्राप्त करना चाहिए क्योंकि सूर्य भेषज है,

---

[33] दैनिक भास्कर 13 फरवरी 2021
[34] तैत्रिरीय संहिता

चिकित्सक है। सूर्य, चन्द्रमा इत्यादि देव अपनी–अपनी सीमाओं में आबद्ध होकर नियमबद्ध तरीके से परिचालित है वैसे ही मनुष्य को इन प्राकृतिक तत्वों के संरक्षण के प्रयत्न करने चाहिए। और हम भगवान सूर्यदेव से प्रार्थना करते है–

आदित्याय विद्महे सहस्रकिरणाय धीमहि। तन्नः सूर्यः प्रचोदयात्।

अर्थात् हम भगवान आदित्य को जानते हैं, पूजते हैं, हम सहस्र (अनन्त) किरणों से मण्डित भगवान सूर्यनारायण का ध्यान करते हैं, वे सूर्य देव हमें प्रेरणा प्रदान करें।

**Professor,
Department of Sanskrit,
G.D.Govt. College for Women, Alwar,
Rajasthan**

11. Legal Frameworks for Environmental Sustainability and Sustainable Development Goals

Dr. Sheikh Inam Ul Mansoor

I. Abstract

This paper aims to analyse how environmental law and the "Sustainable Development Goals" (SDGs) connect and evaluates the contribution of legal frameworks to the advancement of environmental sustainability. The study examines the connection between the concepts of "sustainable development" and "Environmental legislation," giving an account of their development. The legal frameworks at the national and international levels for environmental sustainability are also examined in the study, along with important legal concepts and guidelines.

The "sustainable development Goals" (SDGs) are carefully examined, and the study investigates how "Environmental legislation" might aid in the accomplishment of these objectives. To demonstrate how "Environmental law" may aid in promoting "sustainable development," specific examples are given. These examples include safeguarding biodiversity and ecosystems, preventing pollution, and promoting the use of renewable energy sources.

The study also takes into account the obstacles that limited institutional competence and a lack of resources provide to the implementation of legislative frameworks for environmental sustainability. These frameworks may be strengthened in a number of ways, including through improved stakeholder cooperation and partnerships, the use of creative strategies, and the emergence of new "Environmental law" trends.

The main conclusions of the study are outlined in the paper's conclusion, along with their implications for further study and practise. In order to achieve environmental sustainability, the study advises policymakers and stakeholders to improve the application and enforcement of current "Environmental laws" and regulations, encourage more stakeholder engagement, raise public awareness and education, expand institutional capacity, and adopt new ways.

Ultimately, this study emphasises how crucial legal frameworks are to advancing environmental sustainability and realising the SDGs. Policymakers and stakeholders may contribute to building a more resilient and sustainable future for both the present and future generations by addressing the issues and taking advantage of the chances to develop these frameworks.

II. Introduction

The health and welfare of humans, animals, and ecosystems are all at risk due to environmental degradation and "unsustainable development" practises, which are now major global problems. Air and water pollution, climate change, and the extinction of species have all been brought on by human activities such as industrialisation, deforestation, and the combustion of fossil fuels.[35]

The "sustainable development Goals" (SDGs), a collection of 17 interlinked objectives aiming at eradicating poverty, safeguarding the environment, and ensuring prosperity for everyone, were approved by the United Nations in 2015 to address these issues.[36] The SDGs' emphasis on environmental sustainability stems from the fact that it is essential to attaining several of the objectives, notably those pertaining to climate action, access to clean water and sanitation, and the development of sustainable cities and communities.[37] By setting guidelines, benchmarks, and procedures to avoid and mitigate environmental harm, legal frameworks play a

---

[35] Intergovernmental Panel on Climate Change (IPCC). (2018). Global Warming of 1.5°C. Retrieved from https://www.ipcc.ch/sr15/

[36] United Nations (UN). (2015). Transforming our world: The 2030 Agenda for Sustainable Development. Retrieved from https://www.un.org/ga/search/view_doc.asp?symbol=A/RES/70/1 &Lang=E

[37] United Nations (UN). (2018). The Sustainable Development Goals Report 2018. Retrieved from https://unstats.un.org/sdgs/ files/report/2018/TheSustainableDevelopmentGoalsReport2018-EN.pdf

crucial part in fostering environmental sustainability.[38] Yet, weak implementation and enforcement, a lack of political will, and competing interests sometimes restrict the efficacy of legislative frameworks for environmental sustainability.[39]

In order to better understand how "Environmental law" and "sustainable development" objectives interact, this article will concentrate on the legal frameworks that support environmental sustainability. This study aims to explore potential and difficulties for developing legal frameworks for environmental sustainability and attaining the SDGs by examining the link between "Environmental law" and "sustainable development".

III. Importance of Examining the Intersection of "Environmental law" and "Sustainable Development" Goals

In order to ensure the health and welfare of people and the earth, "environmental law" and "sustainable development" are two interrelated topics that are crucial. Although "sustainable development" aims to advance economic, social, and environmental sustainability, "environmental law" provides a legal framework for tackling environmental concerns including pollution, climate change, and biodiversity loss.[40] With numerous objectives directly connected to environmental preservation, such as SDG 13 on climate action, SDG 14 on life below water, and SDG 15 on life on land, the "Sustainable Development Goals" (SDGs) emphasise the significance of environmental sustainability for attaining

---

[38] United Nations Environment Programme (UNEP). (2017). Environmental Rule of Law. Retrieved from https://www.unenvironment.org/resources/report/environmental-rule-law

[39] United Nations Development Programme (UNDP). (2020). Human Development Perspectives. Retrieved from http://hdr.undp.org/sites/default/files/hdr2020.pdf

[40] United Nations Environment Programme (UNEP). (2017). Environmental Rule of Law. Retrieved from https://www.unenvironment.org/resources/report/environmental-rule-law

"sustainable development".[41] Achieving the SDGs, however, necessitates the creation of new legal frameworks and "sustainable development"-supporting policies, as well as their effective implementation and enforcement.[42]

Consequently, it is necessary to look at how "environmental law" and "sustainable development" objectives interact for a number of reasons:

- To recognise weak areas and potential for environmental sustainability legislative frameworks:
- By analysing the connection between "Environmental law" and "sustainable development," we may find inconsistencies and overlaps in the current legal systems and create fresh legal frameworks that promote environmental sustainability.
- To encourage good environmental law implementation and enforcement: Environmental laws are only effective when they are correctly applied and upheld. We may find obstacles to implementation and enforcement and create plans to get around them by looking at the junction of "Environmental law" and "sustainable development".
- To assist in achieving the SDGs: The SDGs include environmental sustainability as a major goal. We may find methods to include environmental sustainability into policies and strategies intended to achieve the SDGs by looking at how "Environmental law" and "sustainable development" overlap.

Multidisciplinary methods are necessary to tackle environmental concerns since they are complicated. By exploring the relationship between "Environmental law" and "sustainable development," we may encourage cooperation amongst legal professionals, legislators,

---

[41] United Nations (UN). (2015). Transforming our world: The 2030 Agenda for Sustainable Development. Retrieved from https://www.un.org/ga/search/view_doc.asp?symbol=A/RES/70/1 &Lang=E

[42] United Nations Environment Programme (UNEP). (2017). Environmental Rule of Law. Retrieved from https://www.unenvironment.org/resources/report/environmental-rule-law

scientists, and other stakeholders to create practical responses to environmental problems.[43]

Purpose and Scope of the Paper

This author's aims are to study how environmental law and sustainable development principles overlap, as well as to investigate the legal processes and controls that promote environmental sustainability. This paper will primarily:

- Outline the main ideas and tenets of "Environmental law" and "sustainable development," as well as how they relate to one another.
- Analyse how the SDGs and international "Environmental legislation" contribute to environmental sustainability.
- Examine the prospects and difficulties of putting "environmental laws" into effect and enforcing them in order to achieve environmental sustainability.
- Describe the new legal frameworks and tactics, such as environmental rights, green constitutionalism, and the circular economy, that support environmental sustainability.
- Provide examples of real-world situations where "environmental legislation" and "sustainable development" objectives overlap.
- The analysis in this article will include examples and case studies from many parts of the world because of its worldwide breadth. Also, the presentation will concentrate on current issues and advancements in "Environmental legislation" and "sustainable development," such as how the COVID-19 epidemic affects environmental sustainability.

VI. Definition and Evolution of "Environmental law"

"Environmental law" refers to the body of legislation that governs the relationship between humans and the natural environment. It includes a wide range of legal doctrines, laws, agreements, and rules intended to safeguard the environment and advance "sustainable development".[44] Over time, "environmental legislation" has changed

---

[43] Ibid

[44] Birnie, P., Boyle, A., & Redgwell, C. (2009). International law and the environment (3rd ed.). Oxford University Press.

to reflect shifting cultural perspectives on the environment and rising environmental consciousness. At the beginning, the main goals of "Environmental law" were to control pollution and safeguard public health. With the passage of the "Clean Air Act" and "Clean Water Act" in 1972, as well as the "National Environmental Policy Act" in 1970, the United States was one of the first nations to pass comprehensive environmental laws.[45]

The term "environmental law" grew in scope over the ensuing decades to include larger topics like biodiversity preservation, climate change, and "sustainable development". The Earth Summit, often referred to as the "United Nations Conference on Environment and Development" (UNCED), which took place in Rio de Janeiro in 1992, is seen as a turning point in the development of "Environmental law" since it resulted in the passage of the "Rio Declaration" on Environment and Development and the "United Nations Framework Convention on Climate Change" (UNFCCC).[46] Recent years have seen a continual evolution of "environmental law" in response to fresh opportunities and problems, such as the need to deal with the interconnected problems of pollution, climate change, and biodiversity loss. The development of new legal frameworks and tactics as a result has led to the acknowledgment of environmental rights, ecosystem-based methodologies, and circular economy ideas.[47]

VII. The Concept of "Sustainable Development"

The term "sustainable development" first appeared in the 1980s in response to rising worries about environmental destruction and the negative social and economic effects of development. Development that satisfies current demands without jeopardising the capacity of future generations to satisfy their own needs is referred to as "sustainable development" by the Brundtland Commission, also

---

[45] Fowler, D. (2020). Environmental law: A very short introduction. Oxford University Press.

[46] Hofmann, C. (2018). International environmental law and policy. Cambridge University Press.

[47] Birnie, P., Boyle, A., & Redgwell, C. (2009). International law and the environment (3rd ed.). Oxford University Press.

known as the International Commission on Environment and Development.[48] The concept of "sustainable development" is founded on the understanding that social justice, economic growth, and environmental preservation are all intertwined and dependent on one another. It aims to strike a balance between these three aspects of "sustainable development" that will advance everyone's long-term wellbeing while protecting the ecological processes that sustain life on Earth.[49]

The United Nations' "sustainable development" Goals (SDGs), the Paris Agreement on Climate Change, and the Convention on Biological Diversity all contain references to "sustainable development," which has grown to be a widely acknowledged notion in international policy-making.[50] Yet, there is continuous discussion and criticism over how "sustainable development" has really been put into reality and if it has been successful in balancing environmental preservation, social development, and economic progress.[51]

VIII. The link between "Environmental law" and "Sustainable Development"

"Environmental law" provides the legal foundation for putting "sustainable development" ideas and objectives into practise, hence the two concepts are closely related.[52] Natural resource preservation, pollution control, and the promotion of sustainable resource use are all supported by "environmental law," which serves as the legal framework for these actions. The term also refers to international

---

[48] World Commission on Environment and Development. (1987). Our Common Future. Oxford University Press.

[49] United Nations Environment Programme. (n.d.). Sustainable Development. Retrieved from https://www.unep.org/explore-topics/sustainable-development

[50] Ibid

[51] Fischer, F. (2017). The contested meaning of sustainability. The Oxford Research Encyclopedia of Environmental Science. Oxford University Press.

[52] Kiss, A., & Shelton, D. (2007). International environmental law. Transnational Publishers.

agreements that establish "sustainable development" as a worldwide objective, such as the "Convention on Biological Diversity" and the "United Nations Framework Convention on Climate Change".[53]

The concepts of "sustainable development," in turn, serve as the foundation for "environmental legislation," stressing the need to strike a balance between environmental preservation and social and economic advancement. Sustainable development objectives, like the "United Nations" "sustainable development" Goals, encourage a comprehensive approach to environmental preservation and seek to include environmental, social, and economic factors into legislation and policy.[54] The development of new legal strategies, such as environmental impact assessment and strategic environmental assessment, which aim to include environmental concerns into decision-making processes and guarantee that development activities are carried out in a sustainable manner is another way in which "Environmental law" and "sustainable development" are related.[55]

IX. National legal Frameworks for Environmental Sustainability

A crucial element of the worldwide legal framework for environmental sustainability is national legal frameworks. They give countries' ability to execute international environmental accords and control activities that have an impact on the environment while under their control. In order to fulfil "sustainable development" objectives, it has become increasingly apparent in recent years that national legislative frameworks for environmental sustainability must be strengthened.[56]

---

[53] ibid

[54] Hofmann, C. (2018). International environmental law and policy. Cambridge University Press.

[55] Birnie, P., Boyle, A., & Redgwell, C. (2009). International law and the environment (3rd ed.). Oxford University Press.

[56] Kamga, C. (2021). National legal frameworks for environmental sustainability: Lessons learned from Africa. Journal of Environmental Law and Practice, 2(1), 11-26.

Several techniques have been used by nations to create national legal frameworks for environmental sustainability. Some have created specialised laws for certain environmental challenges, such air or water pollution, while some have enacted complete "Environmental laws" that encompass all facets of environmental preservation. To monitor the application and enforcement of "Environmental legislation," several nations have also formed administrative or judicial authorities.[57] National legislative frameworks for environmental sustainability may be effective or ineffective depending on a number of variables, including political will, institutional capability, and public involvement. Goals for "sustainable development" are more likely to be attained in nations with solid legal systems and efficient implementation procedures.[58] Adoption of laws and policies that mirror the "sustainable development" Objectives of the "United Nations" is one recent trend in country legal frameworks for environmental sustainability. As an illustration, several nations have passed legislation to support renewable energy sources, lower greenhouse gas emissions, and save wildlife. Also, there has been a rising movement to incorporate environmental factors into other legal disciplines, including human rights, investment, and trade law.[59]

X. International legal Frameworks for Environmental Sustainability

Global sustainability goals can only be attained with the help of international legislative frameworks for environmental sustainability. The international community has created a variety of legislative structures to assist these initiatives because it recognises the necessity for concerted action to solve environmental concerns.[60]

---

[57] ibid

[58] Ibid

[59] Boyd, D. R. (2017). The environmental rights revolution: A global study of constitutions, human rights, and the environment. UBC Press.

[60] United Nations Framework Convention on Climate Change (UNFCCC). (1992). Retrieved from https://unfccc.int/resource/docs/convkp/conveng.pdf

The "United Nations Framework Convention on Climate Change" is one of the most important international legal frameworks for environmental sustainability (UNFCCC). The UNFCCC, which was adopted in 1992, offers a framework for international collaboration to combat climate change. All 197 parties, including the "European Union" and all "United Nations" members, have approved it. The UNFCCC lays forth broad guidelines and goals for combating climate change and offers a platform for discussions on mitigation and adaptation strategies.[61]

Another significant international legislative framework for environmental sustainability is the "Paris Agreement," which was established in 2015 under the UNFCCC. The Paris Agreement seeks to pursue efforts to keep the temperature increase to 1.5 degrees Celsius and to keep global warming to far below 2 degrees Celsius over pre-industrial levels. To reduce greenhouse gas emissions, prepare for the effects of climate change, and help developing nations financially and technologically, it lays out precise goals and actions.[62]

The Stockholm Convention on Persistent Organic Pollutants, the Basel Convention on the Regulation of Transboundary Movements of Hazardous Wastes and Their Disposal, and the Convention on Biological Diversity (CBD) are further international legal frameworks for environmental sustainability (POPs). The management of hazardous waste, the regulation of hazardous substances, and concerns connected to biodiversity protection are all addressed by these frameworks, in that order.[63] The relationship between "sustainable development" objectives and global legal frameworks for environmental sustainability is also crucial. A comprehensive framework for "sustainable development" is

---

[61] United Nations. (2015). Paris Agreement. Retrieved from https://unfccc.int/sites/default/files/english_paris_agreement.pdf

[62] Convention on Biological Diversity (CBD). (1992). Retrieved from https://www.cbd.int/convention/

[63] Basel Convention on the Control of Transboundary Movements of Hazardous Wastes and their Disposal. (1989). Retrieved from https://www.basel.int/the-convention/

provided by the 2030 Agenda for "sustainable development," which was adopted by the UN General Assembly in 2015. It has 17 "sustainable development" objectives (SDGs). The Sustainable Development Goals (SDGs) focus on a variety of environmental challenges, including climate change, biodiversity preservation, and sustainable water and land use.[64]

Cooperation and coordination between nations are necessary for the effective application of international legislative frameworks for environmental sustainability, as well as the participation of a number of stakeholders, such as civil society, the corporate sector, and indigenous peoples. In order to facilitate the execution of international responsibilities, it also calls for the establishment of efficient institutional and legal structures at the national level.[65]

XI. Key legal Principles and Instruments for Environmental Sustainability

While analysing the junction between "Environmental law" and "sustainable development" objectives, it is crucial to take into account a number of significant legal concepts and tools for environmental sustainability. At the national and international levels, "Environmental laws" and policies are developed and put into effect using these ideas and tools.[66]

The precautionary principle, which urges taking action even in the lack of scientific certainty to avert harm to the environment and human health, is one important guiding concept. A number of international legal documents, such as the "Convention on

---

[64] Stockholm Convention on Persistent Organic Pollutants (POPs). (2001). Retrieved from http://www.pops.int/TheConvention/ Overview/tabid/3351/Default.aspx

[65] United Nations General Assembly. (2015). Transforming our world: The 2030 Agenda for Sustainable Development. Retrieved from https://sustainabledevelopment.un.org/post2015/ transfor mingourworld

[66] United Nations. (1992). Rio Declaration on Environment and Development. Retrieved from https://www.unep.org/documents/ 20126/0/Rio_Declaration.pdf/2b2a493c-591c-4a3a-bcd5- 6bf9b93e9b9c

Biological Diversity" and the "Rio Declaration on Environment and Development," contain the precautionary principle as a tenet.[67] The idea that people who pollute or harm the environment should pay for repair and restoration is known as the "polluter pays" principle. This idea is mirrored in several "Environmental legislation" and regulations at the national and international levels, notably the Environmental Liability Directive of the European Union.[68]

There are a number of important legislative frameworks that assist environmental sustainability in addition to these principles. An example of one of these tools is the Environmental Impact Assessment (EIA), which demands that the possible environmental effects of proposed projects or activities be evaluated before they are approved. EIAs are required by legislation in many nations for specific project categories, such mining or major infrastructure development.[69] The Convention on International Trade in Endangered Species of Wild Fauna and Flora (CITES), which governs the worldwide trade in endangered species, is another significant legal document. Protecting endangered species and fostering ethical wildlife usage have both benefited from CITES.[70]

---

[67] Convention on Biological Diversity. (1992). Retrieved from https://www.cbd.int/convention/

[68] European Union. (2004). Environmental Liability Directive. Retrieved from https://eur-lex.europa.eu/legal-content/EN/TXT/PDF/?uri=CELEX:32004L0035&from=EN

[69] United Nations Environment Programme. (n.d.). Environmental Impact Assessment. Retrieved from https://www.unenvironment.org/explore-topics/resource-efficiency/what-we-do/policy-and-advocacy/environmental-impact-assessment

[70] Convention on International Trade in Endang United Nations Environment Programme. (n.d.). Environmental Impact Assessment. Retrieved from https://www.unenvironment.org/explore-topics/resource-efficiency/what-we-do/policy-and-advocacy/environmental-impact-assessmentered Species of Wild Fauna and Flora (CITES). (n.d.). Retrieved from https://www.cites.org/eng/disc/what.php

Other significant legal frameworks for "environmental sustainability" include the "Paris Agreement" and the "United Nations Framework Convention on Climate Change" (UNFCCC). By lowering greenhouse gas emissions and fostering adaptation to climate change's effects, these accords seek to combat global warming.[71] To promote sustainability, several nations have created "Environmental laws" and regulations at the national level. For instance, the "Clean Air Act" and the "Clean Water Act" of the "United States" restrict, respectively, air and water pollution. The Law on Prevention and Control of Air Pollution was created in China with the intention of enhancing air quality and lowering pollution.[72]

An overall framework for resolving environmental issues and advancing "sustainable development" is provided by the major legislative concepts and tools for environmental sustainability. Governments, civic society, the commercial sector, and indigenous peoples must all be involved for these ideas and tools to be implemented effectively.[73]

XII. Overview of the "Sustainable Development" Goals (SDGs)

As a component of the 2030 Agenda for "sustainable development," the "United Nations General Assembly" established the 17 "sustainable development" Goals (SDGs) in 2015.[74] By 2030, the SDGs seek to eradicate poverty, safeguard the environment, and guarantee everyone's prosperity. The SDGs include a variety of

---

[71] United Nations Framework Convention on Climate Change (UNFCCC). (1992). Retrieved from https://unfccc.int/resource/docs/convkp/conveng.pdf

[72] United Nations. (2015). Paris Agreement. Retrieved from https://unfccc.int/sites/default/files/english_paris_agreement.pdf

[73] United States Environmental Protection Agency. (n.d.). Clean Air Act. Retrieved from https://www.epa.gov/laws-regulations/summary-clean-air-act

[74] United Nations. (2015). Transforming our world: The 2030 Agenda for Sustainable Development. Retrieved from https://www.un.org/en/development/desa/population/migration/generalassembly/docs/globalcompact/A_RES_70_1_E.pdf

economic, social, and environmental challenges and are linked. Goal 13 of the SDGs places a special emphasis on addressing climate change and urges swift action to mitigate its effects. Additional objectives, including Goal 6 (clean water and sanitation) and Goal 14 (life below water), also have significant effects on the sustainability of the environment. The SDGs offer a framework for global "sustainable development" collaboration and are meant to direct national and global policy and decision-making. Moreover, the SDGs are meant to be incorporated into already-existing legal frameworks, such as international environmental treaties and national laws and regulations.

It's crucial to look into how the SDGs and "Environmental law" interact. The SDGs, especially Goal 13 on climate action and other goals relating to environmental sustainability, can be accomplished with the help of "environmental legislation," which can play a significant role in this regard.

On the other hand, the SDGs can also offer a framework for bolstering "Environmental legislation" and increasing its efficacy.The SDGs signify a change in the focus of international development towards a more comprehensive and integrated approach to sustainability.[75]The SDGs seek to promote "sustainable development" in all of its forms and to address the underlying causes of poverty, inequality, and environmental degradation. The universality concept, which stresses that all nations have a duty to contribute to the accomplishment of the objectives, is one of several important ideas that serve as a framework for the SDGs. The concept of "leaving no one behind" is another guiding principle for the SDGs, emphasising the need of attending to the needs of the most marginalised and disadvantaged groups.[76]

---

[75] Nilsson, M., Griggs, D., & Visbeck, M. (2016). Policy: Map the interactions between Sustainable Development Goals. Nature, 534(7607), 320-322.

[76] United Nations Framework Convention on Climate Change. (1992). United Nations Framework Convention on Climate Change. Retrieved from https://unfccc.int/resource/docs/ convkp/ conveng.pdf

The "United Nations Framework Convention on Climate Change" (UNFCCC) and "the Paris Agreement," which offer a framework for global cooperation on climate change, are only two of the international legal instruments that support the SDGs. By fostering biodiversity protection and sustainable use, the "Convention on Biological Diversity" (CBD) and the "Convention on International Trade in Endangered Species" (CITES) also aid in the fulfilment of the SDGs.[77] In addition, a number of financial institutions, such as the Global Environment Facility and the Green Climate Fund, contribute funding to assist the achievement of the SDGs. Also, the SDGs are included in the "sustainable development" Goals Atlas of the World Bank, which offers statistics and details on the global status of the objectives.[78]

To sum up, the SDGs provide a huge opportunity to advance "sustainable development" and environmental sustainability. At both the national and international levels, the SDGs serve as a framework for international collaboration and serve to direct policy and decision-making. The SDGs may serve as a framework for bolstering "Environmental law" and increasing its efficacy, while "Environmental law" itself can play a significant role in supporting the attainment of the SDGs.[79]

XIII. The Role of "Environmental law" in achieving the SDGs

In order to safeguard the environment, preserve natural resources, and advance "sustainable development," "environmental legislation" plays a critical role in accomplishing the SDGs. The term "environmental law" refers to a broad variety of legal instruments,

---

[77]United Nations Framework Convention on Climate Change. (2015). Paris Agreement. Retrieved from https://unfccc.int/sites/default/files/english_paris_agreement.pdf

[78] Convention on Biological Diversity. (1992). Convention on Biological Diversity. Retrieved from https://www.cbd.int/ doc/legal/cbd-en.pdf

[79] Convention on International Trade in Endangered Species of Wild Fauna and Flora. (1973). Convention on International Trade in Endangered Species of Wild Fauna and Flora. Retrieved from https://www.cites.org/eng/disc/text.php

such as international treaties, domestic laws and regulations, and regional and municipal policies and initiatives.[80]

"Environmental legislation" can help the SDGs be achieved in a number of ways. By way of illustration, "environmental laws" can create legal frameworks for environmental management and protection, including the preservation and sustainable use of natural resources. These can include rules and regulations that support the preservation of biodiversity, environmentally sound forestry and ocean management, and waste and pollution abatement.[81] "Environmental legislation" can facilitate the incorporation of environmental concerns into other industries, including infrastructure development, agriculture, and the energy industry. To identify and resolve environmental risks and consequences related to development projects and to support "sustainable development" objectives, for instance, environmental impact assessments and strategic environmental assessments might be helpful.[82]

Furthermore, by supplying legal foundations for their implementation and enforcement at the national level, "environmental law" can help the execution of international environmental accords and pledges, such as the "Paris Agreement" and the "Convention on Biological Diversity".[83] The promotion of public involvement and access to justice in environmental decision-making can also be facilitated by "environmental legislation," which

---

[80] United Nations Environment Programme. (2017). Global Environmental Outlook 6: Healthy Planet, Healthy People. Nairobi, Kenya: United Nations Environment Programme.

[81] United Nations Development Programme. (2018). Environmental Governance for Sustainable Development: A Guide for Implementing the Goals of the 2030 Agenda for Sustainable Development. New York, NY: United Nations Development Programme.

[82] United Nations Environment Programme. (2015). Environmental Rule of Law: An Analysis. Nairobi, Kenya: United Nations Environment Programme.

[83] Kysar, D. A. (2016). The Future of Environmental Law. Journal of Environmental Law and Litigation, 31(1), 1-28.

can play a significant role in this regard. This might involve the establishment of legislative frameworks for public participation in environmental impact assessments and other decision-making procedures, as well as enabling access to justice in situations involving environmental injury or destruction.[84]

XIV. Specific Examples of how "Environmental law" can Support the SDGs

The SDGs may be supported by "environmental law" in a number of ways, such as through establishing legal frameworks for environmental management and protection, encouraging the integration of environmental concerns into other fields, assisting in the execution of international environmental accords, and fostering public engagement and access to justice. These are a few particular instances:

By establishing legal frameworks for the management and preservation of water resources, "environmental law" can assist in achieving SDG 6 (Clean Water and Sanitation). For instance, the Water Framework Directive of the "European Union" creates a legislative framework for the preservation and wise use of water resources throughout the EU and contains rules for the mitigation and prevention of water pollution.[85]

By encouraging the incorporation of environmental factors into urban planning and development, "environmental legislation" can aid in the fulfilment of SDG 11 (Sustainable Cities and Communities). For instance, the Canadian city of Vancouver enacted a "Greenest City Action Plan" that outlines a number of efforts to support sustainable urban development, such as the

[84] Faure, M., & Peeters, M. (2015). Environmental Law and Sustainable Development: A Comparative Study of Environmental Law in Developing and Developed Countries. Cheltenham, UK: Edward Elgar Publishing.
[85] European Union. (2000). Directive 2000/60/EC of the European Parliament and of the Council of 23 October 2000 establishing a framework for the Community action in the field of water policy. Official Journal of the European Communities, L327, 1-72.

promotion of green buildings, the reduction of carbon emissions, and the preservation of green areas.[86]

By establishing a framework for the management and preservation of marine and coastal ecosystems, "environmental legislation" can assist in achieving SDG 14 (Life Below Water). For instance, the National Marine Sanctuaries Act of the United States creates a legislative framework for the preservation of marine biodiversity and the protection of marine ecosystems.[87]

By establishing statutory frameworks for the preservation and wise use of terrestrial ecosystems, "environmental law" can aid in the attainment of SDG 15 (Life on Land). For instance, the Wildlife and Countryside Act of the United Kingdom creates legal safeguards for native species and ecosystems and contains clauses for the creation and administration of protected areas.[88]

By encouraging the execution of international environmental accords like the Paris Agreement on climate change, "environmental legislation" can aid in the attainment of SDG 13 (Climate Action). For instance, the Clean Air Act of the United States offers a legislative framework for the control of greenhouse gas emissions and other air pollutants, and it has been utilised to promote the national implementation of the Paris Agreement.[89]

Overall, "environmental law" is essential to advancing the SDGs because it provides legal frameworks for environmental

---

[86] City of Vancouver. (2011). Greenest City Action Plan. Retrieved from https://vancouver.ca/files/cov/Greenest-city-2020-action-plan.pdf

[87] National Oceanic and Atmospheric Administration. (2020). National Marine Sanctuaries Act. Retrieved from https://sanctuaries.noaa.gov/about/pdfs/nmsa.pdf

[88] United Kingdom. (1981). Wildlife and Countryside Act 1981. Retrieved from http://www.legislation.gov.uk/ukpga/1981/69

[89] United States Environmental Protection Agency. (2016). The Clean Air Act and the Paris Agreement. Retrieved from https://www.epa.gov/paris-agreement-and-clean-power-plan/clean-air-act-and-paris-agreement

management and preservation, encourages the incorporation of environmental concerns into other fields, aids in the execution of international environmental accords, and fosters public engagement and access to justice.

XV. Challenges facing the Implementation of Legal Frameworks for Environmental Sustainability

Although there are several legislative frameworks for environmental sustainability, their implementation faces a number of difficulties. The lack of political will on the part of governments to implement "Environmental laws" and policies is one of the main obstacles. Conflict is frequently brought on by conflicting goals like economic expansion and growth, which can result in the exploitation of natural resources and environmental deterioration.[90] The lack of money for environmental protection is another issue, which might restrict how well legislative frameworks operate to achieve sustainability objectives. This is especially true for developing nations, which might not have the financial means to put "Environmental laws" and policies into effect and enforce them.[91]

In addition, a comprehensive and integrated approach to policy creation and execution is necessary due to the complexity and diversity of environmental challenges. Yet, the ineffective implementation of legislative frameworks may be hampered by a lack of coordination and collaboration across various sectors and parties.[92]

---

[90] Ogwueleka, T. C. (2016). Environmental laws and factors affecting their implementation in Nigeria. Journal of Environmental Protection, 7(6), 877-890. doi: 10.4236/jep.2016.76080

[91] Tebabal, D., & Mohammed, C. (2018). Challenges and opportunities of sustainable development goals for Ethiopia. Sustainability, 10(5), 1405. doi: 10.3390/su10051405

[92] Hens, L., & Jansen, B. (2015). Challenges for implementing the sustainable development goals: The role of sustainability indicators. Sustainability, 7(12), 16583-16600. doi: 10.3390/su71215888

Additionally, the efficiency of legislative frameworks may be hampered by a lack of public understanding and education on environmental concerns. Achieving sustainability objectives and enforcing "environmental laws" and regulations may be challenging without public support and involvement.[93] The application of legislative frameworks for environmental sustainability may also be hampered by a lack of international coordination and collaboration. As environmental challenges frequently cross international borders, effective international collaboration is required.[94] Overall, overcoming these obstacles is essential to achieving the SDGs and effective application of legislative frameworks for environmental sustainability.

XVI. Opportunities for strengthening Legal Frameworks for Environmental Sustainability

In order to successfully accomplish the "sustainable development" Objectives, there are opportunities to increase the legal frameworks for environmental sustainability (SDGs). The increased understanding and appreciation of the significance of environmental sustainability among governments, non-governmental organisations, and the commercial sector is one such opportunity. Strong "Environmental laws" and regulations may be created and put into effect as a result of improved political will and support.[95] The development of technology presents another chance, which may be used to increase environmental sustainability. To combat criminal operations like deforestation and animal trafficking, for instance, the

---

[93] Mrema, G. C., & Otieno, R. O. (2012). Environmental education and public awareness for sustainability: Some African experiences. Journal of Education and Practice, 3(5), 27-34.

[94] Kivuva, J. M., & Njeri, W. G. (2018). The role of international environmental law in achieving the sustainable development goals. Journal of Environmental Management, 222, 324-332. doi: 10.1016/j.jenvman.2018.06.054

[95] Lopes da Silva, R., Pereira, H. M., Gómez-Baggethun, E., Magalhães, M. F., & Santos, R. (2020). Legal frameworks for nature-based solutions: From challenges to opportunities. Ecosystem Services, 45, 101136.

adoption of block chain technology can improve the transparency and traceability of supply chains.[96]

Moreover, coordination and international cooperation might make it easier to put environmental sustainability regulatory frameworks into place. This involves assistance with capacity-building initiatives in developing nations as well as the sharing of best practises and international experiences.[97] Including stakeholders in the creation and application of "Environmental laws" and regulations can also result in more fair and productive results. To guarantee that their viewpoints and knowledge are taken into consideration, this involves interacting with local communities, indigenous peoples, and civil society groups.[98] Overall, these possibilities show how legislative frameworks for environmental sustainability and attaining the SDGs should be strengthened. To reach their full potential, they also need coordinated efforts from several entities, such as governments, the commercial sector, and civil society.

XVII. Emerging Trends in "Environmental law" and "Sustainable Development"

The legal frameworks for "environmental sustainability" are continually changing in response to new developments in "Environmental law" and "sustainable development". One trend is the growing acceptance of local communities' and indigenous peoples' rights in environmental decision-making. The "United Nations Declaration on the Rights of Indigenous Peoples," which was approved in 2007, acknowledges indigenous peoples' rights to their lands, territories, and resources as well as the necessity of

---

[96] Cohen, J., & Das, S. (2020). Blockchain for environmental sustainability: Opportunities and challenges. Business Horizons, 63(3), 311-319.

[97] Zalik, A., & Jenkins, M. (2019). Global environmental governance and sustainable development: The case of transnational wildlife crime. Environmental Politics, 28(2), 231-251.

[98] Lehmann, C. (2021). The role of environmental law in achieving the sustainable development goals: The case of access and benefit-sharing. Journal of Environmental Law, 33(1), 69-92.

obtaining their free, prior, and informed permission before moving forward with any initiatives that may have an impact on them.[99] The rising significance of international environmental courts and tribunals in upholding "Environmental law" and guaranteeing adherence to international accords is another trend. Institutions like the "International Court of Justice" and the "International Criminal Court" are two instances of how environmental considerations are becoming more and more important in decision-making.[100] A third trend is the acceptance of non-state players, such as enterprises, international organisations, and civil society groups, in environmental governance. In order to execute environmental legislation and realise "sustainable development" objectives, partnerships between governments and non-state entities are becoming more and more widespread.[101]

Last but not least, another significant development in "environmental law" and "sustainable development" is the employment of cutting-edge tools and strategies for environmental governance, such block chain and smart contracts. The openness, accountability, and traceability of environmental decision-making processes might be improved by these technologies.[102]

---

[99] UN General Assembly. (2007). United Nations Declaration on the Rights of Indigenous Peoples. https://www.un.org/development/desa/indigenouspeoples/declarat ion-on-the-rights-of-indigenous-peoples.html

[100] Schrijver, N. (2015). The Role of International Environmental Courts and Tribunals in Ensuring Compliance with International Agreements. Review of European, Comparative & International Environmental Law, 24(2), 142-153.

[101] Haas, P. M. (2018). Epistemic Communities and Environmental Governance. In The Oxford Handbook of Governance and Limited Statehood (pp. 243-257). Oxford University Press.

[102] Lundmark, M., & Persson, E. (2019). Blockchain and Smart Contracts for Environmental and Natural Resources Governance. In Environmental and Natural Resources Law (pp. 329-348). Springer.

These new changes provide both possibilities and difficulties for enhancing "environmental sustainability" legal frameworks. They need a flexible and adaptable legal framework that can take into account shifting conditions and developing norms. "Environmental legislation" can continue to be a key component in attaining "sustainable development" objectives by keeping up with these changes and resolving the difficulties they provide.

XVIII. Conclusion

In conclusion, attaining environmental sustainability depends on the convergence of "Environmental legislation" and "sustainable development" objectives. Although "sustainable development" objectives give a vision for achieving social, economic, and environmental well-being, "environmental legislation" offers a framework for safeguarding the environment. The SDGs must be implemented with the help of the legal tools and ideas outlined in this article, such as the precautionary principle and the polluter pays principle. However there are various obstacles that prevent the effective application of legislative frameworks for environmental sustainability, including weak enforcement mechanisms and little resources. Notwithstanding these obstacles, there are ways to better judicial systems, such by using new technology and including stakeholders in the decision-making process. Developing tendencies also present significant opportunities for boosting environmental sustainability, like the blending of human rights and "Environmental law" and the rising use of alternative dispute resolution procedures. It is obvious that in order to handle new possibilities and problems and create a sustainable future, legislative frameworks for environmental sustainability must continue to develop and adapt.

XIX. Summary of the Key Findings

The key findings of this paper are:

Although "sustainable development" objectives give a vision for achieving social, economic, and environmental well-being, "environmental legislation" offers a framework for safeguarding the environment.

The SDGs must be implemented with the help of the legal tools and ideas outlined in this article, such as the precautionary principle and the polluter pays principle.

The efficacy and enforcement methods of national legislative frameworks for environmental sustainability differ.

The efficacy of international legal frameworks for environmental sustainability depends on the desire of governments to execute them, yet they serve as a foundation for international collaboration and coodination.

By tackling challenges like climate change, biodiversity preservation, and access to clean water and sanitation, "environmental legislation" may promote the SDGs.

Implementing legislative frameworks for environmental sustainability is difficult because there are insufficient enforcement mechanisms, few resources, and competing interests.

Incorporating new technology, including stakeholders in decision-making processes, and fostering international collaboration are opportunities to develop legal frameworks for environmental sustainability.

The incorporation of human rights and "Environmental law," the growing use of other conflict resolution procedures, and the requirement to address the environmental effects of developing technology are some of the new developments in these fields.

In order to achieve environmental sustainability, this study emphasises the significance of looking at how "environmental law" and "sustainable development" goals overlap. While possibilities and problems are present, ongoing development and adaption of legal frameworks will be required to handle brand-new opportunities and challenges for a sustainable future.

XX. Implications for Future Research and Practice

The study emphasises a number of implications for ongoing research and application in the area of environmental sustainability legal frameworks. Secondly, more empirical research is required to evaluate the efficacy of present legislative frameworks and spot implementation shortcomings. Case studies, comparative assessments, and the evaluation of policy tools might all be a part of this study.

Second, future research and practise should examine creative solutions to the problems associated with implementing legislative frameworks for environmental sustainability, including incorporating new technology, involving stakeholders, and employing market-based procedures.

Finally, governments, institutions, and other stakeholders need to have stronger capacities for enforcing "Environmental laws" in an efficient manner. This could entail initiatives to improve capacity, training, and public awareness campaigns.

Fourthly, the report emphasises how in order to fulfil the SDGs and promote environmental sustainability, there has to be more cooperation and coordination across different stakeholders, including governments, civil society, academia, and the commercial sector.

Furthermore, there is a need to encourage increased openness and accountability in the use of legislative frameworks for environmental sustainability. This might entail creating frameworks for monitoring and assessment, bolstering institutional and legal structures, and encouraging public involvement in decision-making. Overall, the implications for this field's future study and practise are crucial for advancing environmental sustainability and the SDGs, and they call for a multidisciplinary and collaborative approach.

XXI. Recommendations for Policymakers and Stakeholders

The following recommendations is offered for policymakers and stakeholders based on the main results and implications for further study and application:

To guarantee that current "Environmental legislation" and regulations are in line with the SDGs, they should be strengthened for national and international application and enforcement.

To encourage the creation and adoption of efficient legislative frameworks for environmental sustainability, foster stronger collaboration and partnerships among stakeholders, including governments, civil society groups, businesses, and academic institutions.

Educate and raise public consciousness about the value of environmental sustainability and the contribution of "environmental legislation" to the achievement of the SDGs.

Increase the ability of the institutions and parties involved in the administration and management of the environment, including through offering technical help and training.

Take use of novel strategies and developing trends in "environmental law" and "sustainable development," such the application of cutting-edge technology, alternate conflict resolution procedures, and participatory decision-making techniques.

Policymakers and stakeholders may contribute to building a more resilient and sustainable future for both the present and future generations by putting these ideas into practise.

Assistant Professor of Law,
School of Law,
Presidency University Bangalore.
Karnataka

12. Histology of Leucophyllum Frutescens (Berl.) I.M. Johnst, (Scrophulariaceae) Leaf.

Poonam Sethi

Abstract

Leaf anatomy or histology of Leucophyllum was studied. Trichomes ,dendroid non glandular and mesophyll with calcium oxalate crystals. Trichomes are 110-160µm in height. The lateral spines are 100 µm long the cells of main axis are15µ m in height and 20µm breadth .Others to be mentioned are TPM (Transcurrent Palisade Mesophyll). Thus the above-mentioned leaf features are of great taxonomic significance, this genus is sometimes placed in the family Myoporaceae, hence the present study.

Keywords : anatomy,histology, epidermal, leaf, Leucophyllum,

Introduction

India is one of the countries in the world where medicinal plants form the backbone of traditional systems of medicine in India, thousands of tribal communities still use plants for treatment of various diseases. The great interest in the use and importance of medicinal plants in many countries has led to intensified efforts on the documentation of ethnomedical data of medicinal plants 1. Earlier there were a few or no synthetic medicine and species of higher plants were the main sources of medicines for the world 2. Medicinal plants are the rich source of novel drugs that forms the ingredients in traditional systems of medicine, modern medicines, nutraceuticals, food supplements, folk medicines, pharmaceutical intermediates, bioactive principles and lead compounds in synthetic drugs 3 Many plants synthesize substances that are useful to the maintenance of health in humans and animals. The experimental plant Leucophyllum frutescens (Scrophulariaceae) is given for dysentery, fever, cough, asthma, liver injury, cataracts.. Hence the present investigation was undertaken.

Materials and Method

The whole plant was collected from Velachery , Chennai of Tamilnadu, India identified by botanist of CSMDRIA

Chennai,Tamil Nadu. Fresh hand sections were taken and treated with chloral hydrate and phloroglucinol and HCl .Microscopical characters were studied 4. Trichomes were studied in epidermal peels of plant parts such as lamina .The material was first soaked in the warm water in order to soften the tissues. The peelings were removed with the help of razor and then stained with dilute solution of saffranin and mounted in 50% glycerine. Epidermal tissues were studied from paradermal sections of lamina in surface view. Micro hotographs were taken with thehelp of Nikon (ECLIPSE E400) research microscope.

Results

i. Botanical Description

Leucophyllum frutescens is an evergreen shrub in the figwort family, Scrophulariaceae native to the state of Texas in United States. Popularly called as silver leaf is a shrub with arching branches and woolly, silvery gray leaves. In summer, it bears solitary, bell-shaped rose-purple flowers [Fig.1].

ii. Anatomical Characters of Leaf

The leaf is bifacial with flat adaxial and semicircular abaxial side.The palisade mesophyll cel bundle(TPM).The ground tissue in the abaxial part of the midrib is collenchymatous.Vascular bundle large centrally placed,collateral surrounded by large circular parenchymatous bundle sheath cells.The xylem elements are narrow,angular and thick walled,phloem below the xylem,small and compact.

ls of the lamina are horizontally transcurrent inbetween the adaxial epidermis and vascular bundle(TPM).The ground tissue in the abaxial part of the midrib is collenchymatous.Vascular bundle large centrally placed,collateral surrounded by large circular parenchymatous bundle sheath cells.The xylem elements are narrow,angular and thick walled,phloem below the xylem,small and compact.

Discussion

The family Myoporaceae is characterised by glandular trichome, 5while Leucophyllum has non glandular dendrite trichome. The epidermal cells are not wavy, stomata anomocytic in myoporaceae while Leucophyllum has anisocytic stomata with anticlinal cell wall pattern epidermal cells in abaxial side. Cuticle conspicuous in Myoporaceae while absent in members of Scorphulariaceae. Curved to wavy epidermal walls, striated surface, absence of mucilaginous cells on the leaf abaxial side. The above characters supports the genus to Scorphulariaceae,the fig wort family rather than Myoporaceae .

References

1. Dhar, ML., Dhar, MM., Dhawan, BN. and Ray, C. (1968). Screening of Indian plants for biological activity – Part I. Indian J. Ex. Bio. 6: 232-247.
2. Duke, JA. (1990). Promising phytomedicinals Advances in newcrops Janick J and Simon JE (eds.) Timber Press Portland 491-498.
3. Ncube, NS., Afolayan, AJ. and Okoh, A. (2008). Assessment techniques of antimicrobial properties of natural compounds of plant origin: current methods and future trends. African journal of Biotechnology 7 (12): 1897 – 1806.
4. Evans, WC., Trease and Evans. (1997). Pharmacognosy (14th Ed), Harcourt Brace and Company. Asia Pvt. Ltd. Singapore 343.
5. Sauren Das , Chiou-Rong Sheue , Yuen-Po Yang (2013). Leaf micromorphology and leaf glandular hair ontogeny of Myoporum bontioides A. Gray. Feddes Repertorium 124, 50– 60:4.

Figures
FIGURE:1 The Experimental Plant

FIGURE : 2 Leaf Anatomy of The Experimental Plant

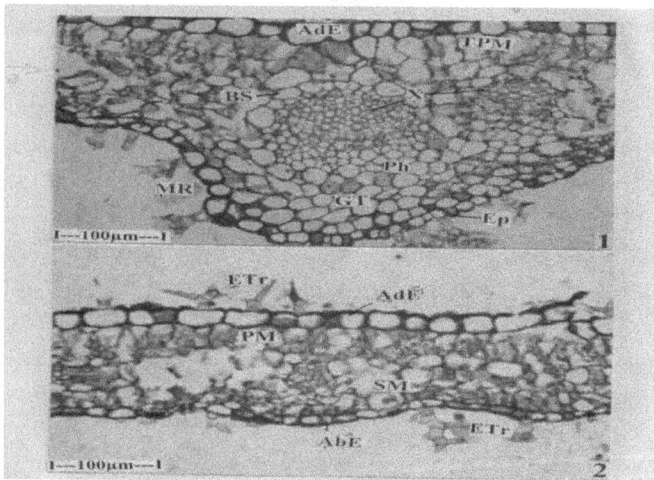

Assistant Professor,
Guru Nanak College,Chennai.
email : poonam123.73@rediffmail.com

13. आधुनिक हिन्दी कविता में मानवाधिकार की संकल्पना

डॉ. ज्योति शर्मा

शोध सारांश

मानव-मूल्यों व मानवाधिकारों का आपसी घनिष्ट सबंध है। मानवाधिकार संविधान देता है और उनका संरक्षण मानव-मूल्य करते हैं। वर्तमान समय में मानवाधिकार साहित्य चिन्तन का प्रमुख विषय है। आधुनिक हिन्दी कविता मानव को मूल्य बोध करवाते हुए, भारतीय संस्कृति के साथ जीवन यापन का संदेश देती है। कविता मानव-मूल्यों के संरक्षण के माध्यम से मानवाधिकारों की सुरक्षा व संरक्षण के दायित्व का निर्वाह करती है। कविता का धरातल मानवीय है, जिसका ध्येय सत्य, अंहिसा, करुणा, मैत्री और विश्व-बंधुत्व के साथ ही मानवाधिकार के महामंत्र-स्वतंत्रता, समता और न्याय का आह्वान है। भारतीय जीवन-मूल्यों से ओतप्रोत हिन्दी कविता मानव को समरसता, समानता के मार्ग पर प्रशस्त करती है। प्रस्तुत शोध आलेख आधुनिक हिन्दी कविता में मानवाधिकारों व मानव-मूल्यों के परिप्रेक्ष्य में चिन्तन करने का एक प्रयास है।

बीज शब्द:

मानवाधिकार, मानव-मूल्य, भारतीय संस्कृति व संविधान

इक्कीसवीं सदी में मानवाधिकार साहित्य चिन्तन का प्रमुख विषय है जिसका केन्द्र बिन्दु मानव-मूल्य है। मानवाधिकार से अभिप्राय मौलिक अधिकारों एवं स्वतंत्रता से है, जिसके हक्कदार सभी मानव है। मानवाधिकार की संकल्पना प्राचीन है जो मानव जीवन को विविध रूपों से संरक्षण प्रदान करती है। आधुनिक युग में 10 दिसम्बर 1948 को संयुक्त राष्ट्र संघ ने मानव अधिकारों का सार्वभौमिक घोषणा पत्र स्वीकार किया जिसमें नस्ल, रंग, लिंग, भाषा, धर्म आदि के आधार पर भेद समाप्त कर सामाजिक, धार्मिक, राजनीतिक व सांस्कृतिक अधिकार प्रदान किये गये। स्वतंत्रता पश्चात भारत ने भी अपने संविधान में मौलिक अधिकारों के रूप में मानवाधिकारों को शामिल किया। भारतीय संविधान में सभी व्यक्तियों को विभिन्न जाति, धर्म, लिंग, वर्ण तथा रंग के बावजूद समान माना गया तथा सभी व्यक्तियों को सामाजिक, राजनीतिक, धार्मिक तथा सांस्कृतिक अधिकार प्रदान किये गये। डॉ .जयराम उपाध्याय के अनुसार- *"मानव अधिकार वे न्यूनतम अधिकार है जो प्रत्येक व्यक्ति को*

123

आवश्यक रूप से प्राप्त होना चाहिए क्योंकि वह मानव परिवार का सदस्य है।" संविधान प्रदत्त अधिकारो का संरक्षण भी संविधान करता है और मानव उसकी पालना करके समाज में परस्पर समता, प्रेम, सहयोग की भावना से आगे बढ़ता है।

मानव-मूल्यों व मानवाधिकारों का आपसी घनिष्ठ सबंध है। मानवाधिकार संविधान देता है और उनका संरक्षण मानव-मूल्य करते हैं। मानवाधिकारों के उद्भव का इतिहास वैदिक संस्कृति से रहा है। वैदिक वाड्.मय में ऋषियों ने धर्मयुक्त कर्त्तव्य पालन के निर्देश देकर, कर्म सिद्धांत की स्थापना की थी, जिससे मानव अधिकारों की सुरक्षा होती थी। इसी परम्परा में भारतीय वाड्.मय का सृजन हुआ है। आधुनिक हिन्दी कविता भी वैश्विक एकता, समानता, शिक्षा, स्वतंत्रता और विश्व बधुत्व की भावना को साथ लेकर चलती है। सत्य, अहिंसा, प्रेम दया क्षमा, धृति, करुणा, त्याग इत्यादि मानव-मूल्यों को मानवधिकारों के परिप्रेक्ष्य में संपोषण तत्व के रूप में स्वीकार कर सकते हैं, क्योंकि मूल्यों के बिना अधिकारों की बात उठाना स्वभाविक नहीं है। मूल्य और अधिकार एक दूसरे के पूरक है। मानव-मूल्य मानव के आत्मत्व है और मानवाधिकार बाह्य तत्व, मानवाधिकारों की संकल्पना में आत्मतत्वों भी महत्ती भूमिका रहती है क्योंकि इन्हीं मानव-मूल्यों से विश्व में मानव सत्ता का आपसी सामंजस्य, भातृत्व व सहयोग रहता है। साहित्य समाज तथा युग की परिस्थितियों का स्पष्ट प्रतिबिम्ब होता है। साहित्यकार युगीन परिस्थितियों से नितांत निरपेक्ष होकर साहित्य सर्जन नहीं कर सकता है। इसी दृष्टि से आधुनिक कवि और उनकी कविता समता सहयोग और समभाव के मापदण्डों पर आधारित है। उसमें शक्ति, ओज, औदार्य, अध्यात्म, राष्ट्रीयता, मंगलाषा, त्याग करुणा, दया, प्रेम आदि मूल्यों की चेतना है।

भारतीय समाज में पूँजीपति ज़मींदार शक्तिशाली लोग कमज़ोर तथा ग़रीब लोगों का शोषण करते हैं उनसे दुर्व्यापार करते हैं। आर्थिक कुचक्र ने समाज को बुरी तरह कुचल दिया है। स्त्री, औरत व बच्चों को दलित द्राक्षा की तरह चूस कर, समाज के किनारे पर रख कर, उनके अधिकारों का सरेआम हनन हो रहा है। कवि प्रशन उठाता है कि रोटी की तलाश करता भूख से व्याकुल पेट कहाँ अधिकारों की बात करेगा-

"औरतें बांधे हुए उरोज पोटली के अन्दर है भूख आसमानी चट्टानी बोझ ढो रही हैं पत्थर की पीठ लाल मिट्टी लकड़ी लालछोर दांत मटमैले इकटक दीठ कटोरे के पेंदे में भात गोद में लेकर बैठा है बाप खा रहा है उसको चुपचाप"[2]

संविधान प्रदत्त 'शोषण के विरुद्ध मानवाधिकार' बलात् श्रम व बेगार को रोकता है। आधुनिक हिन्दी कविता जाति धर्म की जंजीरों को तोड़कर समता की बात करती है। यह समता तभी सम्भव है जब सब मिलकर जाति-पाँति की दीवारों को तोड़कर एक हो जाये अर्थात् सम्पूर्ण मानवता एक हो जाये। कविता शोषक और शोषितों का यथार्थ चित्रण कर शोषण के विरुद्ध अधिकार को बढ़ावा देती है। इसलिए कवि आह्वान करता है-

"जातिधर्म की तोड़ शृंखला खुली हवा में आओ दुनिया के शोषित मिलकर अब एक सभी हो जाओ पूंजीवाद मिटा दो समता तभी विश्व में होगी मनुष्यवाद मिटा दो दुनिया से तो मानवता पनपेगी"[3]

सामाजिक असमानता के शिकार, शोषित कमज़ोर वर्ग के लिए मानवाधिकार की माँग करते हुए, कविता एक ऐसे समाज की रचना चाहती है जो भेदभाव से मुक्त, समता पर आधारित हो। सभी मानवों का अपना जीवन है। उन्हें जीवन जीने की स्वतंत्रता मिले, विचार व्यक्त करने की स्वतंत्रता मिले, आर्थिक स्वतंत्रता मिले जिससे सभी मानव समाज की मुख्य धारा में आ सके। अपने धरातल को पहचान कर, सुनिश्चित व सुनियोजित तरीक़े से स्वयं का विकास कर सके। अपने परिवार व बच्चों का भविष्य सुरक्षित करते हुए, एक स्वस्थ सामाजिक परम्परा युक्त समाज का निर्माण कर सके। इसी विचारधारा का निर्वाह करते हुए; स्वतंत्रता की चाह, जीवन की आस्था और विवेक के मूल्यों के साथ कवि सर्वेश्वरदयाल सक्सेना कवि दायित्व सम्भालते हैं-

"कलम उठाते ही/हमें मासूम बच्चे/निरीह औरतें/मेहनतकश भोले ग़रीब इन्सान/सब हमसाया नजर आते हैं/उनकी दहशत/हमारी दहशत होती है/उनकी मौत/हमारी मौत/चाहे वे शत्रु देश के ही क्यों न हों/हर बेकसूर आदमी की लाश/हमारी कलम की स्याही में/उतर आती है/और हम सिर झुका/उस अनन्त प्रार्थना में डूब जाते हैं/जो इन्सान के लिए अक्ल की भीख माँगती है।"[4]

हिन्दी कविता स्वतंत्रता समता और बधुत्व की भावना से युक्त मानवीय गुणों को संरक्षण प्रदान करते हुए "सर्वे भवन्तु सुखिनः" की कामना करती है। मानव कल्याण की चिन्ता कवियों को है। वे ऐसे समाज की कल्पना करते हैं, जहाँ ऊँच-नीच के भेदभाव ना हो और न ही जाति व वर्ग हो, सभी स्वतंत्रता का उपभोग करे और सुखी हो। कवि भूपेन्द्र नाथ शुक्ल स्वतंत्रता के नव निर्माण और विषमता को दूर करने के लिए ही "जियो और जीने दो" के सिद्धांत का प्रतिपादन करते हैं-

"खुद जियो और जीने दो का सिद्धांत मानवीय चित्र बने। मानव-मानव ही धरती पर बस यहाँ बसे या वहाँ बसे।"[5]

मानवीय समानता में सभी मनुष्य समान हैं उनमें न कोई छोटा है और न कोई बड़ा सभी भातृभाव को धारण करते हुए उन्नति के लिए मिलकर कर्म करते आगे बढ़ते हैं। जब सब समान हैं तो भेदभाव कैसा। आधुनिक हिन्दी कविता कामना करती हैं कि सबका हृदय सदा प्रेम सहित और विरोध रहित होकर एक समान हों। मन एक समान हों। जिससे बल सामर्थ्य एक-दूसरे की सहायता से खूब बढ़े। वस्तुतः मानव-मानव की धरती, मानव के बीच की दीवारों की तोड़कर विश्व की सम्पूर्ण मानवता को एक सूत्र में बाँधकर एक ऐसे विश्व का निर्माण चाहती है जो अन्याय से मुक्त हो। अन्याय से मुक्ति मानव को न्याय का मानवाधिकार दिलाती है। इसी विश्व-बंधुत्व का कवि नगार्जुन संदेश देते हैं- *विषमता के प्रति घृणा का अनोखा उपहार लो/विश्व मानव के लिए मनुहार लो।*[6] महाप्राण कवि निराला भी मानव मात्र को पंथ, वर्ण-जाति लिंग आदि के संकुचित घेरे से बाहर निकलकर समानता की अकांक्षा करते हैं और मानव को नैतिक मूल्य प्रदान करते हैं-

"दूर हो अभिमान, संशय वर्ण-आश्रम-गत महामय जाते-जीवन हो निरामय वह सदाशयता प्रखर दो"[7]

इक्कीसवीं सदी वैश्वीकरण व भूमंडलीकरण की है। सम्पूर्ण विश्व एक घर बन गया है। वैश्वीकरण के इस युग में निजीकरण एवं उदारीकरण को बढ़ावा दिया जा रहा है, जिससे मानवाधिकारों का हनन विविध रूपों में सामने आ रहा है। विश्व में उदारीकरण, वैश्वीकरण एवं बाज़ारवाद के माध्यम से अधिक से अधिक आर्थिक विकास के प्रयास किये जा रहे हैं। सांस्कृतिक मूल्यों के विघटन व परिवर्तन के कारण परिस्थितियाँ विषम होती जा रही है। अधिकारों की आड़ में मानव-मूल्यों का ह्रास हो रहा है। अर्थप्रधान संस्कृति में मानव मशीनी-सा जीवन जी रहा हैं। जिसके सामने संवेदना, सहयोग व सद्भावना कमज़ोर पड़ रही है। यह अंधेरा ईर्ष्या, द्वेष, जलन, घुटन, कुण्ठा, पीड़ा के धुएं का है। प्रसिद्ध साहित्यकार एवं कवि धर्मवीर भारती, भवानी प्रसाद मिश्र, प्रसाद, पंत, निराला, नागार्जुन, रघुवीर सहाय, निर्मल वर्मा, रामदरश मिश्र, केदारनाथ अग्रवाल, त्रिलोचन, कुंवर नारायण, शमशेर बहादुर सिंह, ऋतुराज, चन्द्रकांत देवताले, नरेश मेहता, विजयदेव नारायण साही जैसे अनेक साहित्यकारों ने अपनी कलम से मानव-मूल्यों का संरक्षण करते हुए, उग्र स्वरों में

काव्य सृजना की हैं। रामदरश मिश्र मानव-मूल्यों की पुनर्स्थापना मानवहृदय में कर मानवाधिकारों के सरंक्षण की दिशा दी है-

"ऐसे कब तक चलते रहेंगे? धुआँ फेंकते हुए अलग-अलग कब तक जलते रहेंगे? आओ अपनी-अपनी आँच को जोड़कर एक बड़ी सी मशाल जला लें"[8]

दरअसल अलग-अलग जलना टूटने का संकेत है। मशाल की कल्पना एकता का संकेत है। जो मानव को जीवन बोध कराते हुए उसको एक नई दिशा देती है। सुख-दुख, ताप, अनुभूति, प्रेम, साहस, आस्था, विवेक, निष्ठा आदि आत्मरस हैं। जिन्हें कवि विविध रूप देकर मानव हृदय में स्थापित करने का प्रयास करता है। इन्हीं के पोषण से हृदय को समरसता की ओर ले जाना हिन्दी कविता का दायित्व हैं। रघुवीर सहाय का काव्य-संग्रह 'आत्महत्या के विरुद्ध' मानव-मूल्यों के परिप्रेक्ष्य में मानवधिकारों का घोषणा पत्र कहा जा सकता है। कवि स्पष्ट शब्दों में कहता है कि आज का मानव केवल स्वार्थी ही नहीं है स्वार्थांध भी है। दूसरों के प्रति उसकी आत्मीयता शून्य हो गयी है। मानव आत्मकेन्द्री बनकर 'मैं' में लिप्त हो रहा है। कवि-हृदय त्रासद होकर बोल उठता है-

"अब ऐसा वक्त आ गया है जब कोई किसी का झुलसा हुआ चेहरा नहीं देखता है, अब न तो किसी का खाली पेट देखता है, न थरथराती हुई टांगे और न ढला हुआ सूर्यहीन कंधा देखता है, हर आदमी सिर्फ अपना धंधा देखता है सबने भाईचारा भुला दिया है।"[9]

आधुनिक हिन्दी कविता जन-जीवन की पीड़ा को मुख्य स्वर देती हैं, अन्याय का विरोध कर न्याय का पक्ष लेती है और शोषित-पीड़ित मानव को न्याय दिलाने के लिए कविता प्रतिबद्ध है। कवि नागार्जुन 'प्रतिबद्ध हूँ' कविता में मानव को न्याय मानवाधिकार दिलाने के पक्ष में खड़ें है-

"प्रतिबद्ध हूँ,जी हाँ प्रतिबद्ध हूँ- बहुजन समाज की अनुपल प्रगति के निमित्त संकुचित 'स्व' की आपाधापी के निषेधार्थ................... अविवेकी भीड़ की। 'भेड़िया-धसान' के खिलाफ..................... अंध-बधिर व्यक्तियों' को सही राह बतलाने के लिए............. अपने आप को भी 'व्यामोह' से बारम्बार उबारने की खातिर प्रतिबद्ध हूँ, जी हाँ, शतधा प्रतिबद्ध हूँ!"[10]

आज के जीवन में बढ़ती हुयी व्यावसायिक प्रवृत्ति का सामाजिक सम्बन्धों पर बहुत दुष्प्रभाव पड़ा है। कम समय में अधिक से अधिक सम्पत्ति अर्जित करने की होड़,

127

स्वार्थपरता, भोगपरक जीवन शैली, अनाचार, अत्याचार व अन्याय को बढ़ावा दे रहे हैं। इन सब दुष्परिणामों से बचने के लिए हमें पुनः संस्कृति के अमृत तत्व को आधार मानकर उस पर चलना श्रेयस्कर है। अन्याय के विरुद्ध संघर्ष का एक अहिंसक साधन सत्याग्रह है। भारत की स्वतंत्रता प्राप्ति के लिये उसका सफल प्रयोग भी किया गया है। यह अहिंसा भारतीय मूल्य का अन्याय के विरुद्ध संघर्ष के लिए विनियोजन करने का सुन्दर उदाहरण है। रामधारी सिंह दिनकर अपनी काव्य-कृति कुरुक्षेत्र में मनुज के समता विधायक की माँग उठाते हैं-

"श्रेय होगा मनुज का समता विधायक ज्ञान। स्नेह सिंचित न्याय पर नव विश्व का निर्माण"11

समकालीन परिवेश में मानव के व्यक्तित्व निर्माण, स्वतंत्रता के सम्मान और मानवधिकारों की भावना को प्रबल करने में शिक्षा का विशेष योगदान है। मानवीय जीवन से जुड़े हर पहलू को उजागर करके सामाजिक न्याय और उत्तम सामाजिक व्यवस्था को प्रभाव में लाने में शिक्षा महत्वपूर्ण भूमिका निभाती है। शिक्षा धार्मिक विरोध समाप्त कर, अंधविश्वास, कुरीतियों का खण्डन कर मानव को सही दिशा देती है। शान्ति, सद्भावना और सहिष्णुता का पाठ पढ़ाती हैं। संविधान के अनुसार शिक्षा को प्रत्येक बालक के लिए अधिकार का रूप दे दिया गया हैं। हिन्दी कविता मानव-जीवन में शिक्षा को विशेष स्थान देती हैं। ग्रामीण क्षेत्र में कृषक, मज़दूर, घुमक्कड़ प्रवृत्ति के लोगों को भी शिक्षित करने के लिए युवकों को प्रेरणा देती है। शिक्षा ही एक ऐसी जागृति है, जो सभी मानवाधिकारों का संरक्षण करती जान पड़ती है।

निष्कर्षतः

आधुनिक हिन्दी कविता मानव-मूल्यों के संरक्षण के माध्यम से मानवाधिकारों की सुरक्षा व संरक्षण के दायित्व का निर्वाह करती है। कविता का धरातल मानवीय है, जिसका ध्येय सत्य, अहिंसा, करुणा, मैत्री, और विश्व-बंधुत्व के साथ ही मानवाधिकार के महामंत्र-स्वतंत्रता, समता और न्याय का आह्वान है। भारतीय जीवन-मूल्यों से ओतप्रोत हिन्दी कविता मानव को समरसता, समानता के मार्ग पर प्रशस्त करती है। संविधान प्रदत्त मानवाधिकारों की पालना में मानव मन की समरसता एक शक्ति के रूप में कार्य करती है जो बिना किसी बल, दण्ड और शक्ति के मानवाधिकारों को बराबर समाज में, काल-समय के सापेक्ष में, जाति-धर्म के विभेद में और लिंग-रंग-वर्ण के भेद में, स्वतंत्रता तथा नैतिकता के साथ पालना करवाती है। यथार्थ है कि आधुनिक

हिन्दी कविता 'वसुधैव कुटुम्बकम्' के आधार पर सम्पूर्ण विश्व को 'देहो देवाल्यो' नाम प्रदान करती है।

संदर्भ :
1. उपाध्याय, जयराम, मानवाधिकार, पृ. 16
2. सहाय, रघुवीर, आत्महत्या के विरुद्ध, पृ. 33
3. लक्ष्मीनारायण, उत्पीड़न की यात्रा, पृ. 61
4. सक्सेना, सर्वेश्वरदयाल, कुआनो नदी, पृ. 84–85
5. शुक्ल, भूपेन्द्र, माधवी, पृ. 119
6. नागार्जुन, पुरानी जुतियों का कोरस, पृ. 30
7. निराला, सूर्यकान्त त्रिपाठी, अणिमा, पृ. 08
8. मिश्र, रामदरश, मिश्र, स्मिता, रामदरश मिश्र रचनावली, खण्ड–एक, जुलूस कहाँ जा रहा है, पृ. 34
9. सहाय, रघुवीर, सीढ़ियों पर धूप में, पृ. 83
10. पांडेय, सं. मैनेजर, नागार्जुन चयनित कविताएं, पृ. 01
11. दिनकर, रामधारी सिंह, कुरुक्षेत्र, पृ. 118
12. डॉ. दयाराम, मानव मूल्यों के परिप्रेक्ष्य में, शोधालेख 2017

सहायक आचार्य (हिंदी)
श्री रतनलाल कंवरलाल पाटनी गर्ल्स कॉलेज किशनगढ़,
अजमेर (राजस्थान)
महर्षि दयानंद सरस्वती विश्वविद्यालय द्वारा संबद्ध
email : jyoti9sharma1983@gmail.com

14. GIS Mapping of Municipal Solid Waste Sources, Transportation Routes and Disposal in Bikaner City, Rajasthan, India

Hemlata Sahel[1*],
Mamta Sharma[2],
Anil Kumar Chhangani [1]

Abstract

In recent past many developing countries are facing serious problem of Municipal Solid Waste Management (MSWM). Waste management is defined as beneficial management of managing waste that is good for sustainable development. Population growth levels, exponential economic growth and higher living standards in the community have increased the rate of municipal solid waste (MSW) in urban areas of Indian towns and cities. Inadequate solid waste management poses risks to residents and impacts the natural environment negatively. In India, the volume of waste generation has been increasing rapidly over the last few years. According to the "Swachchh Sandesh Newsletter" by the MOHUA, as of January, 2020 about 147,613 metric tonnes (M.T.) of solid waste generated by India. The aim of this work was to develop a methodology for the optimization of the waste collection and transport system based on GIS technology. The methodology was applied to the Municipality of Bikaner city based on real field data. Bikaner City is situated between the parallels of 28°1'North latitude and 73°19'East Longitude in western Rajasthan. The city area covers 28, 466 Sq. km with about 8, 62,000 human populations. The study was conducted to discover the attributes of the types of Municipal solid waste and analyze the various sources, routes, collection and dumping sites of Bikaner city. The Arc Geographic Information System (GIS) network has been used with the help of Global Positioning System (GPS), to retrieve analyze the various sources, transportation routes, collection points, disposal sites and refilling sites of municipal solid waste. The generation rate of MSW has been approximated at 0.46 kg/capita/day and the total amount has been noted as 300 metric tons per day of MSW in Bikaner city. However the present system is not effectively managed by the city authorities in absence of systematic collection, segregation, transportations and disposal for proper disposal for all 80 wards of the city. The focus of the study is to come out with GIS mapping of the waste sources, collection, transportation, segregation and disposal sites for better and effective waste management.

Keywords : Solid Waste, Arc GIS, GPS, Waste collection point, Disposal site, Refill site.

Introduction

Solid waste management is the one of the major problem faced by today's world. There is an increase in commercial, residential and infrastructure development due to the population growth and it leads to negative impact on the environment. Municipal solid waste management (MSWM) is a greatest challenge before environment scientists, urban planners and decision makers of the world (Tripathi, *et. al.* 2022). Urban solid waste management is considered as one of the most tedious environmental problems facing by municipal authorities in developing countries. Collection of municipal solid waste (MSW) is an important step in every waste management program. It is one of the greatest challenges facing waste managers worldwide. Irrespective of the waste management method to be employed, the waste must first be collected. Collection processes may be tailored to meet the goal of the intended waste management method such as resource recovery or land filling. MSW collection usually involves people and a means of transport to a transfer station, treatment facility, or final disposal site (Worrell and Vesilind, 2012). Collection trucks then pick up containers, empty them at a final disposal site and return the containers to their locations. However, this collection system is associated with difficulties leading to uncollected waste as a result of overflow, ground dumping at collection sites, and open/indiscriminate dumping at unauthorized places.

The rapid growth of population and urbanization decreases the non renewable resources and disposal of effluent and toxic waste indiscriminately, are the major environmental issues posing threats to the existence of human being (Allen, *et. al.* 1997). The most common problems associated with improper management of solid waste include diseases transmission, fire hazards, odor nuisance, atmospheric and water pollution, aesthetic nuisance and economic losses. GIS can recognize, analyze and correlate the spatial relationship between mapped phenomenon the software also has provision for querying thereby enabling policy makers to link disparate sources of information, perform sophisticated analysis, visualize trends, project outcomes and strategize long term planning goals (Malczewski, 1996). Waste collection Route optimization Collection and transportation is responsible for 70-80% of total waste management cost have proposed a GIS based collection and transportation model for MSMW and test checked it for Bikaner municipality. Generally municipal solid waste is collected and deposited in sanitary landfill, such unscientific disposal attract birds, rodents and fleas to the waste dumping site and create unhygienic conditions (Suchitra, 2007). About 60 to 70% of this amount is spent on collection, 20 to 30% on transportation and less than 5% on final disposal of waste. The utilization of Geographic Information Systems (GIS) and Global Positioning Systems (GPS) to capture and analyze spatial data is well known; and is growing in municipal solid waste management (MSWM) (Hua, 2003 and Sarptas, *et. al.* 2005). Information on geographic locations of municipal solid waste collection/dump sites (MSWCS) can help decision-making in MSWM, including collection route planning, dumps cleanup, and future sitting of collection sites. Although few studies have mapped solid waste collection systems (Chalkias and Lasaridi, 2009). The environment is heading towards a potential risk due to unsustainable waste disposal. It is a sensitive issue, which concerns about serious environmental problems in today's world. The present situation of direct dumping of the waste without proper inspection and separation leaves a serious impact of environmental pollution causing a tremendous growth in health related problems. Domestic, industrial and other wastes, whether they are low or medium level wastes, they are causing environmental pollution and have become perennial problems for mankind. Use of these techniques in solid waste management supports in capturing, handling, and transmitting the required information in a prompt and proper manner (Singh, 2019). The Geographical Information System (GIS) can provide an opportunity to integrate field parameters with population and other relevant data or other associated features, which help in selection of sites. Site selection procedures can benefit from the appropriate use of GIS.

Study Area : Bikaner City is situated between the parallels of 28° 1' 22.566" North Latitude and 73° 18' 42.8976" East Longitude. The city area covers 28, 466 Sq. km with about 8, 62,000 human populations as shows in (Figure 1). Bikaner city is divided into five Zones and further subdivided into 80 wards by the municipal authorities. Bikaner city is spread over the area of 28, 466 Square Kilometer out of which the area of Bikaner Municipal Corporation (BMC) is about 155 sq. km. (BMC, 2020). Every year BMC spends on average 18% of its total budget on solid waste management. It is situated in the Thar Desert, Bikaner was considered an oasis on the trade route between Central Asia and the Gujarat coast as it had adequate spring water. The strategic location of Bikaner on the ancient caravan routes that came from West/Central Asia made it a prime trade centre in that times *(http://rajasthantourism.gov.in)*.

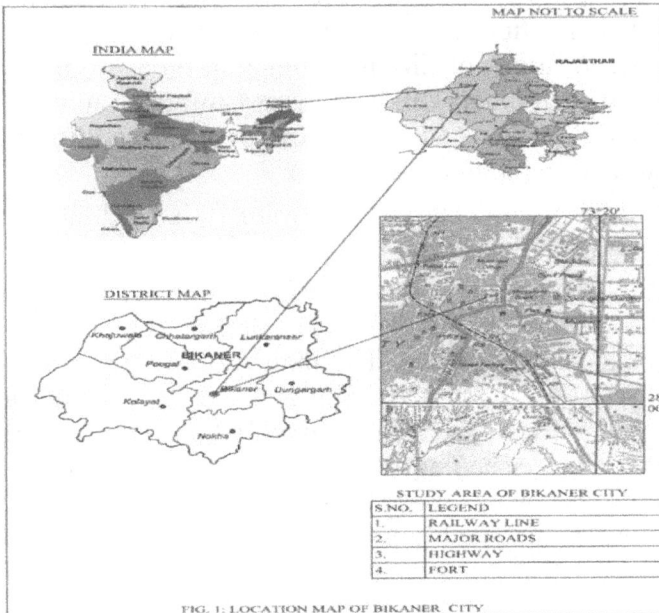

Figure 1 Location of the Study Area in the Bikaner City, Rajasthan, India

133

Methodology :

The aim of this work was to understand the present practices of the solid waste sources collection transport system and disposal and mapping with based on GIS technology. The methodology was applied to the Municipality of Bikaner city based on real field data (Karadimas, 2008).

GIS (Geographic Information System) : It is a computer tool used for capturing storing querying analyzing and displaying spatial data from real world for a particular set of purposes. This technique is used to generate optimal route for collecting solid wastes. GIS is a tool that not only reduces time and cost of site selection, but also provide a digital data bank for future monitoring program of site. Show cased application of GIS in solid waste management for Bikaner city (Shobha and Rasappan, 2013). A geographic information system (GIS) is a computer system for capturing, storing, checking, and displaying data related to positions on Earth's surface. GIS can show many different kinds of data on one map. This enables people to more easily see, analyze, and understand patterns and relationships. With GIS technology, people can compare the locations of different things in order to discover how they relate to each other. GIS can use any information that includes location. The location can be expressed in many different ways, such as latitude and longitude.

A) Data Entry : Arc View GIS software 10 is used to create maps and for analysis of data base.

B) Mapping Technique : The Bikaner city map was obtained from the District Town Planning office. The details were identified using the geographical coordinates. The map was scanned using the HP Precision scan jet 5200c at 600dpi and the scanned images were stored as JPEG files, which were edited wherever necessary, using MS Photo Editor. Scanning results in the conversion of the image into an array of pixels thereby producing an image in the raster format. A raster file is an image in a series of dots called pixels or picture element that are arranged in rows and columns in a matrix format.

The raster images were opened in Arc view GIS as a raster layer using JPEG interchange format. Later this image was projected using projection of geographic latitude and longitude. Registration and Transformation was done to convert the image to real world coordinates. There are two types of transformation techniques, where the first one involves the X and Y co-ordinates recorded in Notepad or dbase being opened in Arc View. The option "Add Table" presents in Arc View adds the X, Y coordinates in the Notepad or dbase to the map, out of which the points were created. The created points were coordinated to that of the raster layer.

Similar features to that of the points were identified in the raster layer and a source point was selected in the raster map. Using that, the destination point was given to the text / dbf map. The raster later was thus assigned the real world coordinated or the ground control points of the study area. On completion of the transformation with the above method, over the raster layer, a new layer is digitized with special points. The entire layer was saved as a shape file.

C.Thematic Mapping : For the present study natural break classification techniques were used to classify sources, routes, disposal sites for thematic mapping.

Results and Discussion :

GIS Mapping of Municipal Solid Waste Different Sources :

A total of 7 Municipal Solid Waste Management (MSWS) (including 320 households, 583 hotel and restaurants, 15 markets, shops and offices, 40 Hospitals) were main sources of Municipal solid waste in Bikaner City. BMC has provided container bins in the major market areas for storage of waste. Main market places in Bikaner city are Rani Bazaar, Super/ Main Market, Kote Gate, Bada Bazar they consist 2.5 % out of total waste. Considering that there are about 583 numbers of hotels and restaurants in the city there would be around 5.68 tonnes of waste each day. The Bikaner city is estimated to have total roads of about 458 km in BMC limits spread across all the 60 wards. On an average each sweeper sweeps around 700-800 Sq meters in per day. Health care facilities operating in Bikaner have obtained connectivity with M/s E-Tech Project covers area is about 150 Km. Total quantity of biomedical waste collected from 264 hospitals, whereas bed capacity is 4503 from member health care facility. GIS mapping of selected total 40 hospitals according to their bed capacity in the study areas shown in Figure 3. Total generated biomedical waste is 2600kg /day out of which 520 kg/day treated by incretion, 6.5 kg/day by Autoclaving, 3 kg/day by shredding and 200L/ day effluent treated.

The resulting feature layer was employed to develop a Solid waste different sources mapping of vegetable markets, Hospitals. According to GIS mapping 6 major vegetable markets in the city these are Daga Building KEM Road, Baido Ki Pirol, Rani Bazar, Phad Bazar, Kote Gate, Pugal Road they contribute vegetables, cartoon, plastic, polythene. Residue vegetable eatable for cows of the city and rest of other waste are carried by rag pickers and sell to whole sailor of waste as shown in Table 1 and Figure 2.

Table 1: Estimation of the Municipal Solid Waste in Bikaner City (%)

Sources of Waste	Percentage
Households	39.3%
Hotel and Restaurants	36.5%
Street Sweeping	10.8 %
Markets	2.5%
Shops and Offices	2.7%
Hospital	8.2%
Total	**100%**

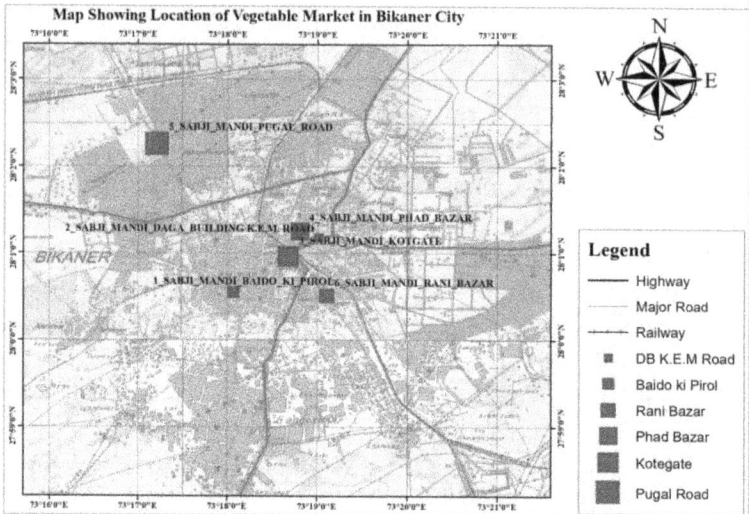

Figure 2: location of Vegetable market in Bikaner city

136

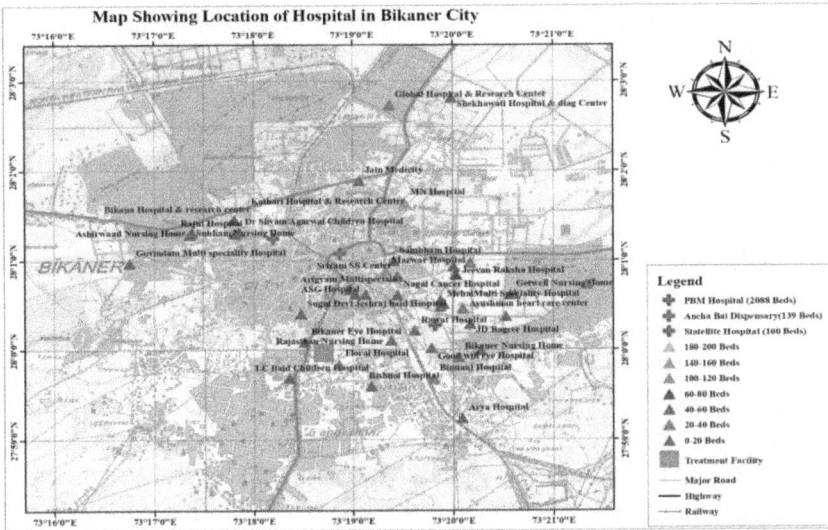

Figure 3: Location of the Hospitals in Bikaner City generating biomedical waste.

GIS Mapping for Municipal Solid Waste Collection and Transportation :

The results of this analysis are shown in Figure 4. Out of the 55 transported routes, 11 (about 50%) had containers and no ground dumping of waste, 24 (39% approximately) had containers with ground dumping of waste, and 20 (nearly 27%) are without containers with ground dumping. Overall, about 67% of MSWCS are experiencing ground dumping, which suggests poor MSWM.

Plate 1: Collection of waste by JPG and loaded in waste Tractor near Dungar college road

The 14 sites experiencing open dumping appear relatively located out of inner town suggesting that the collection system is mostly concentrated in the inner city. There are 132container bins of 3 cum, 2.5 cum, 1.1 cum containers. These container depots are considered as part of the transport system. There is no intermediate transfer station in Bikaner. Records from the waste managers of Bikaner Municipality showed that 37 container sites were in the town. It may be that these managers are not aware of the dumping going on in most of the 14 sites without containers. This map and its relational database could be a great resource to help these waste managers identify the 14 sites for proper management. The collection bins are of size 3 cum, 2.5 cum, 1.1 cum capacity and there are 132 bins spread across the city. There is an active sweeping, secondary collection and transport systems operational with an assessed efficiency of collection of about 90%. Considering that each bin of 3 cubic meter sizes contains a waste of 1.5 tons, around 25-30 tons of market waste is generated each day from markets. The street sweeping work is carried out from 6.00 AM to 12.00 PM in the morning hours.

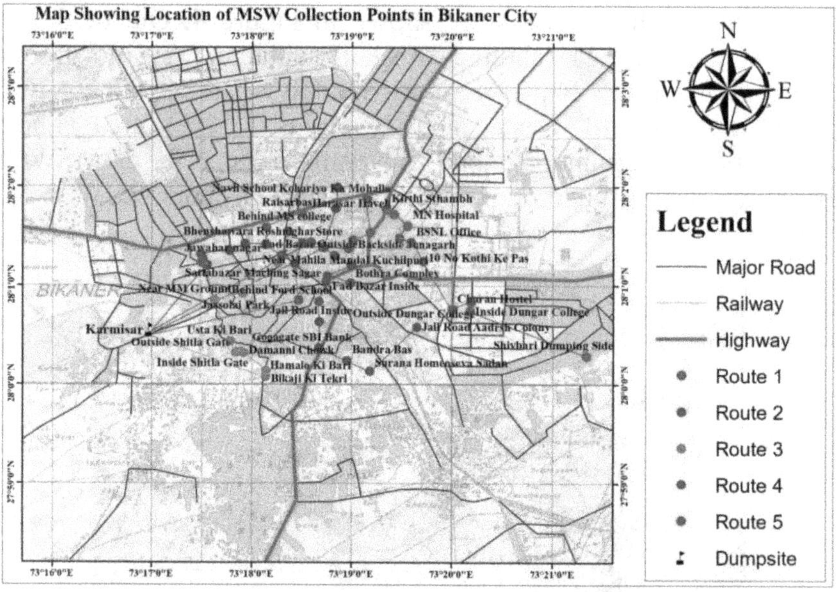

Figure 4: Location of Municipal solid waste collection points in Bikaner city

Transportation of the solid waste generated in the city presently is being managed by Bikaner Municipal Corporation BMC. Primary transportation refers to transporting of waste generated from waste generators to the waste storage depot. Primary transportation of door to door waste collection is done through 1.11 cum small vehicles in Bikaner. There are no intermediate storage depots in Bikaner except container bins. Secondary transportation refers to collection of waste from intermediate storage points like dumper bins and open points to disposal unit. BMC is presently managing the secondary transportation with its vehicles. Compactor, dumper placers and tractor trailers are used as secondary transportation vehicles.

MSWC geodatabase, which can help in planning and management decision making on MSW, is non-existent in Bikaner City. Thus, the creation of this database should be a useful tool toward improving the MSW collection system in Bikaner Municipality.

GIS Mapping of Municipal Solid Waste Disposal Site :

Some routes sites not having containers and ground dumping are an indication that those sites have inadequate containers and may need additional containers to eliminate or minimize ground dumping. Though we lacked adequate resources to quantify ground dumping during the field survey, it is worth noting that dumped waste range from young to matured and low to relatively higher in volume. BMC has set up Municipal Solid Waste disposing site at Goga gate, Karmisar Shiv valley, Vallabh Garden as shown in Fig 5. Existing Vallabh Garden dumping site is located at a distance of about kms from the city center. The total area of the landfill site is about 2 acre approx. area. The landfill site is walled on all sides.

Plate 2: Waste dispose at Vallabh garden dumping site in Bikaner city

The facility has been provided with a watchman's room. BMC has deployed trip entry recorders for the trips of each vehicle on all days. The disposal site is being provided with a 24 hour watch man and weighing bridge. The waste brought to the depot by compactors, dumper placers and tractors is dumped inside and JCB is deployed to form heaps of the waste. The waste heaps are not covered with inert material and no scientific waste processing is done on site.

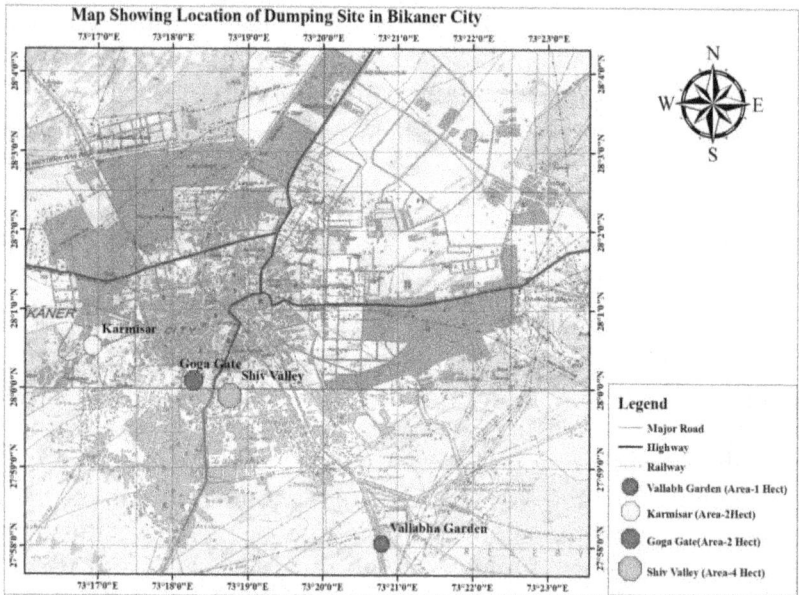

Figure 5: Location of Dumping Sites in Bikaner City

Plate 3: Weighing of loaded waste in tractor at Pandit Dharam Kanta in Bikaner City

Table 2: Types of transportation vehicle to carry the Municipal Solid Waste per day in MT

Types of vehicles	No of Units	Shift	Average no. of trip per day	Capacity (metric tons)	Total waste transported daily (metric tons)
Pvt.Tractor	35	Morning	105	1.05	157.05
Pvt. Tractor	20	Evening	40	1.05	60.00
Govt. Tractor	07	Morning	21	1.05	31.05
Dumper	11	Morning	33	2.05	82.05
Dumper	02	Evening	04	2.05	10.00
Auto tripper	04	Morning	12	0.25	03.00
Refuse Container	01	Morning	11	05.00	05.00

Note Total waste transported by vehicles is 349.00 tonnes per day according to BMC (Nagar Nigam, 2020).

Refill Site: Use of GIS Mapping in the management of Solid Waste, Route, Dumping Site, Collection site, Refilling Site. Recently house to house and transported to waste city dumping yard presently at Vallabh Garden area is about 9 hector approx. areas. Open dumping site is occurred in many parts of the city. The refill station concept could do significantly reduce packaging waste without compromising the price or quality of liquid products as shown in table 3 and Figure 7. In Bikaner city every corner rag pickers use thrown plastic bottles and other recyclable material for selling and its help for their livelihood.

Table 3 Proposed refilling site for municipal waste management in Bikaner city

S.No.	Longitude	Latitude	Area (HA)	Location
1	73.3826E	28.0939N	25.94593955	KG Mines Beechhwal Rural
2	73.3801E	28.0785N	50.62061272	Beechhwal Rural
3	73.4376E	28.0436N	22.20699222	Ridmalsar Purohitan
4	73.4619E	28.0470N	8.15370869	Himtasar
5	73.4682E	28.0486N	4.05275834	Himtasar 1

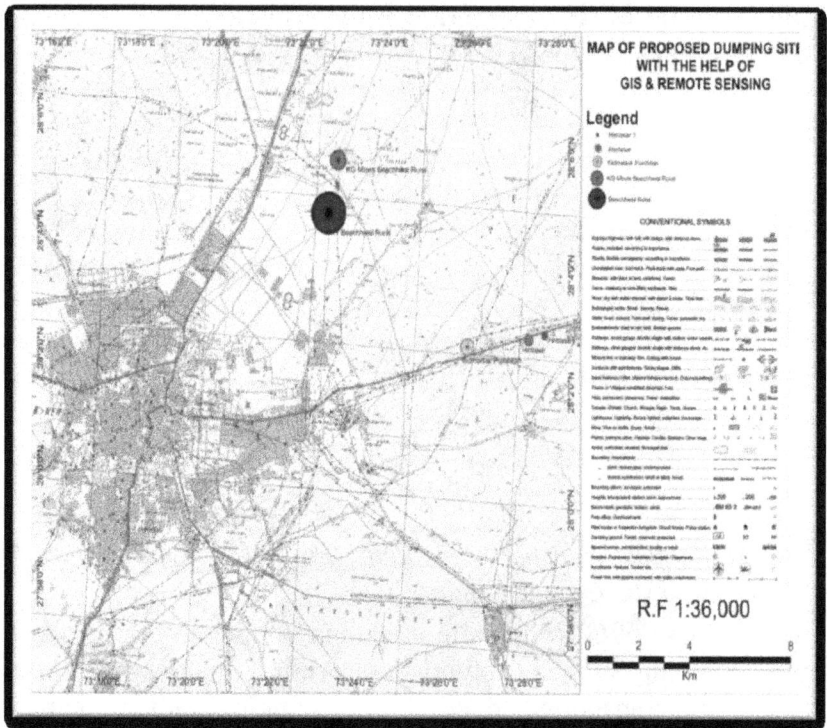

Figure 6: Location of dumping at existed mining area in and around city

The creation of GIS maps for Bikaner town can be utilized for MSW generation sources for sustainable waste management. From the data collected, an analysis of collection efficiency of the Bikaner Municipal collection system was conducted based on communal container availability and ground dumping of waste. The spatial relationship between Transfer routes, dumping sites was examined. The findings show high concentration of MSWCS in the inner city of Bikaner. significant percentage of container sites characterized by ground dumping and higher number of open dumps in Bikaner town were also observed, suggesting weakness in the MSW collection system. This study illustrated that MSWM in developing counties could be improved using GIS technology. The approach used for Bikaner city could be replicated in many other cities and urban towns in Bikaner as well as other developing countries with similar MSWM problems to enhance policy and decision making.

Conclusion :

According to study used of GIS the selection of most suitable site for disposal of solid waste in Kolkata city (Paul, 2014). A well as another study held in Pondicherry its stated that GIS useful for ensure minimum damage to the environment and geology water supply resources, land use, sensitive sites, air quality ground water quality from testing GIS system (Sumathi, 2008). Another study conducted in Sfax city in Tunisia outcome of this study is developed to improve efficiency of waste collection and transportation by the help of Arc GIS network tool (*www.smartcitiescouncil.com*). Collection of Municipal Solid Waste (MSW) is important in every waste management program. Communal container collection systems appear most prevalent in many developing countries. However, this collection system is associated with problems such as overflow of waste containers, ground dumping at collection sites, and open/indiscriminate dumping at unauthorized places. The spatial distribution of these activities present potential contamination challenges to water resources. Spatial information on Municipal Solid Waste Collection/Dump Sites (MSWCS) is essential for Municipal Solid Waste Management (MSWM) decision-making, including sources and collection route planning, and dumps cleanup. This study demonstrated how GIS and GPS can be used to enhance decision making on MSW and water management.

As the main aim of this work is the application of an operational waste collection scheme, future work will focus on the enhancement of the proposed approach. Advanced sectorization can be further investigated, since it is a significant aspect of the collection procedure. GIS technology can be used at local level for the optimization of the waste collection procedure, with considerable financial and environmental savings. The municipal officers and local workers involved in solid waste management should be clear about the function and their role in terms of managing cities effectively with help of GIS system. Thematic maps will help to identify and monitor more generated waste. The assignment of waste management comes to be more unpredictable as the populace increments. The moving capability of GIS in taking care of extensive volume of geospatial information requires its inclination to the utilization of accepted technique for waste management. In this study GIS innovation was utilized for the advancement of a strategy for the optimization of blended MSW gathering. The system employments different geographical information (way organize, area of waste canisters, arrive utilizes and so on) in co-operation with progressed spatial dissection GIS instruments. There is need to improve waste management practices better data monitoring and management with the help of GIS. GIS can be also used at various levels in MSW management in various cities of India. Promoting waste markets and recycling would also create awareness to reduce the total volume of waste at the landfill. This study demonstrated how GIS mapping can be used to enhance the waste management in the urban areas.

Acknowledgment :

We would like to acknowledge the organize of ICMSD, 20222, Raj rishi Government Autonoms College, Alwar, Rajasthan and give warmest thanks to our Professor V.K. Singh Vice chancellor and Head, Department of Environmental Science, Maharaja Ganga Singh University, Bikaner, Rajasthan for providing facilities in the department. We would also like to thank Geomin solution Pvt. Ltd. Member as Geologist Suraj Bhan Singh for creating Map from ArcGIS and sanitary inspector Om Prakash of Nagar Nigam of Bikaner City.

References :
Allen AR, Dillon AM, O'Brien M. (1997). Approaches to landfill site selection in Ireland. Engineering Geology and the Environment. Balkema, Rotterdam pp 15691574.
Bikaner Nagar Nigam, 2019.
BMC. (2020). Nagar Nigam Bikaner. Door to Door MSW collection & Transportation for Bikaner city Report.
Chalkias, C. and Lasaridi, K. (2009). A GIS Based Model for the Optimization of Municipal Solid Waste Collection: The Case Study of Nikea, Athens, Greece. Technology, 1, pp.11-15.
http://rajasthantourism.gov.in.
Hua, H.Z.X. (2003). Application of GIS System into the Management of Municipal Solid Waste. Liaoning Urban and Rural Environmental Science & Technology, 4, pp.0-18.

Karadimas N.V and Loumous V.G. (2008). GIS based modeling for estimation of municipal solid waste generation and collection. Waste management and research, 26, pp. 337-34.

Malczewski, J. (1996). A GIS based land use suitability analysis, a critical overview, Program. Plan. 62(1) pp. 3-65.

Paul, K., Dutta, A. & Krishna, A. P. (2014). A comprehensive study on landfill site selection for Kolkata City, India. Journal of the Air & Waste Management Association, Volume 64 Issue (7), pp. 846–861.

Rasappan, S. K. (2013). Application of GIS in solid waste management for Coimbatore City. International Journal of Scientific and Research Publications Volume (3), Issue 10 pp 1-5.

Sarptas, H., Alpaslan, N. and Dolgen, D. (2005). GIS Supported Solid Waste Management in Coastal Areas. Water Science & Technology, 51, pp. 213-220.

Singh, A. (2019). Remote sensing and GIS applications for municipal waste management. Journal of Environmental Management. . Elsevier, 243, pp 22-29.

Suchitra, M. (2007). Outside: Burnt or buried, garbage needs land. Down to Earth, 15 March, pp. 22–24.

Sumathi, V.R., Natesan, U. and Sarkar, C. (2008).GIS-based approach for optimized sitting of municipal solid waste landfill. Waste Management, Volume 28, Issue, 11 pp. 2146-2160.

www.smartcitiescouncil.com.

Tripathi, D. K., Kumar, M.and Biswas, V. (2022). Spatial Modeling for Municipal Solid Waste Management Using Remote Sensing and Geographic Information System. Advances in Geographical and Environmental Sciences. Springer Book , 483-497.

Worrell, W.A. and Vesilind, P.A. (2012). Solid Waste Engineering. 2nd Edition, Cengage Learning, Stamford. ISBN-13: 978-1-4390-6215-9.

[1]Department of Environment Science, MGS University, Bikaner, Rajasthan.
[2]Department of zoology, RR Government Autonomous College, Alwar, Rajasthan
* email : sahalhem88@gmail.com

15. Human Rights and Education

Dr. Pooja Bagri

Abstract

The human rights refer to all rights that are present in our existing society. Without human rights one cannot live as human beings in our existing society. Human rights are the basic rights that a person irrespective of race, caste, gender, creed, religion or any other background cannot be denied anywhere and or at any condition. Rights are provided in Part III of the Indian Constitution as fundamental rights. The Constitution guarantees six fundamental rights to Indian citizens as follows: right to equality, right to freedom, right against exploitation, right to freedom of religion, cultural and educational rights, and right to constitutional remedies. Education is the most powerful tool which can shape the destiny of an individual as well as the whole nation. The right to education is a fundamental human right under the right to freedom. It is also central to realizing other human rights. The Indian Constitution has provisions to ensure that the state provides education to all its children. The Indian Constitution in its original enactment defined education as state list subject. In 1976, the 42nd Constitutional amendment was added and education became a concurrent list subject which enables the central government to legislate it in the manner suited to it. The 86th Constitutional amendment making education a fundamental right was passed by Parliament in 2002under the article 21A. The Right of Children to Free and Compulsory Education Act (RTE Act), a law to enable the implementation of the fundamental right was passed by Parliament in year of 2009. Both the Constitutional amendment and the new law came into force from 1st April 2010. On Constitutional basis, the present paper highlights the fundamental human rights and right to education of the children.

Keywords : Human Rights, Right to Education, Indian Constitution, Children.

Introduction

Every human being has dignity. The principles of human rights were drawn up by human beings as a way of ensuring that the dignity of everyone is properly and equally respected. The human rights refer to all rights that are present in our existing society. Without human rights one cannot live as human beings in our existing society. Human rights are the basic rights that a person irrespective of race, caste, gender, creed, religion or any other background cannot be denied anywhere and or at any condition. Human rights are commonly understood as basic fundamental rights that a person cannot be denied by any individual or any government simply because he or she is a human being. President Franklin Roosevelt of USA, in his famous message to the Congress in 1941, for the first time used the term 'Human rights' and stressed that the world should be founded on four essential freedoms – freedom of speech, freedom of religion, freedom of want, and freedom of fear. In 1948, the UN General Assembly adopted the Universal Declaration of Human Rights Which had 30 articles most of which had been drafted by Rene Cassin who was later on awarded Nobel Prize in 1968. This Universal Declaration of Human Rights has been the most outstanding and the most fundamental landmark in the history of the concept of Human Rights in the world. The 30 articles of the Declaration together form a comprehensive statement covering economic, social, cultural, political, and civil rights. Every year 10th December is celebrated as Human Rights Day.

There are a large number of human rights problems, which cannot be solved unless the right to education is addressed as the key to unlock other human rights. The right to education is clearly acknowledged in the United Nations' Universal Declaration of Human Rights (UDHR), adopted in 1948, which states:

"Everyone has the right to education. Education shall be free, at least in the elementary and fundamental stages. Elementary education shall be compulsory. Technical and professional education shall be made generally available and higher education shall be equally accessible to all on the basis of merit." - Article 26(1).

"Education shall be directed to the full development of the human personality and to the strengthening of respect for Human Rights and fundamental freedoms. It shall promote understanding, tolerance and friendship among all nations, racial or religious

groups, and shall further the activities of the United Nations for the maintenance of peace." Article 26(2).

The right to education is one of the fundamental rights proclaimed in the UDHR under Article 26. It is considered by the Declaration not only as a right in itself but also as a means of promoting peace and respect for human rights and fundamental freedoms generally.

Human Rights and Indian Constitution

Rights are claims that are essential for the existence and development of individuals. In that sense there will a long list of rights. Whereas all these are recognized by the society, some of the most important rights are recognized by the State and enshrined in the Constitution. Such rights are called fundamental rights. These rights are fundamental because of two reasons. First, these are mentioned in the Constitution which guarantees them and the second, these are justifiable, i.e. enforceable through courts. Being justifiable means that in case of their violation, the individual can approach courts for their protection. If a government enacts a law that restricts any of these rights, it will be declared invalid by courts. Such rights are provided in Part III of the Indian Constitution. The Constitution guarantees six fundamental rights to Indian citizens as follows: (I) right to equality (II) right to freedom(III) right against exploitation (IV) right to freedom of religion (V) cultural and educational rights and (VI) right to constitutional remedies.

Originally, there were seven Fundamental Rights in the Constitution. Besides the above mentioned six rights, there was the Right to Property also. Since this Right created a lot of problems in the way of attaining the goal of socialism and equitable distribution of wealth, it was removed from the list of Fundamental Rights in 1978 by 44th constitutional amendment. However, its deletion does not mean that we do not have the right to acquire, hold and dispose of property. Citizens are still free to enjoy this right. But now it is just a legal right and not a Fundamental Right.

(I) Right to Equality

(II) Article14 : Equality before law: The State shall not deny to any person equality before the law or the equal protection of the laws within the territory of India.

Article15 : Prohibition of discrimination on grounds of religion, race, caste, sex or place of birth.

Article 16 : Equality of opportunity in matters of public employment.

Article 17 : Abolition of Untouchability: "Untouchability" is abolished and its practice in any form is forbidden. The enforcement of any disability arising out of "Untouchability" shall be an offence punishable in accordance with law.

Article 18 : Abolition of titles.

(II) Right to Freedom

Article 19 : Protection of certain rights regarding freedom of speech, etc.

Article 20 : Protection in respect of conviction for offences.

Article 21 : Protection of life and personal liberty.

Article 21 A : Right to education.

Article 22 : Protection against arrest and detention in certain cases.

(III) Right against Exploitation

Article 23 : (1) Traffic in human beings and beggar and other similar forms of forced labour are prohibited and any contravention of this provision shall be an offence punishable in accordance with law.

(2) Nothing in this article shall prevent the State from imposing compulsory service for public purposes, and in imposing such service the State shall not make any discrimination on grounds only of religion, race, caste or class or any of them.

Article 24: No child below the age of fourteen years shall be employed to work in any factory or mine or engaged in any other hazardous employment.

(IV) Right to Freedom of Religion

Article 25 : Freedom of conscience and free profession, practice and propagation of religion

Article 26 : Freedom to manage religious affairs

Article 27 : Freedom as to payment of taxes for promotion of any particular religion

Article 28 : Freedom as to attendance at religious instruction or religious worship in certain educational institutions

(V) Cultural and Educational Rights

Article 29 : Protection of interests of minorities

Article 30 : Right of minorities to establish and administer educational institutions

Article 31 : [Repealed.]

Saving of Certain Laws

Article 31A : Saving of Laws providing for acquisition of estates, etc.

Article 31B : Validation of certain Acts and Regulations

Article 31C : Saving of laws giving effect to certain directive principles

Article 31D : [Repealed.]

(VI) Right to Constitutional Remedies

Article 32 : Remedies for enforcement of rights conferred by this Part

Article 32A : [Repealed.]

Article 33 : Power of Parliament to modify the rights conferred by this Part in their application to Forces, etc.

Article 34 : Restriction on rights conferred by this Part while martial law is in force in any area.

Article 35 : Legislation to give effect to the provisions of this Part.

Education and Indian Constitutional Perspectives

To ensure global and international covenant on education, earnest struggle is made and essential amendment are brought in constitution of India to safeguard educational right to all citizen in light of global principle. The Indian constitution has provisions to ensure that the state provides education to all its citizens. The Indian constitution in its original enactment defined education as state subject. In 1976, the 42nd Constitutional amendment was added and education became a concurrent list subject which enables the central government to legislate it in the manner suited to it. The Fundamental Rights and Directive Principles of State Policy (DPSP) & Fundamental Duties of the Indian Constitution provide the framework for rights to education.

I. Right to Education and Human Fundamental Rights (Part III)

Article 21A : The Right of Children to Free and Compulsory Education Act (RTE, Right to Education): The Right of Children to

Free and Compulsory Education Act' or 'Right to Education Act also known as RTE', is an Act of the Parliament of India enacted on 4thAugust 2009, which describes the modalities of the importance of free and compulsory education for children between 6 and 14 in India under Article 21A (Article 21is the Fundamental Right to Life under Right to Freedom) of the Indian Constitution. India became one of 135 countries to make education a fundamental right of every child when the act came into force on 1 April 2010. "The State shall provide free and compulsory education to all children of the age of six to fourteen years in such manner as the State may, by law, determine".

II. Right to Education and the Directive Principles of State Policy (Part IV)

Article 41: *Right to work, to education and to public assistance in certain cases.* The State shall, within the limits of its economic capacity and development, make effective provision for securing the right to work, to education and to public assistance in cases of unemployment, old age, sickness and disablement, and in other cases of undeserved want.

Article 45 : *Right for Early Childhood Care and Education (ECCE) to all children until they complete the age of six years.* This article is considered as a directive principle of state policy. It states "The State shall endeavour to provide, within a period of ten years from the commencement of this Constitution, for free and compulsory education for all children until they complete the age of fourteen years".

The Government of India has included ECCE as a constitutional provision through the amended Article 45(as per the 86th Amendment of December, 2002 and passed by Parliament in July 2009) which directs that "the State shall endeavour to provide Early Childhood Care and Education for all children until they complete the age of six years".

Article 46 : *Promotion of the economic and educational interests of the Scheduled Castes, Scheduled Tribes and other weaker sections:* The State shall promote with special care the educational and economic interests of the weaker sections of the people, and, in particular, of the Scheduled Castes and the Scheduled Tribes, and shall protect them from social injustice and all forms of exploitation.

It is laid down in Article 46 as a directive principle of State policy that the State should promote with special care the educational and economic interests of the weaker sections of the people and protect them from social injustice. Any special provision that the State may make for the educational, economic or social advancement of any backward class of citizens may not be challenged on the ground of being discriminatory. Special efforts are being made for education of the backward classes. Scholarships, hostel facilities, ashram residential schools, relaxed norms for admission, reservation of seats are efforts to achieve universal education in case of backward classes.

III. Right to Education and Fundamental Duties (Part IVA)

By the Constitution (Eighty-Sixth Amendment) Act, 2002, (w.e.f 1.4.2010) adding a new clause (k) under Article 51A (fundamental duties), making parent or guardian responsible for providing opportunity for education to their children between six and fourteen years.

Conclusion

There is no doubt that education has a major role to play for protection and promotion of human rights. HRE is considered as one of the major tools to stop the violations against human rights. Education should be imparted to each and every one so that they understand the importance of human rights. Equality shall be the primary consideration in actions concerning children, respect for the views of the child are the general principals of the Convention on the Rights of a child. Education in their own mother language about human rights will make the learners more prompt about their values and ways to use them in their day to day life. The values of cultural diversity and social diversity should be inculcated as a basic teaching. For integration of human rights, the relevant subjects at the primary stage are languages & environmental studies. Stories, poems and songs concerning human rights values will have to be selected. Education should impart gender equality, respect for human dignity and rights.

References

1. **Alam K. & Halder U. K. (2018).** Research Article Human Rights and Right to Education in India
2. **Ghosh, S. &Mohan, R. (2016).** Education in Emerging Indian Society the Challenges and Issues. PHI Learning Private Limited.
3. **Gupta, M. & Lata, P. (2013).**Protection of Child Rights in India: Role of Teachers and Parents, Educationia Confab, 2(3).36-44.
4. **Mahapatra, N. (2012).**Role of Education in Promotion and Protection of Human Rights, Odisha Review, 26-30.
5. **Naseema, C. (2008).** Human Rights Education Theory and Practice. Shipra Publications, Delhi.
6. **Naseema, C. (2012).** Human Rights Education Conceptual and Pedagogical Aspects. Kaniska Publishers Distributors, New Delhi.
7. **Puar, S.S. (2012).** Right to Education Act: A Critical Analysis. International Journal of Educational and Psychological Research (IJEPR), 1(2), 27-30.
8. **Ruhela, S.P. & Nayak, R.K. (2011).**Value Education and Human Rights Education. Neelkamal Publications Pvt. Ltd.
9. **Ruhela, S.P. & Nayak, R.K. (2011).**Value Education and Human Rights Education. Neelkamal Publications Pvt. Ltd.
10. **The Constitution of India,** Govt. of India, Ministry of Law and Justice.
11. **Viswanath, M. (2014).** Right to Education using Human Rights Based Approach: A Policy Perspective for India. IOSR Journal of Humanities and Social Science (IOSR-JHSS), 19(6), 46-54.

Assistant Professor of Education
Shri Ratanlal Kanwarlal Patni Girls's College Kishangarh,
Ajmer
(Affiliated to MDS University Ajmer)
email : poojatanw@gmail.com

16. Histopathological Changes in The Intestine of *Aetomylaeus Nichoffii* (Bloch & Schnaider, 1801) with special reference to Helminthic Infection

Vasant Dongare

Abstract

Studies of histopathological changes on gastrointestinal tract of infected cestode parasite of *Gymnorhynchus* in the intestines of fish *Aetomylaeus nichoffii* (Bloch & Schnaider, 1801) from Alibag Coast, Dist. Raigad (M.S.) India. This parasite caused significant histological changes in the fish intestine, such as weakened villi, villi shortening, inflammation, hyperplasia, normal structural degradation, intestinal lumen widening, and an increase in the number of mucous cells. Damage occurs to both the mucosal and submucosal layers in case of severe infection. There was also obvious compression and absence of intestinal villi.

The present paper deals with the histopathological changes showed the intestine of marine water fish *Aetomylaeus nichoffii* infected with cestode Parasite *Gymnorhynchus*

Keywords : *Marine Fish, Aetomylaeus nichoffii, Infected Intestine, Cestode Parasite*

Introduction

Intestinal helminthes of vertebrates can includes inflammation of the host digestive tract, resulting in altered gastrointestinal function, namely enhanced secretion and propulsive motility of the gut (Palmer & Greenwood-Van Meerveld, 2001). Furthermore, helminthes seriously disrupt structures of the gut wall and interrupt communications between the nervous and endocrine system (Fair-weather, 1997). One of the most important factors in the pathogenesis of gastrointestinal parasite infections is a reduction in the host feed intake (Houtert & Van Sykes, 1996; Mercer et al., 2000). Moreover, gut parasites also increase endogenenous protein 136 and fat losses thus affecting growth rate of the host (Hiscox & Brocksen, 1973).

The host-parasite relationship results in the gain of one organism and the loss of another and leads to various diseases and disorders. Naturally, it is important to study this relationship, not because of their parasitological value but for the relative existence of humankind. These studies may have considerable intrinsic interest and raise fundamental question, common to other areas of biology, at a molecular, cellular, tissue and whole organism level. Several studies on the effect of intestinal parasites have shown that the main detrimental consequences for the host species are localised at the site of infection (Hoste, 2001)

Material and Methods :

Marine fish *Aetomylaeus nichoffii* (Bloch & Schnaider, 1801) were brought to the local laboratory alive and sacrificed just before examination. During the parasitological examination, the intestines were cut open and examined under stereomicroscope to see the degree of infection. The tapeworms were collected, placed in saline solution, freed from the adhering mucus by gentle shaking, they were flattened, processed and stained for morphological studies and were identified as *Gymnorhynchus shindei n. sp.* within short time 2 to 3 cm long pieces of proximal intestinal segments containing tapeworms were fix in Bouin's solution for 24 hrs, as the tissue undergoes autolysis rapidly after death and rapid fixation is essential.

The fixed material was transferred and processed through ascending grades of alcohol, dried in a wax miscible agent and impregnated in wax (M. P. 58°-60°C). Sectioning was carried out on a rotary microtome at 6μm. Sections were floated on warm water at 48°C and mounted on chemically cleaned slides coated with egg albumin. The mounted, unstained sections were dewaxed in three stages of xylene at 1 minute each and stained with most widely used standard haematoxylin and eosin stain, staining was carried out using haematoxylin and eosin staining technique (Bullock, 1978). This stained is often sufficient for identification of larger parasites such as helminthes, in this method the nuclei of cells are stained by the haematoxylin; the cytoplasm is coloured by the eosin. 139 Stained mounted section were examined under light microscope for good ones that were selected for photomicrography.

**Histopathological sections of intestine from
Aetomylaeus nichoffii (Bloch & Schnaider,1801)
infected with *Gymnorhynchus shindei* n.sp.**

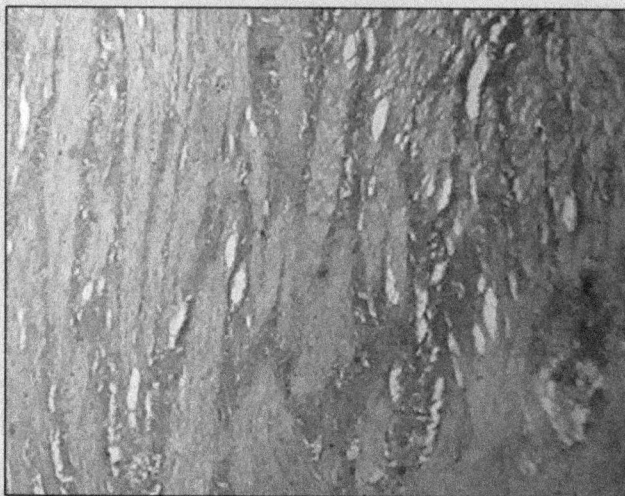

T.S. of non-Infected intestine

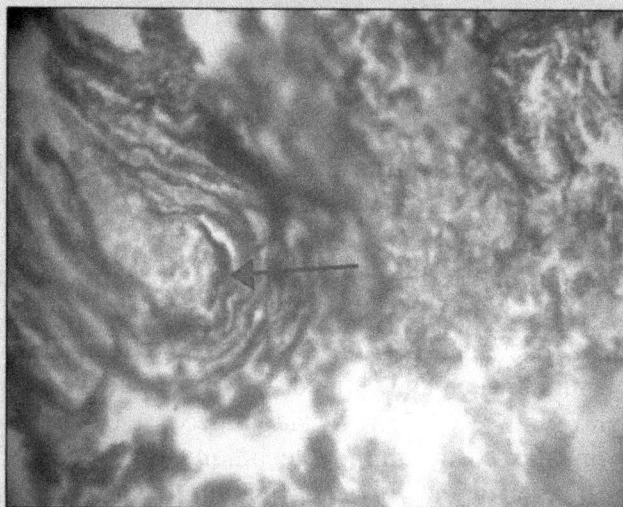

T.S. of Infected intestine with attached Parasite

Results and Discussion

Histopathology of *Gymnorhynchus shindei n. sp* infection of the intestine *Aetomylaeus nichoffii* (Bloch & Schneider, 180), specimen of cestode *Gymnorhynchus shindei* n. sp.were found on several occasions during the dissection of *Ateomylaeus nichoffii*. Submitted for routine diagnostic examination from At. Dighi coast, Dist Raigad (M. S) India in the period of October 2005 to December 2007.

Histopathological examination reveals a variety of pathological changes, depending upon the number of parasites and extent of damage of intestinal wall. Moderate infection of *Gymnorhynchus shindei* n. sp. causes to the submucousa. However, servere infection damage shape, size and colour of the villi, thickening and necrosis of mucosal layers. Besides this, hemorrhagic lesions have been observed in submucosa. Mucosa was infiltrated with eosinophil, lymphocytes and plasma cells. The worm *Gymnorhynchus shindei n. sp* is having penetrative type of scolex, hence; they have only close intimate contact with intestinal tissue of its host *Ateomylaeus nichoffii*. In transverse section of intestine of Ateomylaeus nichoffii, it has been observed that the worm attached to the mucosa layer of intestine and slowly invades the host tissue, causing less damage but destroys the intestinal epithelium showing that moderately pathogenic. Thus, it can be concluded that the rich environment of host intestine, is favorable for the development and growth of the worm.Hence, the parasites maintaining good host pathological relationship with its host

Refrences :

Chincholikar, L. N. & Shinde, G. B. (1977a): A new species of cestode Gymnorhynchus
cybiumi (Gymnorhynchidae Dollfus, 1935) from a marine fish at Ratngiri, India. Rivista di
parasitologia.XXXVIII (2/3): 161- 164.
Cuvier, G. (1817): Le Regne animal distribute d'Apres son organization.4VolsParis

Fairweather, J. Peptides., (1997): An emerging force in host response to parasitism, in pathogens: effects on host hormones and behavior. Beckage N.e.9ED0, Chapman & Hall, New York, 113-139.

Hoste H. (2001): Adaptive physiological processes in the host during gastrointestinal parasitism. International Journal for228 Parasitology, 31, 231-244.

Houtert, M. F. J. and Van Sykes, A. R. (1996): Implications of nutrition for the ability of ruminants to withstand gastrointestinal nematode infections. International Journal for Parasitology, 26,1151-1168.

Hiscox, J. I. and Brocksen, R. W. (1973): Effects of a parasitic gut nematode on consumption and growth in juvenile Rainbow trout (Salmo gairdneri). Journal of the Fisheries Research Board of Canada, 30: 443-450.

Linton, E. (1924): Notes on cestode parasites of sharks and rays. Proceeding of the united stataes National Museum 64: 1-114.

Palmer, J. M. & Greenwood – van meerveld, B. (2001): Integrative immunomodulation of gastrointestinal function during enteric parasitism. Journal of Parasitology, 87, 483-504.

Pramanik and Manna (2007): New species Gymnorhynchus barsai ns.p National journal of life science pp15-18

Robinson, E. S. (1959): Some new cestode from New Zealand marine fishes. Transactions of
the Royal Society of New Zealand 86:381-392.

Southwell, T. (1929): A monograph of cestodes of the order Trypanorhyncha from Ceylon
and India pt. I. Ceylon J.sci. 15, pt. III 169-312.

Yamaguti, (1952): Studies on the Helminth fauna of Japan part 49 cestodes of fishes
II Acta medicine. Okayama, 8 (1): 1-76.

Yamaguti, S. (1959): Systema Helminthum Vol.II. The cestode of vertebrates.
Interscinence publ. New York & London: 1-860.

Yamaguti, S. (1960): Studies on the helminth fauna of Japan, part 56, cestode of
Fishes III. Publ.Seto Mar. Biol. Lab. 8(1):41-50.

Yamaguti, S. (1934): Studies on the Helminth fauna of Japan part 49 Cestode of
fishes.Japan, J. Zool. 6: 1-112.

Department of Zoology,
Sundarrao More College of Arts, Commerce & Science
Poladpur-Raigad

17. Anita Desai's *Cry, The Peacock* : A Cry for Women's Liberation

Dr. Harish G. Tapadia

Abstract

Anita Desai is one of the prominent Indian writers who has supported the feminist cause by dealing with various women's issues in her works. Her novel *Cry, the Peacock* portrays the tragic life of Maya who suffers because of an unhappy marriage and her own superstitious beliefs. Desai excellently brings out the inner life of Maya who ends up murdering her husband and then commits suicide. After getting married to Gautama, her thirst for love remained unquenched due to his unemotional nature. She is haunted by the astrologer's prophecy that either she or her husband would die within four years of their marriage. The combined effect of her superstitious belief in the prophecy and her mis-matched conjugal life push her towards neurosis. This paper attempts to study the feminist perspective in *Cry, the Peacock* while detailing Maya's journey from sanity to insanity.

Keywords : Anita Desai, Sensibility, Feminism, Maya, Gautama

Introduction

Anita Desai is undoubtedly one of the best Indian women novelists of the twentieth century. Some of her best known novels are *Bye-Bye, the Black-bird, In Custody, Voices in the City and Cry, the Peacock*. Preoccupation with expressing feminine sensibility is the most important feature of her works. *Cry, the Peacock*, her first novel (1963), portrays the tragic life of Maya who suffers because of an unhappy marriage and her own superstitious beliefs. Anita Desai excellently brings out the inner life of Maya who ends up murdering her husband and then commits suicide. The combined effect of her superstitious belief in the prophecy and her mis-matched conjugal life push her towards neurosis. This paper attempts to study the feminist perspective in *Cry, the Peacock* while detailing Maya's journey from sanity to insanity.

The gender-wise division of society has been a worldwide phenomenon. According to Claude m. Steiner, as men and women, human beings are socialised to develop certain parts of their personalities while suppressing the development of other parts. (Steiner, 1980) The socio-cultural programming of sex roles trained women to suppress their faculties of controlling and rationality and develop those of nurturing and intuition. This gave rise to an exploited and oppressed society of women. Simone de Beauvoir aptly comments that femininity is a cultural construct as one isn't born a woman, but becomes one. (Beauvoir, 1975) The situation began to change slowly in the latter half of the nineteenth century with the efforts of the social reformers and writers. The feminist movement revolted against male domination and tried to restore women to their rightful place in society. Eminent feminist scholar, Toril Moi observes, "The words 'feminist' or 'feminism' are political labels indicating support for the aims of the new women's movement which emerged in the late 1960s." (Moi, 1986) Along with Shashi Deshpande, Nayantara Sehgal, Bharti Mukherjee and Uma Vasudev, Anita Desai is one of the prominent Indian writers who have supported the feminist cause by dealing with various women's issues in their works.

Anita Desai's *Cry, the Peacock* is divided into three parts, first part being the prologue and third part the epilogue. The first part deals with the death of Toto, Maya's pet dog and the contrasting reactions of Maya and Gautama to this incident. The second part is divided into seven chapters, each dealing with a different episode and culminates into Gautam's accidental death at the hands of Maya. The third part of the novel elaborates on Maya's feelings of guilt and her subsequent suicide. The title of the novel symbolises Maya's wish for her husband's love and attention. The major characters in the novel are very few. They include Maya's father, her brother, Arjuna, her mother-in-law, her sister-in-law, Nila, in addition to Gautama, her husband. An albino astrologer is another significant character. When Toto dies, Maya is grief-stricken. She wishes for a proper burial for Toto but Gautama just calls the PWD and gets the corpse removed. Maya is deeply wounded by such unemotional attitude which is typical of Gautama. Maya was accustomed to excessive affection and attention of her father who had never allowed her to feel the pangs of being motherless. After getting married to Gautama, her thirst for love remained unquenched due to his unemotional nature. There was quite an age difference between the two which did not help. Moreover, Gautama had misinterpreted the Bhagwat Geeta theory of detachment and used to maintain emotional distance from everybody including his wife.

The second part of the novel highlights Maya's loneliness as she continues to grieve for Toto. She does not agree with Gautama's practice of detachment theory and simultaneous materialistic pursuits. She feels alienated as Gautama disregards her views and wishes. She is haunted by the astrologer's prophecy that either she or her husband would die within four years of their marriage. The combined effect of her superstitious belief in the prophecy and her mis-matched conjugal life push her towards neurosis. Gautama, a busy and prosperous lawyer, is realistic and rational. He fails to understand Maya's deteriorating condition who is left to the solitude and silence of the house. Maya is frightened as the fourth year of her marriage is coming towards its end. Meena Belliappa observes that Anita Desai's *Cry, the Peacock* is "a remarkable attempt to fuse fantasy with perceptual experience". (Belliappa, 1971) In her neurotic state Maya starts believing that either she or Gautama is going to die shortly.

Anita Desai is not a self-declared feminist. The fact that she has delved deep into the problems of women in a patriarchal society in almost all of her novels bears testimony to her strong feminist perspective. She expresses a unique feminine sensibility through the character of Maya, an intelligent, acutely sensitive and emotional woman who feels suffocated being trapped in a love-less marriage and is pushed to the brink of her sanity. In spite of enjoying an affluent lifestyle, her mind knows no peace and she ends up committing a crime. Gautama expected Maya to be contented with the comfortable life which he had given her. She wished for complete satisfaction of her bodily and emotional desires. She refused to suppress her feminine desires and plunged into despair because of her inability to cope with the patriarchal society. If she had been content with her lot just like an ordinary, submissive housewife, her tragic fate could have been avoided. Maya is romantic and Gautama is realistic. Their very names symbolise attachment and detachment respectively. Her being confined to the solitude and silence of the house begins to dent her psyche. Her attempt of getting rid of the negativity by visiting her friends such as Leila or Pom is unsuccessful. The company of her mother-in-law and her sister-in-law, Nila cheers her spirits for a while. When they leave, she is again surrounded by her loneliness and anxiety.

Maya accuses Gautama of not loving her. He replies that her father has pampered her. Even her father advises her that she should try to adjust with Gautama. Her obsession with the prophecy continues to grow in the alienated and neurotic state in which she finds herself. She feels that if one of them has to die, it should be Gautama as life and death is alike to him, whereas, she has strong desire to live. Bindu Lata Chaudhary aptly remarks: "The joy of life in her case is the joy of death as the story shows her thirst for life and this is gradually built up only to justify her killing of Gautama." (Chaudhary, 1995) Maya starts to have nightmares. Her tender, feminine heart begins to harden towards her husband. In this state of mind, a fatal incident happens one night. Gautama and Maya are taking a stroll on the roof of the house enjoying the cool atmosphere. Maya is enraptured at the sight of the rising moon. When Gautama moves in front of her obstructing her vision of the moon, she is enraged and pushes him over the parapet and he falls to his death. Everyone believes the incident to be an accident. Maya's in-laws are sympathetic towards her. Maya is grief-stricken and holds herself responsible. She loses her mind completely and commits suicide.

Conclusion

In short, Anita Desai's *Cry, the Peacock* offers a deep insight into feminist consciousness while exploring the tragedy of Maya due to her husband's indifference and neglect and her own neurotic psyche resulting from an obsession with a childhood prophecy. Maya suffers in spirit being devoid of love as Gautama is bereft of emotions. The writer seems to exhort society to give women their just place in order to make man-woman relationships happier and healthier. *Cry, the Peacock* is also a cry for women's liberation which is essential for the creation of a harmonious society.

References

Beauvoir, S. D. (1975). *The Second sex.* Trans. H. M. Parshley. Penguin Books.

Belliappa, M. (1971). *Anita Desai: A Study of Her Fiction.* Writers Workshop.

Chaudhary, B. L. (1995). *Women and Society in the Novels of Anita Desai.* Creative Books.

Moi, T. (1986). "Feminist Literary Criticism". *Modern Literary Theory.* (Ann Jefferson and David Robey Ed). B. T. Bastfold Ltd.

Steiner, C. M. (1980). *Scripts People Live.* Bantam.

Asst. Professor of English,
V. N. Govt. Institute of Arts and Social Sciences, Nagpur
email : harishtapadia@rediffmail.com

18. Green & Sustainable Chemistry

Dr. Sonlata Bargotya

When Pollution Prevention Act was passes in 1990 a newer thought arouse that paved a path to Green Chemistry. By the time the term green chemistry was first coined in 1991 by Prof. Paul T. Anastas to enact sustainable development in chemistry and chemical industry. Elaborating the same green chemistry incorporates two main components. First, it addresses the problem of efficient utilization of raw materials and minimizing hazardous waste. Second, it deals with the health, safety and environmental concerns related to the manufacture, use and disposal or reuse of chemicals and reactants. Therefore, Green chemistry incorporates a new approach to the synthesis, processing and application of chemical substances in such a manner as to reduce threats to health and the environment. Green chemistry applies across the biorhythm of a chemical product starting from its design, manufacture, processing, and usage thereafter it's eventually to its disposal. So, Green Chemistry could also be termed as sustainable chemistry and this is a part of chemical science that targets to reduce or eliminate the use of polluting substances. As a chemical credo, green chemistry is multidisciplinary research area that covers all wide aspects of inorganic chemistry, organic chemistry, physical chemistry, biotechnology, ecology, toxicology, molecular biology, biochemistry and analytical chemistry. Be it in a part of any synthesis, laboratories or industries should create none or minimum by-products which pollute the environmental pollution. Green chemistry can be defined as the practice of chemical science and manufacturing in a manner that is sustainable, safe, and non-polluting and that consumes minimum amounts of materials and energy while producing little or no waste material. Hence "the reduction or elimination of the use or generation of hazardous substances in the design, manufacture and application of chemical products" Green Chemistry theory and Practice - Anastas and Warner "Green Chemistry underlies our commitment to potentially harmful technologies by developing alternative syntheses to prevent environmental pollution."

To be more elaborating this sustainable chemical science includes the practice of manufacturing the products in such a manner that is safe and non-polluting to the ecology by consuming minimum amounts of materials and energy that is minimal of waste material. Hence, it objects in redesigning chemical products with minimizing wastes and dangerous materials. Ignoring the economical profit green chemistry is about promoting innovation while protecting the human health and environment.

The works in Green Chemistry were recognized in 2005 by awarding Yves Chauvin, Robert H. Grubbs, and Richard R. Schrock the Nobel Prize in Chemistry for "the development of the metathesis method in organic synthesis. Frances Arnold won the same 2018, it for the directed evolution of enzymes.

Do We Need Green Chemistry?

- Chemistry is playing undoubtly a crucial role in our day to day lives. Everything we use today is composed of chemicals. Understanding basics of chemical science becomes important and very much essential to make our routine healthy and safe.
- With alarming increasing Environmental pollution novel chemicals are bringing new environmental issues and harmful unexpected side effects, which create a demand for 'greener' chemical products.
- The Green Chemistry props up the inputs from multiple disciplines so; innovation of more eco-friendly green chemical synthetic routes is possible, which significantly reduces the generation of hazardous substances.

Principles of Green Chemistry

12 principles of green chemistry as formulated by P.T. Anastas and J.C. Warner, in *Green Chemistry: Theory and Practice*, 1998.

1. Prevention- It is better to prevent waste formation than to treat/clean up it after it is created.

2. Atom economy- Design synthetic methodologies to maximize incorporation of all material used into final product.

3. Less hazardous Chemical Synthesis- Synthetic methods should, where practicable, use or generate materials of low human toxicity and environmental.

4. Designing safer chemicals- Chemical product design should pronounce efficacy while reducing toxicity.

5. Safer solvents and Auxiliaries- Avoid auxiliary materials - solvents, extractants - if possible.

6. Designs for Energy efficiency- Energy requirements should be minimized: conduct synthesis at ambient temperature and pressure.

7. Use of Renewable feedstock- Raw materials should be renewable rather than depleting.

8. Reduce derivatives- Unnecessary derivatization should be avoided where possible.

9. Smart catalysis- Selectively catalyzed processes are superior to stoichiometric processes.

10. Degradable design- Chemical products should be designed to be degradable to innocuous products when disposed of and not be environmentally persistent.

11. Real-time analysis for pollution prevention- Monitor processes in real time to avoid excursions leading to the formation of hazardous materials.

12. Hazard and accident prevention- Materials used in a chemical process should be chosen to minimize hazard and risk for chemical accidents, such as releases, explosions, and fires.

The Benefits of Green Chemistry

Human health

- Less usage of hazardous chemicals makes minimum exposure to harmful chemicals.
- Less release of hazardous chemical wastes to water leads to safe and clean drinking and recreational water.
- To use safer consumer products of all varieties: new, safer products with less wastage should be promoted.
- Consumption of safer food: Use of toxic chemicals that can enter the food chain and thereafter persists for longer. Safer pesticides that degrade rapidly after use should be emphasized.
- Safety for workers in the chemical industry should be pronounced by less use of toxic materials which has less potential for accidents e.g., fires or explosions.
- Green chemistry ensures minimum release of hazardous chemicals to air leading to less damage on human health.

- Green chemistry promotes treatment of chemical wastes to water leading to fresh cleaner drinking water.
- Use of less hazardous and toxic chemicals in working places ensures accidental safety.
- To ensure safer consumer products of all types promising less waste and safe products. Availability of new, safe products for purchase.
- Safer food consumption by using; safer pesticides that are toxic only to specific pests and degrade rapidly after use. Green chemistry avoids using elimination of persistent toxic chemicals that can enter the food chain.

Environment

- Many chemicals end up in the environment by intentional release during use (e.g., pesticides), by unintended releases (including emissions during manufacturing), or by disposal. Green chemicals either degrade to innocuous products or are recovered for further use
- Plants and animals suffer less harm from toxic chemicals in the environment
- Lower potential for global warming, ozone depletion, and smog formation
- Less chemical disruption of ecosystems
- Less use of landfills, especially hazardous waste landfills

Economy and business

- Higher yields for chemical reactions, consuming smaller amounts of feedstock to obtain the same amount of product
- Fewer synthetic steps, often allowing faster manufacturing of products, increasing plant capacity, and saving energy and water
- Reduced waste, eliminating costly remediation, hazardous waste disposal, and end-of-the-pipe treatments
- Allow replacement of a purchased feedstock by a waste product
- Better performance so that less product is needed to achieve the same function
- Reduced use of petroleum products, slowing their depletion and avoiding their hazards and price fluctuations
- Reduced manufacturing plant size or footprint through increased throughput

- Increased consumer sales by earning and displaying a safer-product label (e.g., Safer Choice labeling)
- Improved competitiveness of chemical manufacturers and their customers.

What is Green Chemistry and Environmental Chemistry?

Green Chemistry is an area that establishes and created a set of guidelines, principles, products, and processes that alleviate or eliminate the utilization and generation of hazardous substances at the source. Green Chemistry is a key to sustainable development, as it directs and drives the scientific community to the remedial and innovative solutions for the existing environmental problems.

Environmental chemistry is the branch of science that focuses on the biochemical process occurring in air, water, aquatic and terrestrial establishments and the impacts of pollution and other anthropogenic activities on them.

Hence, it is the study of the impacts, source points, reactions, destination of chemical species in the air, water, and land, transport, and the impact of human actions on various components of environment, such as hydrosphere, atmosphere, lithosphere, and biosphere.

While environmental chemistry is associated with the impact of polluting chemicals on the natural resources, green or sustainable chemistry as a branch of chemical science focuses on design of chemical processes and products that minimize generation of hazardous chemical substances. It studies the impact of environmental factors or attributes with respect to chemistry, reduction in the consumption of conventional resources and technological solutions for preventing pollution.

While environmental chemistry is associated with the impact of polluting chemicals on the natural resources, green or sustainable chemistry focuses on the impact of environmental factors or attributes with respect to chemistry, reduction in the consumption of conventional resources and technological solutions for preventing pollution.

Both the concepts are different from each other.

Conclusion

Although many things are tried and approaches are increasing but still needs some strict rules and regulations to stop misuse, negligence, and many more. We need to provide a repeated encouraged education about chemical hazards, use, handling, renewable approaches, carefulness, safety and many more things to the small children to higher grade students through curriculum. Those wills repeatedly strikes their mind not to misuse, not to be careless and others and generate responsibility towards environment. If public awareness is high and cultured motivation, then it will lead to a better adaptation to the greener concepts and the approaches. To get a sustainable chemistry, the grow of GC over the past decades should be accelerated more towards the diverse sector of chemistry from education, research to core practice and adaptation by the industry in greater aspects. We may not need to worry about the consequences and have a greener environment in future. We should make it as our everyday practice and natural reflection. For that, we need to grow the future chemists with the good moral knowledge of Green Chemistry. For a small lab if a researcher did some malpractice, it could be seen as a small but let's think in a global scenario, there are millions of chemists who are working every day and a mistake made by a single person per day effects in a wider way. So let's take a step and be responsible for ourselves.

References :
1. P.D. Sharma , A text book of "Ecology and Environment", 12th edition, Rastogi Publication, Meerut.
2. R.D. Saini, The role of green chemistry in controlling environment and ocean pollution, International Journal of Ocean and Oceanography, 11(2), 2017, 217-229.
3. P. Sharma, M. Kumar, A. Sharma, Anoverview of green chemistry, World journal of pharmacy and pharmaceutical sciences, 8(5), 2020, 202-208.
4. http://en.wikipedia.org/wiki/green-chemistry.

5. P.T. Anastas, J. C. Warner, Green Chemistry, Theory and Practice, Oxford university press, New York, 1998, 30.
6. http://www.epa.gov/grenchemistry/pubs.whats_gc.html

Assistant Professor, Chemistry
Govt. College, Tonk,
Rajasthan

19. The Study of Preffered Breeding Sites for Aedes Species in Urban Area of Hanumangarh

Ishwer Lal Jal, Dr. Kailash Kumar Swami

Abstract

Introduction : Dengue is a mosquito-borne viral disease occurring in tropical and subtropical areas which is spread by *Aedes aegypti*. Dengue fever infection is one of the most important arboviral diseases in humans. The main objective of the study was to detect breeding habitat diversity of *Aedes aegypti* in urban area of Hanumangarh.

Methodology : The adult *Aedes aegypti* were collected with the help of aspirator of different size from various breeding habitats while larval stages collected and identified in laboratory.

Result: - A total of 710 containers were studied from outdoor and indoor sites of 8 breeding habitats. Most of the *Aedes aegypti* were found form the outdoor breeding sites as compared to indoor one. The most common breeding sites for *Aedes aegypti* was containers in house, tyres, mud pot, jerrican, bird water pots, cattels water pots, plastic drum, pipe leakage and stagnant water etc.

Conclusion : These studies indicates that the *Aedes aegypti* has adapted to breed in clean and clear water (tap and/or rain water).

Keywords : *Aedes aegypti*, breeding site, arboviral, dengue.

Introduction

Dengue is a mosquito-borne viral disease occurring in tropical and subtropical areas which is spread by *Aedes aegypti*. Dengue fever infection is one of the most important arboviral diseases in humans. The main objective of the study was to detect breeding habitat diversity of *Aedes aegypti* in urban area of Hanumangarh.

Globally *Aedes* has 950 species out of which 115 species of *Aedes* has been reported from India. *Aedes albopictus* also has similar area of distribution in Asia and played vector for Dengue and Chikunguniya [1].

The district headquarter Hanumangarh is situated on the bank of Ghaggar River which is the present form of the last mythological river Saraswati. Ghaggar River, which is called as 'Nali' in local dialect divides the district headquarter into two parts. In the north of Ghaggar River, Hanumangarh Town and in the south the habitation of Hanumangarh Junction is situated.

Originating in Africa, *Aedes aegypti* probably invades other transcontinental via trading and transport ships that resupplied in Africa ports during the fifteen through seventeenth centuries [2, 3]. Currently *Aedes aegypti* is widespread in Asia [4] and following epidemic dengue activity experienced in south-east Asia [5]. Although *Aedes aegypti* currently has a wide distribution in maximum tropical and subtropical region. The current distribution on does not reflect the maximum range of its potential distribution as defined by historical records.

Urban areas with high-density of water storage receptacles are suitable for breeding of *Aedes* mosquitoes [6]. In most of these areas small number of *Aedes* breeding habitats exist even during the adverse months of the year and consistently serve as the primary producers of *Ae. aegypti,* referred as "Key Containers" [7] which are region specific for *Aedes* breeding [8]. Key containers in Philippines include plastic & metal drums and plastic containers [9] while it is roof gutters in Australia [10]. In India, cement tanks and plastic containers were identified as major breeding habitats of *Aedes aegypti* [11–12]. In the capital city Delhi, India overhead tanks and curing tanks were identified as key containers of *Aedes* breeding [12].

Fig 1:- Area map of Hanumangarh

Methodology : The latitude of Hanumangarh, Rajasthan, India is 29.625996, and the longitude is 74.287491. Hanumangarh, Rajasthan, India is located at India country in the Cities place category with the GPS coordinates of 29° 37' 33.5856" N and 74° 17' 14.9676" E. Periodic investigation were undertaken from March 2022 to Feb 2022. Mosquitoes and larval stages were collected with the help of suction tube and torch and dipping method for larval stage. Specimens were reared in laboratory and identified using standard taxonomic keys as given by Roy & Brown (2003) [13].

Mosquito larvae were collected from discarded tires and other artificial containers with a plastic cup, pipette, or classical dipper. To decrease the effect of disturbance, tires and other larger containers were approached cautiously and the cup was immersed fast at the water surface instead of slowly "scooping" the water. For smaller containers the water was transferred to pans for immature stages collection. Water in tires and containers of which the opening was too narrow was sucked up with a pipette.

Result : A total of 710 containers were studied from outdoor and indoor sites of 8 breeding habitats. Most of the *Aedes aegypti* were found form the outdoor breeding sites as compared to indoor one. The most common breeding sites for *Aedes aegypti* was containers in house hold, tyres, mud pot, bird water pots, cattels water pots, plastic drum, pipe leakage and stagnant water etc. (Table 2)

The preffered locations of *Aedes aegypti* was Satipura area (84.75) followed by Civil lines (82.75) Canal Colony (77.75). (Table1)

The preffered breeding habitats of *Aedes aegypti* was House hold (45.00) followed by Bird water points (41.00) Pipe leakage (32.00). (Table 2)

Table 1: Month wise density (No. per man hour) of mosquito *Aedes aegypti* in Hanumangarh city (Jan 2022 to Dec 2022) values are monthly average data of one year

Month	Bus stand and railway Junction area	Satipura	Suresia	Civil lines	P&T Colony	Canal colony
January	NR	NR	1.00	0.00	NR	00

February	NR	NR	2.50	0.00	NR	00
March	3.25	1.25	3.00	1.50	NR	3.25
April	1.25	NR	0.00	0.00	1.50	1.25
May	00	NR	0.00	0.00	1.25	00
June	2.25	3.00	3.00	4.50	NR	2.25
July	6.75	7.00	7.00	8.25	5.25	6.75
August	4.50	8.50	18.50	20.25	6.75	20.25
September	4.00	3.00	31.50	30.00	NR	29.75
October	3.00	2.00	18.25	15.25	3.00	14.25
November	1.00	NR	0.00	3.00	2.25	00
December	NR	NR	0.00	0.00	NR	00

NR: Not reported

Table 2: Occurrence and abundance (No. per man hour) of mosquito *Aedes aegypti* in Hanumangarh city (Values are monthly average of one year data) (Jan 2022 to Dec 2022)

Month	Plastic drum	Mud pot	Tyres	House hold	Bird water point	Stagnant water	Cattles water point	Pipe leakage
January	–	–	–	-	1	–	–	–
February	–	–	–	–	1	–	–	–
March	2	3	4	2	3	–	–	1
April	2	3	5	4	5	–	–	3
May	2	2	3	2	8	–	–	4
June	4	–	–	3	7	–	–	4
July	5	4	3	5	–	–	–	7
August	4	3	2	8	6	2	–	3
September	–	5	4	7	6	3	–	5
October	–	2	2	4	4	1	–	4
November	–	–	–	5	1	1	–	1
December	–	–	–	5	1	–	–	–
Total	19	22	23	45	41	7	–	32

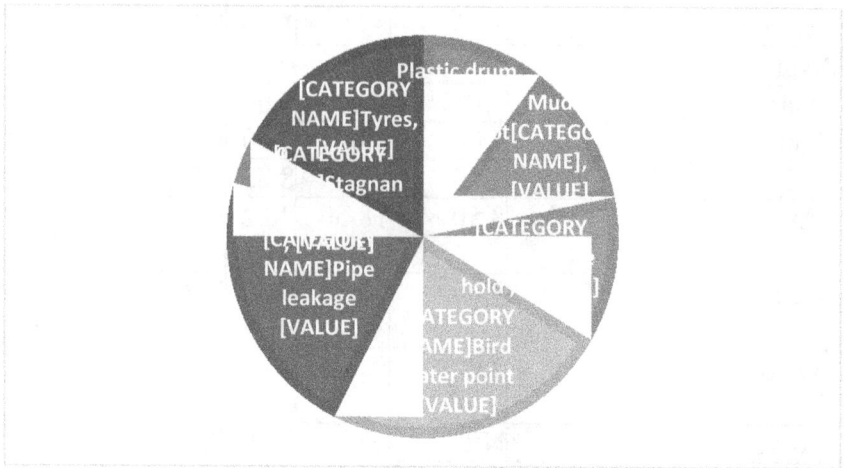

Fig 2:-Occurrence and abundance (No. per man hour) of mosquito *Aedes aegypti* in Hanumangarh city (Values are monthly average of one year data) (Jan 2022 to Dec 2022)

Discussion

Water chemistry of aquatic habitats may also play a critical role in determining the survival rate of mosquitoes [17, 19]. *Aedes aegypti* exhibits a great deal of specialization in breeding site selection and consequently the distribution of this species is limited by those sites [20]. Since the presence of water in containers is probably the most important factor in determining the breeding of mosquitoes, especially *Aedes* and Culex species, a mosquito control programme should be established in Hanumangarh city. For the control of container breeding mosquitoes it is possible to use different methods in integration and these include covering water holding containers [16, 34], using appropriate biological control agents [16], public health education [14, 15, 21], creating knowledge and awareness of the residents on mosquito-borne diseases [21], eliminating water-filled unused containers [14, 15], draining of containers once a week [18], and proper waste management system for all housing areas [15]. However, targeting specific types of water-holding containers would enable a more focused approach to vector control than attempting to eliminate all water-holding containers [22].

Conclusion: - These studies indicates that the *Aedes aegypti* has adapted to breed in clean and clear water (tap and/or rain water). This study involved only collection and identification of mosquito larvae from tires, household containers, and discarded water holding materials so that it needs further investigation to look for mosquito larvae in natural water holding containers and larger water tanks. There has to be a viral isolation through collecting the adult females to look if they harbor the dengue disease pathogen. It also needs awareness creation of the population not to be affected by the disease in case epidemic may occur.

References :
1. Soper FL, 1667. Dynamics of *Aedes agypti* Distribution and Density. Bull. Wld. Hlth. Org. 36:536 – 5538.
2. Christophers SR. *Aedes aegypti* (L.) the Yellow Fever Mosquito; Cambridge University Press: London, UK, 1960.
3. Reiter P, *Aedes albopictus* and the world trade in used tires, 1988e1995: the shape of things to come? Journal of American Mosquito Control Assoc. 1998; 14(1998):83e94.
4. Halstead SB. Dengue in the Americas and Southeast Asia: do they differ? Rev. Panam. Salud. Publication. 2006; 20(2006):407e415.
5. Kamimura K, Matsuse IT, Takahashi H, Komukai J, Fukuda T, Suzuki K et al. Effect of temperature on the development of *Aedes aegypti* and *Aedes Albopictus*. Medical Entomology. Zoology. 2002; 53(2002):53e58.
6. Sinh Vu N.Key container and key premise indices for *Ae. aegypti* surveillance and control. In: Linda S. Lloyd editor. Best practices for dengue prevention and control in the Americas. Strategic Report;2013; pp.51-56.
7. Salamat MSS, Cochon KL, Crisostomo GCC, Gonzaga PBS, Quijano NA, Torio JF, *et al*. Entomological Survey of Artificial Container Breeding Sites of Dengue Vectors in Batasan Hills, Quezon City. Acta Medica Philippina. 2013; 47(3): 63–68.
8. Edillo FE, Roble ND, Otero ND 2nd. The key breeding sites by

pupal survey for dengue mosquito vectors, *Aedes aegypti* (Linnaeus) and *Aedes albopictus* (Skuse), in Guba, Cebu City, Philippines. South- east Asian Trop J Med. Public Health. 2012; 43(6): 1365–1374.

9. Montgomery BL, Ritchie SA. Roof gutters: a key container for *Aedes aegypti* and Ochlerotatusnotoscrip- tus (Diptera: Culicidae) in Australia. American Journal of Tropical Medicine and Hygiene. 2002; 67(3): 244–246. PMID: 12408662

10. Balakrishnan N, Venkatesh S, Lal S. An entomology study on the dengue vector during outbreak of den- gue in Tirupur town and its surroundings, Tamil Nadu, India. J Commun Dis. 2006; 38:164–168. PMID: 17370680

11. Mondal R, Devi NP, Jauhari RK. Occurrence of *Aedes* mosquitoes (DIPTERA: CULICIDAE) in urban areas of doon valley, (Uttarakhand), INDIA. Modern Parasitology. 2014; 28:255–262.

12. Vikram Kumar, Nagpal BN, Pande Veena, Aruna Srivastava, Gupta Sanjeev K,Anushrita, *et al.* Com- parison of *Ae. aegypti* breeding in localities of different socio-economic groups of Delhi, India. Interna- tional Journal of Mosquito Research 2015; 2(2): 83–88.

13. Roy DN, Brown AWA. Entomology. Biotech Books, New Delhi. 2003, 1-413.

14. M. A. Bhat and K. Krishnamoorthy, "Entomological investigation and distribution of *Aedes* mosquitoes in Tirunelveli, Tamil Nadu, India," International Journal of Current Microbiology Application Sciences, vol. 3, no. 10, pp. 253–260, 2014.

15. S. N. R. Saleeza, Y. Norma-Rashid, and M. Sofian-Azirun, "Mosquitoes larval breeding habitat in urban and suburban areas, Peninsular Malaysia," International Journal of Biological Veterinary, Agricultural and Food Engineering, vol. 5, no. 10, pp. 81–85, 2011.

16. A. Philbert and J. N. Ijumba, "Preferred breeding habitats of *Aedes aegypti* (Diptera-Culicidae) mosquito and its public health implications in Dares Salaam, Tanzani," Journal of Environmental Research and Management, vol. 4, no. 10, pp.

344–351, 2013
17. C. D. Chen, H. L. Lee, S. P. Stella-Wong, K. W. Lau, and M. Sofian-Azirun, "Container survey of mosquito breeding sites in a university campus in Kuala Lumpur, Malaysia," Dengue Bulletin, vol. 33, no. 1, pp. 187–193, 2009.
18. A. Hiscox, A. Kaye, K. Vongphayloth *et al.*, "Risk factors for the presence of *Aedes aegypti* and *Aedes albopictus* in domestic water-holding containers in areas impacted by the Nam Theun 2 hydroelectric project, Laos," American Journal of Tropical Medicine and Hygiene, vol. 88, no. 6, pp. 1070–1078, 2013.
19. K. Rajesh, D. Dhanasekaran, and B. K. Tyagi, "Survey of container breeding mosquito larvae (Dengue vector) in Tiruchirappalli district, Tamil Nadu, India," Journal of Entomology and Zoological Studies, vol. 1, no. 6, pp. 88–91, 2013.
20. P. Thangamathi, S. Ananth, and N. Kala, "Seasonal variations and physicochemical characteristics of the habitats in relation to the density of dengue vector *Aedes aegypti* in Thanjavur, Tamil Nadu, India," vol. 5, pp. 271–276, 2014
21. K. D. Thete and L. V. Shinde, "Survey of container breeding mosquito larvae in Jalna City (M.S.), India," Biological Forum, vol. 5, no. 1, pp. 124–128, 2013.
22. T. Chareonviriyaphap, P. Akratanakul, S. Nettanomsak, and S. Huntamai, "Larval habitats and distribution patterns of *Aedes aegypti* (Linnaeus) and *Aedes albopictus* (Skuse), in Thailand," Southeast Asian Journal of Tropical Medicine and Public Health, vol. 34, no. 3, pp. 529–535, 2003
23. Kyle JL, Harris E. Global spread and persistence of dengue. Annu Rev Microbiol 2008; 62:71–92.

**Department of Zoology,
Govt. Dungar College Bikaner,
Rajasthan**

20. Exploratory Factor Analysis : An Approach towards identifying the Perception of Coffee Intake effects

Ms. Divya Vijithaswan Nair[1]
Ms. Tanzim Shahabuddin Shaikh[2]

Abstract

Coffee is one of the most consumed beverages in the world. It is even consumed very much among many parts of India. Various studies concentrate on effects of consuming coffee and consumer's behavior in purchasing products related to coffee. Very less studies focus on their effect among college students. Therefore, the aim of this study was to determine the coffee consumption habits and the perception of its effect among college students in Mumbai. The study was performed using convenient sampling method with a sample of size 234 students studying in different colleges from Mumbai. We collected information about the characteristics of the students participated, coffee intake habits and the perception of its effect on consuming coffee. The maximum students in the study consumes coffee. Using Factor Analysis, we identified the major factors dependent on consuming coffee on daily basis. The consumption of coffee is more during their academics like project work or examination days. Due to the burden of exams and to score best in exams students consume coffee to increase their study hours and academic performance.

Keywords : Coffee, perception, examination, Factor Analysis.

1. Introduction

Coffee is one the most popular drinks consumed in the world. It is considered that coffee serves as the major tool in the delivery of caffeine followed by tea and many energy drinks (Schubert et al., 2017). Caffeine consumption by college students has drastically increasing day by day and of which maximum students prefer drinking coffee followed by tea. Coffee is one the major source which is a caffeinated beverage and it is a type of psychoactive substance that comes from the pharmacological class of methyxanthines (AtikahRamli et al., 2019).

In 2017 – 2018, it was reported that the global production of coffee beans has reached to the peak and achieved USD 200 billion yearly. The highest consumption was reported in Europe of approximately 10 kg of coffee per year (Czarniecka-Skubina et al., 2021). According to Statista Research, Coffee consumption in India amounted to 1.21 million 60 kilograms during the financial year 2022. India ranked seventh in export volumes worldwide and third in Asia after Vietnam and Indonesia. Many studies says that coffee market is widely expanding among Asian countries (AtikahRamli et al., 2019). It is mentioned that in Malaysia drinking coffee has become a part of their culture and now many western countries like United states started following the same culture (AtikahRamli et al., 2019).

Many studies (Cano-Marquina et al., 2013) concentrates on the effect of coffee consumption among consumers health and presence of caffeine is considered to be more among coffee (Schwarz et al., 1994). Based on health, coffee apart from taste and texture it also shows significant effect on cellular level (Czarniecka-Skubina et al., 2021). The consumption of coffee has been found to increase dramatically among adolescents and young adults. Their perception towards consuming coffee may lead to addiction which may cause several negative effects on their health. It's tremendously proved that excessive consumption of coffee may have long term effects on their health and if people consumes 5 cups or more on a daily basis may show significant effect on their health (Czarniecka-Skubina et al., 2021).

Nowadays among young adults consuming coffee is considered as the judgement of their life status. Hanging out with friends usually ends up in consuming coffee. Because of which many coffee shops are expanding their outlets in various parts of the country. Various studies (Sousa et al., 2016) confirms that a cup of coffee naturally give pleasure to the consumers and they feel relaxed after consuming coffee. Consumers find themselves different after consuming coffee or any other caffeinated products. Many studies (Sousa et al., 2016) says that the consumers consume coffee with certain foods such as bakery products.

Additionally, It has even reported that consumption of caffeinated beverages or coffee plays a vital role in appetite control (Schubert et al., 2017). It was also observed that coffee consumed in between 3 – 4.5 hours before a meal had minimal influence on food, while caffeine consumed 0.5 – 4 hours before a meal may cause acute energy intake (Schubert et al., 2017).

Although various studies on coffee intake is published but still there is lack of research related to the consumption of coffee by college students. The coffee consumption habits and the perception of its effects among college students differ person to person. Nowadays, young students are very much keen to consume coffee to get them out of stress and give relaxation to their mind and body. Drinking coffee is a part of their lifestyle. Their party, their enjoyment always starts and ends with a coffee. Their debate with friends, long lasting projects and many more things are interrelated with coffee. They themselves will never know that coffee has become a part of their life. The excessive consumption of coffee may cause long term side effects. To understand the habit and their perception towards consumption of coffee is studied in this research. The available resources related to this research do not cover the topic in a wide way, and they refer to the topic in different perspective. This study fills this research gap.

The largest coffee shops chains such as Bombay Coffee House, KCROASTERS, Starbucks Coffee, Cafe Coffee Day, are increasing their number of outlets all over Mumbai, irrespective of considering the rates of coffee students prefer to consume coffee to maximum extent.

Therefore, this study aims to determine Mumbai college student's habit towards consumption of coffee and their perception towards intake of coffee. The second aim was to understand the reason behind not consuming coffee on daily basis.

The objectives of the study were to address the following parts:

(a) To understand the characteristics of the respondents.

(b) To assess the relation between consumption of coffee with respect to characteristics of the respondents.

(c) To monitor the coffee intake habit among respondents.

(d) To extract the factors based on their perception towards intake of coffee.

(e) To identify the association between coffee intake habits and their perception.

(f) To know the reason behind not consuming coffee on daily basis.

2. Materials & Methods

In order to understand the perception of student's studying at Mumbai towards coffee consumption. A convenience sampling method was used to get the opinions from the students. The questionnaire consists of three parts where Part A consists of student's personal details like Gender, Age (in complete years), Economic status, Highest Qualification and the area they reside. Part B aims to collect data based on their Habits and preference in consuming coffee. Part C totally aims to understand their attitude and perception towards consuming coffee on daily basis. This Part C focuses on getting answers from students based on 5 points Likert Scale.

The questionnaire was assessed by determining its reliability. The Cronbach's alpha was used to understand the validity of the questionnaire. The Inclusion criteria of students were decided based on students age group in between 16 to 30 years who agreed to fill the online questionnaire. The exclusion criterion was students whose highest qualification is above Postgraduate Degree.

The questionnaire was validated based on the concept of reliability. It was estimated on pilot test that participants can finish up the online survey in 5 to 10 minutes. A link to the questionnaire using Microsoft forms was sent to various students studying in different colleges in Mumbai. The information collected from students were kept confidential. The data collected through Microsoft forms were exported to Microsoft Excel, almost 251 samples were collected and then outliers were removed and the respondents belonging to exclusion criteria were also removed. After data cleaning almost 234 samples were collected, this is further used for analysis.

The cleaned data were exported to Statistical Package for Social Sciences (SPSS, Version 23.0, 2015) for data analysis. Some part of data was also analyzed using Microsoft Excel 2007. The validity test of questionnaire was based on Cronbach's alpha represented in Table 1 is indexed at 0.834 and is considered as valid questionnaire since the value of Cronbach's alpha is greater than 0.5.

TABLE 1. CRONBACH'S ALPHA FOR THE SET OF QUESTIONNAIRE

Cronbach's Alpha	Cronbach's Alpha based on Standardized Items	N of Items
0.834	0.831	40

The categorical data are analyzed using frequency distribution and Graphical representation. The associations are obtain using Chi Square Test of association, if the properties of Chi Square Test fail then will proceed to use Continuity Correction for 2 x 2 tables or Fisher's Exact Test for m x n table and the Quantitative data are analyzed using Mean ± Standard Deviation. To determine the factors to understand the perception towards consuming coffee, Factor analysis is used to determine the factor which explains the maximum variation towards the perceptions. The Scree Plot is used to get an idea about the most important factors.

The research was concentrated on 95% Level of Confidence, and its significance level of 5% (p value < 0.05) to interpret the result to reject the hypothesis if p value < 0.05 .

3. Results

3.1 Characteristics of students participated

The characteristics of the students participated are represented in Table 2. The study involved mainly respondents from Junior college and Degree Colleges, living in different area with different economic status. The students were mainly in the age group 16 – 30 years old, who belongs to Mumbai. It is clearly seen that the majority are Coffee Drinker (84.2%) as compared with Non Coffee Drinker (15.8%). The majority was Females (56.0%) and Males (42.3%) and some prefer not to say (1.7%). The maximum number of respondents belongs to age group 16 – 20 years old (59.0%) and belongs to Bachelor Degree (35.0%) or Grade12 (34.6%). The highest group of respondents belongs to Average Economic Status (65%) residing in Urban Area (91.9%).

It is also seen that the moderately enough Coffee Drinkers belongs to Female Category (55.8%) than Male Category (42.1%). The maximum Coffee Drinkers also belongs to age group 16 – 20 (59.4%). The Coffee drinkers are either from Grade 12 (36.0%) and Undergraduate students (35.5%). The economic status of majority of coffee drinkers were Average (64.5%) and residing in urban area (92.4%).

Table 2. Characteristics of the students participated

	Group	Number of Respondents	Percentage of Respondents (%)
Total	-	234	100.0
Drinking styles	Coffee Drinker	197	84.2
	Non Coffee Drinker	37	15.8
Gender	Female	131	56.0
	Male	99	42.3
	Prefer Not to say	4	1.7
Age	16 – 20 years old	138	59.0
	21 – 25 years old	89	38.0
	26 – 30 years old	7	3.0
Education	Grade 11	14	6.0
	Grade 12	81	34.6
	Diploma or Certificate Course	3	1.3
	Bachelor	82	35.0

	Group	Number of Respondents	Percentage of Respondents (%)
	Degree		
	Post Bachelor Degree	54	23.1
	Poor	7	3.0
	Below Average	10	4.3
Economic Status	Average	152	65.0
	Above Average	56	23.9
	Affluent	9	3.8
Area	Rural	19	8.1
	Urban	215	91.9

Furthermore, this study focused on the student's residential area to evaluate whether this parameter affect the consumption of coffee. The Fisher's Exact Test states that there is no association between consumption of coffee with respect to the area of the respondents reside (p value = 0.330). It is also observed that the consumption of coffee has insignificant association with respect to Gender (p value = 1.000), Education (p value = 0.068), Economic Status (p value = 0.780) and Age Group (p value = 0.261). Furthermore, it is also observed that there is significant association between the consumption of Coffee and Non Coffee Drinkers with respect to Age Group (p value = 0.04).

3.2 Coffee Intake Habits Among the respondents
The majority of the respondents consume Coffee and aware of the presence of Caffeine in coffee (97.5%). The Figure 1 states that majority of the respondents (83.2%) drink 2 cups or less coffee per day followed by respondents (12.7%) drink 3 – 4 cups of coffee per day. A smaller percentage (4.0%) of respondents consumed more than 5 cups of coffee per day.

It is also observed that, in the age group 16 – 20 years maximum respondents (82.1%) consumed 2 cups or less coffee followed by the age group 26 – 30 years (80.0%). It was also studied that maximum consumption of coffee (86.7%) is among rural area with 2 cups or less per day. The frequency of consuming 2 cups or less coffee is more among Females (84.5%) as compared with Males (81.9%). However, there is no significant association on frequency of consuming coffee with respect to characteristics of the respondents like Gender (p value = 0.409), Education (p value = 0.953), Economic Status (p value = 0.488), Age Group (p value = 0.964) and economic status (p value = 0.488).

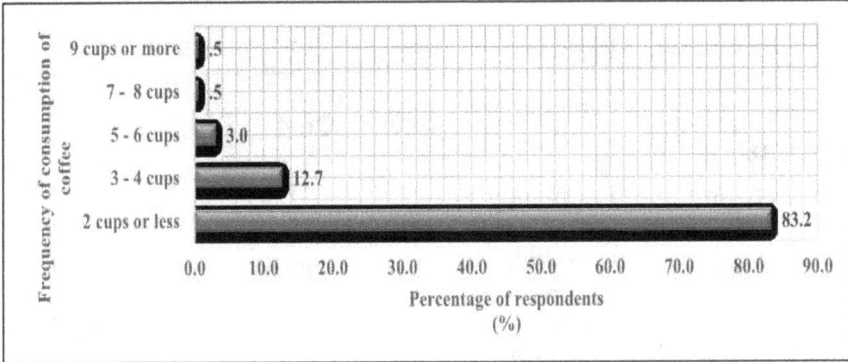

Figure 1. Frequency of Consumption of Coffee by respondents

The Habits of consuming coffee were categorized based on consuming Morning time, Lunch time, with Dinner, during examination days, stressed out, get together with friends and relatives. The respondents were asked to answer the questions based on scaling as Never, Rarely, Often and Always. The respondent's habits of consuming coffee are represented in Table 3.

Table 3. Percentage Distribution of Coffee Intake Habits among respondents

Coffee Intake Habits	Frequency & Percentage distribution of respondents			
	Group	Never	Rarely	Often	Always

Coffee Intake Habits	Frequency & Percentage distribution of respondents				
	Group	Never	Rarely	Often	Always
Consuming after waking up in the morning.	Frequency	59	62	35	41
	Percentage (%)	29.9	31.5	17.8	20.8
Consuming with Breakfast.	Frequency	58	44	43	52
	Percentage (%)	29.4	22.3	21.8	26.4
Consuming During Morning Break.	Frequency	98	52	28	19
	Percentage (%)	49.7	26.4	14.2	9.6
Consuming During Afternoon Break.	Frequency	82	57	31	27
	Percentage (%)	41.6	28.9	15.7	13.7
Consuming During Dinner.	Frequency	171	18	5	3
	Percentage (%)	86.8	9.1	2.5	1.5
Consuming During Bed time.	Frequency	148	36	11	2
	Percentage (%)	75.1	18.3	5.6	1.0
Consuming During Examination Week.	Frequency	40	52	56	49
	Percentage (%)	20.3	26.4	38.4	24.9
Consuming when visited at Friends or Family place.	Frequency	23	86	49	39
	Percentage (%)	11.7	43.6	24.9	19.8
Consuming	Frequency	64	55	40	38

Coffee Intake Habits	Frequency & Percentage distribution of respondents				
	Group	Never	Rarely	Often	Always
while stressed out.	Percentage (%)	32.5	27.9	20.3	19.3

The students (28.4%) consume more amount of coffee during examination week and also maximum respondents (43.6%) consumes coffee when visited at Friends or Family place. The majority of the respondents (86.8%) said that they never consume coffee during dinner and at Bed time (75.1%). The consumption of coffee is also very less during Morning break (9.6%).

3.3 Perception of its effects among the respondents

The perception of the effect on consuming coffee was asked from respondents based on 5 point Likert Scale and the factors are evaluated based on Exploratory Factor Analysis. It was based on two criteria suggested by Costello and Osborne (Costello & Osborne, n.d.),

(i) they should have salient factor loadings (> 0.40) and (ii) small cross loadings (an item loads at less than 0.32 on other factors).

(ii) MacCallum (MacCallum et al., 1999) have demonstrated that when communalities after extraction are above 0.5 then a sample size between 100 and 200 can be adequate. We have a sample of size 197 Coffee Drinkers with all communalities above 0.5, and so the sample size is really adequate. However, the KMO measure of sampling adequacy is 0.878 which is above Kaiser's recommendation (*Kaiser_citation_classic_factor_simplicity.Pdf*, n.d.) of 0.5. This value is also termed as meritorious (Hutcheson, 1999). It is suggested that the sample size is adequate to yield distinct and reliable factors.

The Bartlett's test is performed to test whether the correlation matrix is sufficiently different from an identity matrix. In this case it is significant, χ^2 (153) = 1592.254 (p value < 0.001) indicating that the correlations within the R – matrix are sufficiently different zero to warrant factor analysis. In order to extract factors assessing the perception of effects on consuming coffee, Exploratory Factor Analysis is used. The Table 4 represents the exploratory factor analysis to understand the perception of effects on consuming coffee.

Table 4. Exploratory Factor Analysis

Perception	Academics	Sleep	Choice	Disease	Relax
Coffee consumption increases reading power.	0.820				
Coffee consumption increases self-confidence.	0.803				
Coffee consumption increases recalling power.	0.791				
Coffee consumption increases academic performance.	0.779				
Coffee consumption helps in overnight study.	0.765				
Consumption of Coffee improves group work activity.	0.736				
Consumption of Coffee	0.732				

Perception	Academics	Sleep	Choice	Disease	Relax
increases study hours.					
Coffee consumption increases IQ.	0.711				
Consuming coffee boost up energy.	0.707				
Coffee helps to stay awake.	0.692	0.447			
Consuming coffee gives relaxation.	0.597				0.418
Consuming coffee makes feel important.	0.544				
Difficulty in fall asleep if consumed during day time.		0.581	0.474		
Consuming coffee increases risk of heart diseases.		0.534		0.423	
Consume coffee for the sake of friends.			0.703		
Prefer other de-caffeinated drinks to caffeinated drinks.		0.413	0.613		
Consuming coffee for the				0.719	

Perception	Academics	Sleep	Choice	Disease	Relax
taste.					
Preferred local brands				0.621	0.480

It is observed that Kaiser criterion (*Kaiser_citation_classic_factor_simplicity.Pdf*, n.d.) of extracting factors with eigenvalues greater than 1 is reliable when there are less than 30 variables and even after extracting it should be greater than 0.7 and sample size somewhere above 250. For this study, the sample size was 197 Coffee Drinkers, there are 18 variables, and the mean communality was 0.666, so extracting five factors is really not fruitful. The Figure 2 represents Scree Plot which is another way of extracting factors and it shows clear twist at 1 and 5 factors and so using the scree plot that one major factor can be extracted.

Figure 2. Scree Plot for extracting Factors

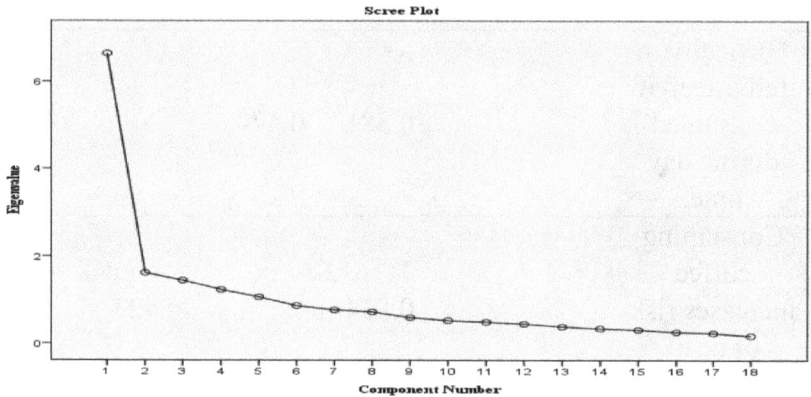

The Scree plot shows inflexion at 1 factor, hence the major factor that can be extracted is related to Academics where respondents feel like Consuming coffee increases their reading power, self – confidence, recalling power, academic performance, helps in overnight study, improves group work activity, increases study hours, increases IQ, boost up their energy, makes feel important, to stay awake and for relaxation.

3.4 Association between perception with respect to coffee intake habits

The Factor analysis extracted factors related to Academics. Several respondents consume coffee during their examination week as their perception is, it will increase study hours and good for academics. The Table 5 represents the association between their perception and coffee intake habits.

Table 5. Association between perception and coffee intake habits

Consuming coffee during Examination week			
Perception	Chi square	value	Association is
Coffee consumption increases reading power.	59.139	0.000	Significant
Coffee consumption increases self-confidence.	60.860	0.000	Significant
Coffee consumption increases recalling power.	44.197	0.000	Significant
Coffee consumption increases academic performance.	59.70	0.000	Significant
Consumption of Coffee improves group work activity.	33.381	0.000	Significant
Consumption of Coffee increases study hours.	83.837	0.000	Significant
Coffee consumption increases IQ.	38.458	0.000	Significant
Consuming coffee boost up energy.	68.870	0.000	Significant
Coffee helps to stay awake.	68.686	0.000	Significant
Consuming coffee gives relaxation.	41.649	0.000	Significant

It is observed that during examination those who always consume coffee agreed that it boost up their energy (59.2%). Along with that (57.1%) it is also agreed that Consuming coffee relaxes them and as the heredity follows during examination week, it often helps them to stay awake (55.4%). This study predicts that there is significant association between their coffee intake habits with respect to their perception. There is strong kind of relation between them.

3.5 Reasons behind not consuming coffee on daily basis.

It is observed from the sample of size 234, 197 (84.2%) were Coffee Drinkers and 37 (15.8%) of respondents were Non Coffee Drinkers. Even though there was lesser number of people who turned up negatively by saying they do not consume coffee on daily basis but they were asked to rank the reasons of not consuming and it was observed that the respondents gave first rank (6.0%) to not consuming because of health reasons followed by the second rank (5.6%) was given to they don't like the taste of coffee and third rank (5.1%) was given to that they don't like the smell of the coffee. Some even expressed their viewpoints that coffee products are really expensive.

By concluding, it is understood that students studying in colleges from Mumbai prefer consuming coffee with less in amount but the consumption pattern increases during their examination days. On an average 60 ± 82.208, the respondents consume coffee from past 5 years (Mean = 60 months and Standard Deviation = 82.208). Some even specified that they consumed it from childhood and some said it is their habit from past one decade. Even though with the current study it couldn't say that the consumption will cause major effect to their health. However, coffee is becoming a major part of life among young adults.

4.Discussion

The major idea of the current study was to understand the coffee consumption habits and perception of its effects among students studying in Mumbai. It is found that very large proportion (84.2%) of the respondents was coffee user. These findings are almost similar to the findings of all other studies (AtikahRamli et al., 2019) describing a high consumption of coffee among young adults (Kharaba et al., 2022). The present study concluded that the majority (83.2%) of the respondents consumes 2 cups or less amount of coffee per day and they prefer drinking coffee during their exam days as according to them consuming coffee increases their reading power, recalling power, academic performance, increases their study hours and many more. Many such perceptions the respondents have towards consuming coffee on a daily basis.

Many studies (Czarniecka-Skubina et al., 2021) states that consuming coffee more than 5 cups per day may cause a long term side effects and may affect their health. The present study for the time being doesn't show any long term side effects which may lead to any addiction. There is still a possibility if the study concentrates only on understanding the pattern of coffee consumption during examination days. The consumption of coffee during break was found very less (28.9%) than other categories. The major factor observed is consuming coffee boosts their energy. Strangely, it is also observed that very less (27.9%) respondents consume coffee while they are stressed out.

The present study was focused on only college going students so may be the factors like stress, consuming coffee during break doesn't reflects much importance. It was also observed that the there is no significant association between consuming coffee with respect to the characteristics of the respondents. The major factor that got extracted was related to academics but along there was some quite less weightage on diseases and relaxation.

Many literature suggests (Maqsood et al., 2020) that moderate way of consuming coffee is relative safe, but that higher consumption of coffee may cause physiological, psychological and behavioral harm.

5. Conclusion

The study concludes that female students had more interest towards consuming coffee than male students. The major perceptions regarding coffee was to boost their energy, increase their recalling power, reading power, academic performance, increases IQ, increases their group activity work, increases their study hours, make them feel important and also give them relaxation. The major perception for not consuming coffee was that due to risk of heart diseases, some doesn't prefer the taste of coffee; some didn't like the smell of the coffee.

For each and every student, education should not depend on consuming coffee and increasing their study hours or their academic performance. There should be proper guidance given to students to make them aware of advantages and disadvantages of consuming coffee. Students should be guided to enhance their learning abilities through various other techniques like stress management or physical exercise to improve their sleep and eating habits.

5.1 Limitation and Future Research

There are certain study limitations. The study is done on the basis of convenience sampling technique, focused on students from Mumbai. Future studies can concentrate on various other statistical methods and can compare it with different countries. Coffee consumption behavior among various students with respect to various countries may bring a wide change in the conclusion. Furthermore, considering the increasing habits of consuming coffee its long term effects on health can be studied. Further studies may also focus on giving some best alternative to coffee while students studying for their examination. It can also focus on how much amount of caffeine in terms of coffee is consumed by students during their project work or exam days. Finally, one can even concentrate on future research based on coffee consumption motives with respect to their lifestyles.

6. Acknowledgment

We express our sincere gratitude to the several Statistics Department in Mumbai who wholeheartedly supported us to distribute the questionnaire and also helped in getting the maximum consistent answers to each and every question. We also thank the Department of Community Medicine, T.N.M.C B.Y.L Nair Ch. Hospital, Mumbai Central and Department of Statistics, V.P.M's B.N Bandodkar College Of Science(Autonomous), Thane for their support and guidance. We would also like to thank our family, friends who helped us a lot in finishing up with this research work.

6.1 Conflicts of Interest

The Authors declare no conflicts of interests.

References

1. AtikahRamli, N. A., Sriperumbuduru, V. P. K., Ghazi, H. F., & Dalayi, N. J. (2019). A Study of Caffeine Consumption Patterns and Dependence among Management and Science University Students. Indian Journal of Forensic Medicine & Toxicology, 13(1), 101. https://doi.org/10.5958/0973-9130.2019.00021.5
2. Cano-Marquina, A., Tarín, J. J., & Cano, A. (2013). The impact of coffee on health. Maturitas, 75(1), 7–21. https://doi.org/10.1016/j.maturitas.2013.02.002
3. Costello, A. B., & Osborne, J. (n.d.). Best practices in exploratory factor analysis: Four recommendations for getting the most from your analysis. https://doi.org/10.7275/JYJ1-4868
4. Czarniecka-Skubina, E., Pielak, M., Sałek, P., Korzeniowska-Ginter, R., & Owczarek, T. (2021). Consumer Choices and Habits Related to Coffee Consumption by Poles. International Journal of Environmental Research and Public Health, 18(8), 3948. https://doi.org/10.3390/ijerph18083948
5. Hutcheson, G. (1999). The Multivariate Social Scientist. SAGE Publications, Ltd. https://doi.org/10.4135/9780857028075
6. Kaiser_citation_classic_factor_simplicity.pdf. (n.d.).
7. Kharaba, Z., Sammani, N., Ashour, S., Ghemrawi, R., Al Meslamani, A. Z., Al-Azayzih, A., Buabeid, M. A., & Alfoteih, Y. (2022). Caffeine Consumption among Various University Students in the UAE, Exploring the Frequencies, Different Sources and Reporting Adverse Effects and Withdrawal Symptoms. Journal of Nutrition and Metabolism, 2022, 1–7. https://doi.org/10.1155/2022/5762299
8. MacCallum, R. C., Widaman, K. F., Zhang, S., & Hong, S. (1999). Sample size in factor analysis. Psychological Methods, 4(1), 84–99. https://doi.org/10.1037/1082-989X.4.1.84
9. Maqsood, U., Zahra, R., Latif, M. Z., Athar, H., Shaikh, G. M., & Hassan, S. B. (2020). Caffeine Consumption & Perception of Its Effects Amongst University Students. Proceedings of Shaikh Zayed Medical Complex Lahore, 34(4), 46–51. https://doi.org/10.47489/p000s344z770mc
10. Schubert, M. M., Irwin, C., Seay, R. F., Clarke, H. E., Allegro, D., & Desbrow, B. (2017). Caffeine, coffee, and appetite

control: A review. International Journal of Food Sciences and Nutrition, 68(8), 901–912. https://doi.org/10.1080/09637486.2017.1320537

11. Schwarz, B., Bischof, H. P., & Kunze, M. (1994). Coffee, Tea, and Lifestyle. Preventive Medicine, 23(3), 377–384. https://doi.org/10.1006/pmed.1994.1052

12. Sousa, A. G., Machado, L. M. M., Silva, E. F. da, & Costa, T. H. M. da. (2016). Personal characteristics of coffee consumers and non-consumers, reasons and preferences for foods eaten with coffee among adults from the Federal District, Brazil. Food Science and Technology, 36(3), 432–438. https://doi.org/10.1590/1678-457X.10015

[1]Assistant Professor in Biostatistics,
Department of Community Medicine,
Topiwala National Medical College & B.Y.L Nair Charitable Hospital,
Mumbai Central, Maharashtra, India,
email : divya.nair421@gmail.com
[2] Assistant Professor in Statistics & Research Scholar,
Department of Statistics,
V.P.M's B.N Bandodkar College of Science (Autonomous),
Maharashtra, Thane, India,
email : tanzimsshaikh@gmail.com

www.ingramcontent.com/pod-product-compliance
Lightning Source LLC
Chambersburg PA
CBHW050222270326
41914CB00003BA/531

.